Fundamentals of Analytics Engineering

An introduction to building end-to-end analytics solutions

Dumky De Wilde, Fanny Kassapian,
Jovan Gligorevic, Juan Manuel Perafan,
Lasse Benninga, Ricardo Angel Granados Lopez,
Taís Laurindo Pereira

Fundamentals of Analytics Engineering

Group Product Manager: Kaustubh Manglurkar
Publishing Product Manager: Apeksha Shetty
Book Project Manager: Aparna Nair
Editor: Juan Venegas
Senior Editor: Vandita Grover
Technical Editor: Kavyashree K S
Copy Editor: Safis Editing
Proofreader: Safis Editing
Indexer: Pratik Shirodkar
Production Designer: Jyoti Kadam
DevRel Marketing Coordinator: Nivedita Singh

First published: March 2024

Production reference: 1220324

Published by Packt Publishing Ltd.
Grosvenor House
11 St Paul's Square
Birmingham
B3 1RB, UK.

ISBN 978-1-83763-645-7

www.packtpub.com

Dedicated to every Xebian who contributed to this book's development!

To **Juan Venegas, for your meticulous and all-encompassing editing work,** *as well as organizing writing workshops that shaped our work. Trust us, the book would not be half as coherent without your help.*

To our teammates: Guillermo Sanchez, Pádraic Slattery, Thom van Engelenburg, and Thomas van Latum, for your work as technical reviewers and proofreaders. Go and follow them on GitHub and check out their conference talks. All of them are world-class analytics engineers!

To Giovanni Lanzani, for your editorial support. We are deeply grateful for the time you took to refine and transform some of our longest chapters into masterpieces. Your contribution has truly elevated the quality of this book.

And to Bram Ochsendorf, for your continuous support and encouragement. Thank you for keeping us sane during the whole journey.

Thank you all for your contributions.

Foreword

Analytics engineering, as a role, is relatively new. Broadly speaking, it encompasses tasks such as ingesting data into a central location, transforming this data into a format valuable for business use cases, and engaging with the wider organization to promote data-driven decisions. The advent of cloud data warehouses, the explosive growth of modern data stack products, and the widespread adoption of dbt have made the tasks of analytics engineers more complex but also more valuable. Given this pace of change, it is impossible to write a book that covers everything you need to know to become a successful analytics engineer, but the core concepts will remain the same regardless of this change.

This book is a curated collection of knowledge from a group of individuals with a wide set of skills who have learned valuable lessons working with data across a variety of industries and roles. Their collected insights will serve as a solid foundation for the success of your own career in analytics engineering.

Over the course of this book, you will find discussions on data modeling techniques, tutorials on how to set up modern cloud tooling, and best practices concerning data transformation. These are among the growing number of tasks falling under the scope of analytics engineering. As such, no two roles are the same, but I believe that the concepts covered will provide you with guidance as you progress on your journey. Whether you are embarking on your first steps in analytics engineering or you have been walking this road for several years, I wish you the best of luck.

Pádraic Slattery

Analytics Engineer

Xebia

Contributors

About the authors

Dumky de Wilde is an award-winning analytics engineer with close to 10 years of experience in setting up data pipelines, data models, and cloud infrastructure. Dumky has worked with a multitude of clients from government to fintech and retail. His background is in marketing analytics and web tracking implementations, but he has since branched out to include other areas and deliver value from data and analytics across the entire organization.

Fanny Kassapian has a multidisciplinary background across various industries, giving her a unique perspective on analytics workflows, from engineering pipelines to driving value for the business.

As a consultant, Fanny helps companies translate opportunities and business needs into technical solutions, implement analytics engineering best practices to streamline their pipelines, and treat data as a product. She is an avid promoter of data democratization, through technology and literacy.

I would like to thank my talented Xebia colleagues – in particular, Padraic for his invaluable technical expertise and Guillermo and Lucy for their precious advice. A special thanks to my parents for their unwavering support and to my beloved sister Flora for her encouragement to pursue my ambitions.

Jovan Gligorevic is an analytics engineer specializing in data modeling and building analytical dashboards. His passion is building and delivering end-to-end analytics solutions and enabling self-service analytics for clients.

Jovan has a background in business and data science. His skills range from machine learning to dashboarding, and he has democratized data in a range of industries, including banking, e-commerce, automotive, FMCG, trading, and a seed production company. He is accustomed to working with different tooling and programming languages and has acquired vast experience working with the modern data stack.

Jovan also likes to deliver training in dbt and Power BI and share his knowledge.

I am grateful to Ivana for supporting me throughout this journey and would like to thank my dear colleagues for the combined effort to make this book a reality.

Juan Manuel Perafan has worked in the realm of analytics since 2017, specializing in SQL, data governance, and **business intelligence (BI)**. He joined Xebia in 2020 as their first analytics engineer, making him an early adopter of this approach.

Besides helping his clients realize the value of their data, Juan is also very active in the data community. He has spoken at dozens of conferences and meetups around the world (including Coalesce 2023). Additionally, he is the founder of the Analytics Engineering meetup in the Netherlands as well as the Dutch dbt meetup.

A Megan, Daniel, Ella, Nugget y a mi querida familia feliz: Gracias por todo el amor y el apoyo en los momentos difíciles ¡Los quiero mucho a todos!

Lasse Benninga has been working in the data space since 2018, starting as a data engineer at a large airline, then switching to cloud engineering for consulting and working for different clients, ranging from healthcare to ride-sharing. Since 2021, he has been working as an analytics engineer at Xebia Data, where he combines his knowledge of cloud engineering with a love for analyzing data.

For Simone.

Ricardo Angel Granados Lopez is an analytics engineer who specializes in data engineering and analysis. With a master's in IT management and a focus on data science, he is proficient in using various programming languages and tools. Ricardo is skilled in exploring efficient alternatives and has contributed to multicultural teams, creating business value with data products using modern data stack solutions. As an analytics engineer, he helps companies enhance data value through data modeling, best practices, task automation, and data quality improvement.

I want to thank my loving wife and daughter for their constant support and encouragement while writing this book. I'm also grateful to my family, colleagues at Xebia Data, and all the coauthors for their help during this project. Thank you all for being there and making this book a reality.

Taís Laurindo Pereira is a versatile data professional with experience in a diverse range of organizations – from big corporations to scale-ups. Before her move to Xebia, she had the chance to develop distinct data products, such as dashboards and machine learning implementations. Currently, she is focusing on end-to-end analytics as an analytics engineer.

With a mixed background in engineering and business, her mission is to contribute to data democratization in organizations, by helping them to overcome challenges when working with data at scale.

To Renske, my loving and patient future wife who supported me immensely during this process. Thank you for your understanding and for motivating me during hard times!

I would also like to thank my colleagues at Xebia that made this book a reality – the coauthors and other team members. Thank you for all your dedication and expertise.

About the reviewers

Kaveh Noorbakhsh is a computer scientist and biomedical engineer who has worked in technology fields for over 20 years. He has a B.S.E in biomedical engineering from Case Western Reserve University and an M.S. in computer science from Kent State University. Kaveh has spent his career building innovative products in the HealthIT, SaaS, and big data spaces. He has worked at companies at various levels, from small, 20-person start-ups to large, multinational firms. His work has been recognized by the awarding of two patents in big data analytics and data pipelines (US 20170206255 and US 20170201556).

I want to thank Shambhavi and Akshay who were patient with me and helped guide me through the review process.

Devanshu Tayal is a highly accomplished data scientist with a master's degree from BITS, Pilani, India. His extensive expertise in data science is evidenced by his contributions to a wide range of industries. Devanshu is deeply committed to mentoring and guiding aspiring data scientists and is an avid researcher of emerging technologies in the field. He is a strong advocate for diversity and inclusion and has shared his insights through various publications. Devanshu is frequently invited to deliver guest lectures at universities throughout India, and his contributions as a technical reviewer have been acknowledged in multiple books. His comprehensive knowledge and experience in the field make him an asset to any team or project.

Table of Contents

Part 1: Introduction to Analytics Engineering

1

2

Part 2: Building Data Pipelines

5

Data Modeling   63

6

Transforming Data   93

7

Serving Data   113

Part 3: Hands-On Guide to Building a Data Platform

8

Hands-On Analytics Engineering   129

Part 4: DataOps

9

Data Quality and Observability   165

10

Writing Code in a Team   187

11

Automating Workflows   223

Part 5: Data Strategy

12

Driving Business Adoption   261

13

Data Governance   271

14

Preface

This book was written by a team of seven analytics engineers from Xebia, an international consultancy company in the Netherlands. As Xebians, knowledge sharing is a key part of our culture. In addition to helping our clients, we organize biweekly knowledge exchange sessions and monthly innovation days. As a result, our colleagues are always actively contributing to open-source software, organizing meetups, speaking at data conferences, and writing books.

While we are colleagues at the same company, each of us brings unique expertise and skills to the table. Analytics engineering is a diverse field, and mastering every aspect is not expected. In this book, each author contributed two or three chapters based on their interests and expertise. The same applies to you as a reader. Depending on your organization's needs, certain chapters may hold greater relevance. Our goal is to provide a comprehensive overview of essential concepts, tailored to the varied demands of this profession.

Since its inception in 2019, analytics engineering has experienced remarkable growth. As its importance continues to be recognized by organizations worldwide, we firmly believe that analytics engineers will become indispensable members of every data team. Through this book, you have the opportunity to become a frontrunner in this evolving field, contributing to its advancement and shaping its future alongside us.

Who this book is for

This book is for data engineers and analysts considering transitioning to analytics engineering, as well as for analytics engineers looking to improve their skills and identify areas for growth.

While introductory in nature, you will benefit from having prior knowledge in key areas such as data analysis processes, including data ingestion, transformation, and visualization, along with database fundamentals such as data modeling, querying, database management, and architecture.

What this book covers

Chapter 1, What Is Analytics Engineering?, traces the history of analytics engineering and its surge in popularity. Dive into its *why* and *what* to understand role responsibilities thoroughly.

Chapter 2, The Modern Data Stack, explores the modern data stack, demystifying SQL and cloud impact. Witness the industry's shift to purpose-built tools for contemporary data management.

Chapter 3, Data Ingestion, explores fundamental techniques, common issues, and strategies for moving data between systems. We break down data ingestion into eight steps and elaborate on common considerations for data quality and scalability.

Chapter 4, Data Warehousing, delves into the core concepts and history of data warehouses. You will gain insights into the evolution of data storage solutions and the impact of cloud technologies on this space.

Chapter 5, Data Modeling, details the proactive design process of establishing relationships between data within information systems. This critical process can reduce costs, enhance computational speed, and elevate user experience.

Chapter 6, Transforming Data, unravels the shift from ETL to ELT pipeline paradigms, the importance of data cleaning and transformation, reusability in query processes, and optimizing SQL queries for modularity.

Chapter 7, Serving Data, discusses presenting data to end users. You will gain insights into exposing data through different means, understanding data as a product, and examining the motivations and challenges associated with achieving self-service analytics in companies.

Chapter 8, Hands-On Analytics Engineering, also describes tools such as Airbyte Cloud for managed ingestion, Google BigQuery for warehousing, dbt Cloud for transformations, and Tableau for visualization.

Chapter 9, Data Quality and Observability, helps you ensure data quality and establish observability in analytics processes. Delving into strategies and tools, this chapter equips you with the skills to maintain data integrity and transparency.

Chapter 10, Writing Code in a Team, focuses on collaborative coding practices within a team setting. With an emphasis on best practices, version control, and effective communication, this chapter focuses on teamwork and efficiency in analytics engineering projects.

Chapter 11, Automating Workflows, concludes the DataOps section by exploring the implementation of continuous workflows. You will be introduced to practices that streamline analytics workflows, optimizing efficiency and productivity.

Chapter 12, Driving Business Adoption, highlights the critical process of collecting and interpreting business requirements. You will be guided through the steps to understand and align analytics initiatives with the unique needs and objectives of the business.

Chapter 13, Data Governance, delves into the principles and practices of data governance. You will gain insights into establishing robust data governance frameworks, ensuring the reliability of organizational data, and aligning analytics strategies with overarching business goals.

Chapter 14, Epilogue, summarizes the learning from this book and gives you extra tips to take your analytics engineering career even further.

To get the most out of this book

Familiarity with Python and SQL will enhance comprehension of *Chapters 8, 10,* and *11.* Additionally, basic knowledge of command-line usage (with tools such as Git and dbt) and familiarity with cloud computing concepts will be beneficial, as this book serves as an introduction to these topics.

The following software/hardware are covered in the book:

Software/Hardware are covered in the book	Operating system requirement
Airbyte Cloud	WindowsOS, macOS, or Linux
dbt Cloud	
Google Cloud, Google BigQuery, Google Sheets	
Tableau Desktop	
Git and GitHub	

Some of these tools have paid versions. To follow the instructions in this book, you can use the free versions or make use of a free trial.

If you are using the digital version of this book, we advise you to type the code yourself or access the code from the book's GitHub repository (a link is available in the next section). Doing so will help you avoid any potential errors related to the copying and pasting of code.

Several chapters in the book feature code snippets designed to showcase best practices. However, executing these snippets may need extra setup, not covered in this book. You should view these snippets as illustrative examples and adapt the underlying best practices to your unique scenarios.

Download the example code files

You can download the example code files for this book from GitHub at `https://github.com/PacktPublishing/Fundamentals-of-Analytics-Engineering`. If there's an update to the code, it will be updated in the GitHub repository.

There are several hands-on guides mentioned in the book, they can be found at `https://github.com/PacktPublishing/Fundamentals-of-Analytics-Engineering/tree/main/chapter_8/guides`.

We also have other code bundles from our rich catalog of books and videos available at `https://github.com/PacktPublishing/`. Check them out!

Conventions used

There are a number of text conventions used throughout this book.

`Code in text`: Indicates code words in text, database table names, folder names, filenames, file extensions, pathnames, dummy URLs, user input, and Twitter handles. Here is an example: "Notice how the next CTE, called `employees`, selects from the `raw_source` CTE."

A block of code is set as follows:

```
def add_numbers(a, b):
    c = a + b
    return c
```

Any command-line input or output is written as follows:

```
on-run-end: "{{ dbt_project_evaluator.print_dbt_project_evaluator_
issues() }}"
```

Bold: Indicates a new term, an important word, or words that you see onscreen. For instance, words in menus or dialog boxes appear in **bold**. Here is an example: "A common application for the ETL process is when organizations have strict requirements regarding **Personal Identifiable Information (PII)**."

> **Tips or important notes**
> Appear like this.

Get in touch

Feedback from our readers is always welcome.

General feedback: If you have questions about any aspect of this book, email us at `customercare@packtpub.com` and mention the book title in the subject of your message.

Errata: Although we have taken every care to ensure the accuracy of our content, mistakes do happen. If you have found a mistake in this book, we would be grateful if you would report this to us. Please visit `www.packtpub.com/support/errata` and fill in the form.

Piracy: If you come across any illegal copies of our works in any form on the internet, we would be grateful if you would provide us with the location address or website name. Please contact us at `copyright@packtpub.com` with a link to the material.

If you are interested in becoming an author: If there is a topic that you have expertise in and you are interested in either writing or contributing to a book, please visit `authors.packtpub.com`.

Share Your Thoughts

Once you've read *Fundamentals of Analytics Engineering*, we'd love to hear your thoughts! Scan the QR code below to go straight to the Amazon review page for this book and share your feedback.

https://packt.link/r/1837636451

Your review is important to us and the tech community and will help us make sure we're delivering excellent quality content.

Download a free PDF copy of this book

Thanks for purchasing this book!

Do you like to read on the go but are unable to carry your print books everywhere?

Is your eBook purchase not compatible with the device of your choice?

Don't worry, now with every Packt book you get a DRM-free PDF version of that book at no cost.

Read anywhere, any place, on any device. Search, copy, and paste code from your favorite technical books directly into your application.

The perks don't stop there, you can get exclusive access to discounts, newsletters, and great free content in your inbox daily

Follow these simple steps to get the benefits:

1. Scan the QR code or visit the link below

https://packt.link/free-ebook/9781837636457

2. Submit your proof of purchase
3. That's it! We'll send your free PDF and other benefits to your email directly

Prologue

In my first job, one of my primary responsibilities was manually filling out an Excel sheet that powered a rudimentary dashboard with the most important KPIs. The dashboard was shown at the standup, which meant arriving early at the office every morning. Back then, I had little to no experience with data. But I was going to do anything in my power to sleep 15 minutes longer.

My plan was to find the right dashboarding tool and learn how to automate this report. That was when I came across Tableau. Very quickly, manually refreshing dashboards became a thing of the past. Honestly, I had a lot of fun building dashboards and torturing the data for insights.

One day, a top-level manager passed by my desk on his way to a meeting. When he noticed I was building a dashboard, he approached me and asked: "Are these the results of the latest campaign?". I nodded. He grabbed a chair, sat next to me, and proceeded to ask me multiple follow-up questions. I will never forget the fascination in his eyes when I opened Tableau and started creating visuals in a matter of seconds. That moment changed the rest of my career.

As the requests started growing, I had to ask for help from my systems and database administrators. Unfortunately, they were always busy with other projects, and I was never on their priority list. Getting access to a system or requesting any change in the data warehouse was always a hassle. Often, it was easier to go to tutorial hell and teach myself how to do it myself.

The level of support from both the IT department and your management team can vary between companies and even roles. However, you can likely relate to this story. Despite this incident occurring almost a decade before the term "analytics engineer" was coined (during a time when the biggest buzzwords were Hadoop and IoT), two enduring lessons emerged: the ability to analyze data makes you indispensable, and enhancing your engineering skills reduces your reliance on the IT department.

Please note that the journey from manual data entry and lack of IT support is not just a story of personal growth; it highlights a broader need within organizations. This book is born from those challenges. At first glance, this book is a roadmap to empower individuals with the skills and knowledge to bridge the gap between data analysis and engineering. On a deeper level, it is about overcoming the technical and human challenges to become a data-driven organization.

Juan Manuel Perafan

Analytics Engineer

Xebia

Part 1:
Introduction to Analytics Engineering

The first two chapters present the fundamental ideas supporting analytics engineering and the Modern Data Stack. They highlight how analytics engineers utilize software engineering principles to structure, modify, verify, implement, and document data in a reusable manner, ultimately streamlining team effort and time. Conversely, the Modern Data Stack prioritizes rapid delivery, cost-efficiency, and data accessibility, yet it can result in multiple tools and fragmented data.

This section has the following chapters:

- *Chapter 1, What Is Analytics Engineering?*
- *Chapter 2, The Modern Data Stack*

1

What Is Analytics Engineering?

In the era of modern data warehousing, the landscape for data teams saw a radical transformation. With affordable storage and the growing popularity of **Extract, Load, and Transform (ELT)**, a new breed of data teams has emerged. No longer dependent solely on data engineers for warehouse management and data transformation, these teams seek to bridge the gap between engineering and business. This change resulted in the rise of a specialized role – the **analytics engineer**.

The first written mention of the term *analytics engineer* appeared in early 2019. Since then, the field of analytics engineering has grown in popularity, demand, and standards.

In this chapter, you will learn what an analytics engineer does and how they can contribute to a solid data strategy. Additionally, we will discuss the shift from **Extract, Transform, and Load (ETL)** to ELT and the difference between the work of data analysts, data engineers, and analytics engineers.

The following main topics will be covered:

- Introducing analytics engineering
- Why do we need analytics engineering?

Introducing analytics engineering

In early 2019, in a blog post from the *Locally Optimistic* community, the term *analytics engineer* emerged to describe the need for a new role born out of new challenges in the data landscape. When working with data at scale, many companies face difficulties with traditional data teams, where data engineers and data analysts' work is often siloed. Shortly after, dbt Labs – the company that developed **dbt (data build tool)**, an open-source data transformation tool – started a community-wide campaign to promote this new job title.

Defining analytics engineering

Although currently there are many definitions of what this role entails, for this book we decided to present our own, backed up by years of consultancy experience in the field.

> **A definition of an analytics engineer**
>
> Analytics engineers are the bridge between business and data engineering. By adhering to software engineering best practices, they build and maintain robust transformation pipelines to produce high-quality datasets. With this process, they improve the accessibility and reliability of data products. The analytics engineer is a center role in empowering end users to make truly data-informed decisions.

Other relevant definitions can be easily found on the internet – the most popular being the one by dbt Labs. We believe that the analytics engineer role goes beyond working with dbt and writing SQL. It includes analytics translation skills, such as effective communication, domain knowledge, project management, and entrepreneurial spirit. These skills are essential when talking to business stakeholders to understand business processes, translate these to relevant data models, and finally build pipelines. By delivering reliable and well-documented datasets to downstream users, analytics engineers are essential to data democratization initiatives in an organization.

From the definition presented, it can be inferred that the analytics engineering field, as the name already suggests, sits at the intersection of data engineering and analytics. From data engineering, it applies its software engineering principles – such as version control, testing, and continuous integration and deployment – to data pipelines, and from analytics, its data modeling techniques. A skilled analytics engineer can balance these two areas of expertise, pairing them up with business understanding.

Why do we need analytics engineering?

Now that you understand the core definition and skills behind the term, it is time to deep-dive into why the role is necessary. Without analytics engineering, data teams often struggle with the quality and reliability of data models. Data engineers might be overworked trying to maintain infrastructure while working on data modeling. Meanwhile, it is hard for analysts to trust the metrics that they report on, since they have limited visibility on the complex transformation process that goes into it. When metrics are wrong, business stakeholders might lose trust in data. Ultimately, it impacts business performance, since it becomes harder to make data-informed decisions.

Let's illustrate this situation with an analogy.

A supermarket analogy

Consider the data team as a supermarket supply chain. The data engineer is responsible for procurement, planning the transportation of products from producers and storage points to the supermarket for delivery. The data analyst, like a store manager, identifies shopping trends and presents them to business owners for pricing and promotional decisions.

Ultimately, the analytics engineer is responsible for store layout design, product grouping, and ensuring customers can easily find items. They oversee inventory, coordinate product arrivals, avoid damaged goods, and ensure proper placement of new products. They also maintain aisle labels, product freshness, and shelf organization to minimize expired products and promote store sales.

These tasks help the data analyst (store manager) monitor supermarket activities, maintain accurate metrics, and create reports on store conditions. It also helps the data engineer (procurement) to meet consumer expectations and provide an overall pleasant shopping experience.

From the analogy, we can take away that the analytics engineer acts as a bridge between the data engineer and the data analyst's work, facilitating a smooth customer experience. In a smaller store without this role, the product stocking task would fall to either one of the two, adding to their responsibilities and increasing their workload. In such a store, customers might struggle to find the products they want, which could be expired, damaged, or out of stock. This situation would negatively impact their experience and delay product delivery. Thus, the analytics engineer plays a central role in enabling a sustainable business operation.

The shift from ETL to ELT

In the recent decades, the rise of cloud computing contributed to scalable and cost-effective compute and storage systems. This resulted in the wide adoption of cloud data warehouses, enabling affordable and efficient storage for large volumes of data. This reduced the need to transform data as much as possible before loading it, contributing to the shift from ETL to ELT.

This shift, in turn, is one of the factors that influenced the increased demand for analytics engineers. In **ETL**, which for so long has been the standard approach, data is extracted from various sources, transformed, and then loaded in a target data warehouse. In this process, data engineers typically own the whole cycle, and data analysts often have limited visibility of the logic used. This might result in siloed knowledge about how the data was processed. Conversely, with **ELT**, raw data is loaded into a data warehouse and transformed afterward. *Figure 1.1* illustrates the ETL process:

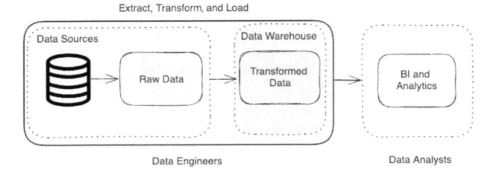

Figure 1.1 – An ETL process

Figure 1.2 displays the ELT process:

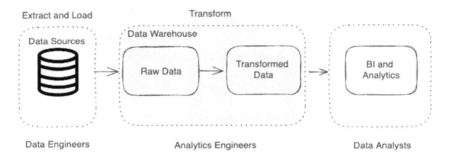

Figure 1.2 – An ELT process

Figure 1.1 and *Figure 1.2* illustrate that the shift from ETL to ELT facilitated data engineers to focus on managing data sources and loading them into data warehouses. With that, the need for a specialized role focused on transformation emerged, creating the demand for analytics engineers. In ELT, they transform the raw loaded data and provide curated datasets for downstream users, such as analysts and business stakeholders.

Since with ELT all raw data is loaded in the warehouse, it is often an improvement in terms of agility and simplicity. Data ingestion is faster, and transformations can be done in SQL instead of complex Python code. Analytics engineers would then own the transformation layer while enabling data analysts to contribute to the SQL models behind it. This process would reduce siloed knowledge between engineers and analysts and streamline metrics definitions.

Moreover, with the availability of raw data, exploration can be done easily, allowing data teams to move fast and correct bugs quickly when necessary. With ELT, since historical raw data is loaded in the target data warehouse, transformations can be easily redone and rerun.

However, it is important to note that ETL is still widely used in many organizations. Whether ETL or ELT – or even **Extract, Transform, Load, and Transform (ETLT)** – is employed depends on the requirements for the data products and team resources and skills. A common application for the ETL process is when organizations have strict requirements regarding **Personally Identifiable Information (PII)**. In this scenario, PII fields need to be deleted or masked before entering the data warehouse. Although ELT has many advantages regarding flexibility and efficiency (especially in terms of data ingestion speed), ETL processes continue to improve in terms of methods and tools.

The difference between analytics engineers, data analysts, and data engineers

Now that the shift from ETL to ELT has been explained, it is time to understand in depth the differences – and in some cases, the overlap – between the work of analytics engineers, analysts, and data engineers.

To start, it is important to highlight that roles can differ significantly between companies, depending on their maturity stage, industry, and organizational structure. Additionally, individual preferences and skills can also influence how job responsibilities are shaped.

Still, although sometimes the lines may be blurry, differences remain between the work of these data professionals.

Hence, if we think about a *data supply chain*, from data collection to information usage – with its intermediary states being cleaned and prepared raw data (equivalent to the **Transform** step in *Figures 1.1 and 1.2*) – analysts' and engineers' core tasks are distinct. However, some responsibilities might overlap, especially in smaller organizations where job specialization is rare.

If their responsibilities can intersect, what about analytics engineers? The following diagram (*Figure 1.3*, Xebia, `https://pages.xebia.com/whitepaper-data-democratization`) builds upon *Figures 1.1 and 1.2* and explores in depth the steps from data capture to information usage (BI and analytics):

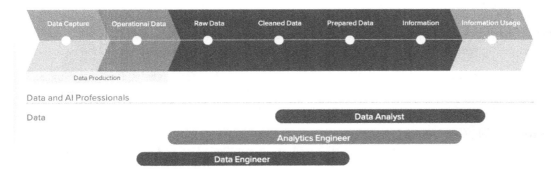

Figure 1.3 – Intersecting the job roles of data engineers , analytics engineers, and analysts

We observe from *Figure 1.3*, data analysts focus on analyzing data, developing dashboards and reports, and uncovering insights that influence business decisions. Their work is centered around descriptive, diagnostic, and prescriptive analytics, requiring constant contact with business stakeholders and often leadership. Because of that, besides technical capabilities such as SQL, Python/R, and BI tools, this type of professionals are expected to possess significant domain knowledge to deliver relevant analyses. In their effort to uncover insights, data analysts are often responsible for cleaning and preparing (modeling) data before information delivery.

Conversely, data engineers are concerned with designing, building, and maintaining the infrastructure that supports analytics engineers and downstream users, such as data analysts and data scientists. They work closely with these roles and other stakeholders to ensure that this infrastructure enables analytics-driven decisions. Data engineers are also often responsible for custom data extraction pipelines that require custom Python code. In terms of technical skills, high proficiency in Python is expected, such as a clear understanding of **Object-Oriented Programming (OOP)** paradigms – SQL, **Continuous Integration/Continuous Development (CI/CD)**, orchestration, and infrastructure as code. Depending on the organization and the tasks involved, other programming languages might be necessary in addition to Python, such as Scala and Java.

Therefore, the analytics engineer serves as a bridge between data engineers and analysts, focusing on the entire data domain of the supply chain – raw, cleaned, and prepared data – up to the point of information delivery. Analytics engineers often leverage tools from the Modern Data Stack, which will be discussed in *Chapter 2, The Modern Data Stack*, to achieve this task. Among these tools, a key one is **dbt**, which allows analytics engineers to transform data using SQL, testing and documenting these transformations while tracking data lineage. For this role, it is necessary to have a high proficiency in SQL, Python, and data modeling techniques, and an understanding of orchestration and CI/CD principles. Finally, business acumen is also essential to understand how to contribute to business value, through relevant data models that represent business processes and enable key decisions.

Summary

In this chapter, you learned how analytics engineers act as the bridge between business, analytics, and data engineering, enabling data democratization through the quality and accessibility of data products. By delivering reliable data models, analytics engineers are a centerpiece of data-informed decisions.

You also learned how the shift from ETL to ELT contributed to the rise of analytics engineering, and how both methods are still applicable currently. Additionally, we discussed how roles can differ across organizations, and how analytics engineers fit in the data supply chain.

In the next chapter, *The Modern Data Stack*, you will get an overview of the collection of tools and technologies that enable this life cycle, and how this shifted roles and technical barriers in the data landscape.

2

The Modern Data Stack

Data's exponential growth and the need to incorporate analytics-driven decision-making have brought new challenges and requirements to organizations. Information must be reliable, scalable, and delivered quickly to remain competitive. In this scenario, a new set of tools, technologies, and processes starts to gain traction – the **Modern Data Stack (MDS)**.

In this chapter, you will learn what the MDS is, the principles that differentiate it from legacy stacks, and its advantages and disadvantages. Although this set of tools brought significant technological advancements versus legacy tightly coupled systems, it is important to be aware of its pitfalls and the recent considerations when choosing this type of stack.

The main topics that are going to be covered are as follows:

- Understanding the Modern Data Stack
- Explaining three key differentiators versus legacy stacks
- Discussing the advantages and disadvantages of the MDS

Understanding a Modern Data Stack

As the name suggests, the MDS represents a technological evolution compared to previous systems widely used in recent decades. From the development of the business data warehouse in the 1980s to the rise of cloud technology with **Amazon Web Services** (**AWS**) in the early 2000s, on-premises legacy data stacks dominated the landscape. These systems had a monolithic IT infrastructure, resulting in complex maintenance. The MDS transformed this scenario – bringing modularity and cloud-native tools. However, before we dive into the details, let's first define what a **data stack** is.

A data stack is a collection of tools and services as part of an extensive technology infrastructure designed to ingest, store, transform, and serve data. It makes data accessible across an organization and is fundamental to delivering business insights through reporting and dashboards, advanced analytics, and **Machine Learning** (**ML**) applications. *Figure 2.1* illustrates an example of a high-level architecture of a data stack.

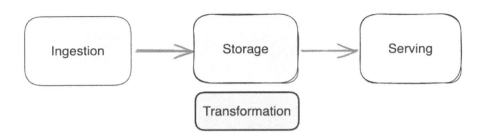

Figure 2.1 – An example of a high-level architecture of a data stack

Here, the data flows from left to right. The raw data is ingested, stored in a data warehouse, transformed, and finally, served to data analysts, data scientists, and business users.

Consequently, the MDS is nothing more than a subset of such architecture – a specific set of tools that democratizes access to the main functionalities of a data stack, reducing the complexity of implementation and improving the scalability of the data life cycle.

In the following table, we compare the main characteristics of the legacy data stack and the MDS.

Characteristic	Legacy Data Stack	Modern Data Stack
Architecture	Monolithic architecture	Modular tools
Servers	On-premises servers	Cloud-based
Maintenance	Complex – many resources required	Simplified, managed solutions
Programming languages	Java/Scala/Python	SQL-first
Data ingestion	ETL-focused	ELT-focused

Table 2.1 – A legacy versus Modern Data Stack comparison

Now that we have seen the definition of the MDS and how it compares to legacy stacks, it is time to see how it looks in practice. In *Figure 2.2*, an example is provided, with an overview of some of the tools that are used for key functionalities within this design:

Figure 2.2 – An example of an MDS

As we can see in *Figure 2.2*, the main blocks of an MDS can be considered as follows:

- **Managed ingestion**: This is responsible for the *EL* in ELT. It helps to streamline data extraction and ingestion through third-party-managed software applications.

- **Data warehouse/lakehouse**: These are cloud-based systems used to store large volumes of data.

- **Transformation**: This is what the *T* in ELT stands for. Transformations help in data cleaning and preparation to meet business intelligence needs.

- **Orchestration**: Orchestration helps in setting up specific tasks to run automatically at a particular event. As an example, an orchestration tool can be paired up with dbt Core for scheduled transformation.

- **Self-service layer**: In this block, reports and analysis are provided to business users, enabling these stakeholders to answer their questions and make data-informed decisions.

With managed ingestion, data teams are less dependent on the work of data engineers. Tools such as Stitch, Fivetran, and Airbyte empower analytics engineers to own end-to-end data pipelines, focusing on data modeling and transformation.

The list of tools and blocks in *Figure 2.2* is not exhaustive. New tools and MDS companies emerge every year. Other common and important blocks are as follows:

- **Data catalog tools** are used for search and discovery tools, helping users to document and democratize access to business logic and data assets. Examples are Atlan, data.world, and DataHub.

- **Data quality and observability tools** are used to monitor pipelines and ensure the overall quality of data. Tool examples are Soda, Datafold, and Monte Carlo.

- **Reverse ETL** is used to retrieve data from a data warehouse and publish it to the systems used by business users, such as CRM software. Key market leaders are Census, Hightouch, and RudderStack.

We will now move our focus to how the modern data stack differs from the legacy stacks.

Explaining three key differentiators versus legacy stacks

The MDS brought a series of technological advancements in comparison with precursor systems (pre-cloud). As demonstrated in *Figure 2.1*, the main differentiators are its SQL-first approach, cloud-native tools, and managed and modular solutions. In this section, we are going to deep dive into the details of these characteristics.

Lowering technical barriers with a SQL-first approach

Developed in the 1970s by IBM researchers, SQL – or *SEQUEL* as it was called originally – was designed to access data in an integrated relational database, by both professional programmers and more occasional database users. Here is a link to the full version of the paper, published by Donald D. Chamberlin and Raymond F. Boyce (1976): `https://doi.org/10.1145/800296.811515`.

Decades later, SQL remains indispensable for this purpose, and its popularity has increased sharply. In the Stack Overflow Developer Survey 2022, it was the third most used programming language, as voted by 49.43% of all respondents – professional and beginner developers.

Despite SQL's popularity, until recent years, big data professionals focused on programming languages such as Java and Scala. Due to their complexity, these languages demand a high technical skill level. SQL, conversely, is simple, accessible, and flexible, contributing to a lower technical barrier for the required skill set to work with data at scale. Therefore, SQL and Python are the main programming languages currently seen in job postings for analytics engineers, data engineers, data analysts, and data scientists.

Not surprisingly, in the MDS, SQL has a fundamental role – with SQL-first tools such as **dbt**, analytics engineers (or, in some cases, data analysts) can own a more significant part of the data life cycle. Through models using this language, these professionals can now execute data transformation pipelines following software engineering best practices, such as version control and modular code – once limited to Java/Scala roles in traditional data teams.

The following screenshot displays a dbt model in dbt Cloud:

```
stg_orders.sql                    ×

models > staging > jaffle_shop > stg_orders.sql
 1
 2    with orders as (
 3
 4        select
 5            id as order_id,
 6            user_id as customer_id,
 7            order_date,
 8            status
 9
10    from {{ source('jaffle_shop', 'jaffle_shop_orders') }}
11
12    )
13
14    SELECT * from orders
```

Figure 2.3 – An example of a dbt model written in SQL

In the figure, through mainly SQL commands, a staging orders table was created referencing a source (raw table), as a pre-step to a more complex data transformation. More on data transformation will be discussed in *Chapter 6, Transforming Data*.

Therefore, the SQL-first character of the MDS is fundamental to the democratization of tasks once limited to technical experts in more complex programming languages.

> **A quick glance at popular technologies**
>
> You can check out the Stack Overflow Developer Survey 2022 at `https://survey.stackoverflow.co/2022/#most-popular-technologies-language` for a quick review of the popular tools and technologies that developers use these days.

Next, you will learn about another key principle – **cloud-native solutions**.

Improving infrastructure efficiency with cloud-native systems

As mentioned in the first section, *Understanding a Modern Data Stack*, legacy systems were often on-premises, making scalability and maintenance harder. With the launch of modern cloud computing systems by Amazon with **AWS** in 2002, this landscape started to change. Since then, new players have emerged, such as Google, Microsoft, and Alibaba.

According to a recent market share report (`https://www.srgresearch.com/articles/q1-cloud-spending-grows-by-over-10-billion-from-2022-the-big-three-account-for-65-of-the-total`) developed by the Synergy Research Group and shared by Statista, AWS has the highest global market share in revenue – 32% in Q1 2023. It is followed by Microsoft Azure, with 23%, and Google Cloud, with 10%. These three largest cloud providers account for 65% of the global market. The report also states that the cloud market continues to grow worldwide, where **EMEA (Europe, Middle-East, and Africa)**, North America, and **APAC (Asia-Pacific)** lead it, with a growth of 20% year over year.

The MDS is cloud-native, meaning that its tools are designed to integrate seamlessly with different clouds. More specifically, they are designed to integrate easily with cloud data warehouses. This type of integration is an improvement on the legacy data stack in the overall system infrastructure. In these systems, connecting new applications to the existing on-premises database was often an arduous task.

In cloud-based environments, adaptability, scalability, and maintenance become less complex, resulting in fewer necessary resources – both in cost and people – when compared to traditional monolithic systems. Lastly, since the MDS tools can be integrated with different clouds, vendor lock-in (such as data warehouse vendors) is also reduced.

Next, it will become clear how the combination of being cloud-based and using out-of-the-box managed and modular tools translates into the speed of delivery and cost advantages discussed in the first section.

Simplifying implementation and maintenance with managed and modular solutions

An important innovation in the MDS is the use of **managed solutions**. *Managed* refers to software applications that are maintained and hosted by third-party service providers, which, in this case, are the companies that own these products.

In the case of managed ingestion, these tools simplify the deployment and maintenance of data pipelines, preventing the need for custom code and custom deployments. With several pre-made connectors available, it is easy and quick to set up a data source and a destination (e.g., a data warehouse or a lakehouse) and have an almost maintenance-free ingestion.

Another important innovation refers to **modularity**. Legacy data stacks were often tightly coupled with a high-level interdependency between components, making this system very resistant to changes. As shown previously, in *Figure 2.2*, in the MDS, different tools serve different purposes, such as ingestion, storage, transformation, orchestration, and business intelligence. With this configuration, it is possible to integrate new functionality faster or change parts of the stack without impacting its core function – to ingest, transform, and serve data. This design reduces vendor lock-in, due to several available options for each block.

Additionally, it is important to note that some managed tools are based on open-source software. This is the case for Airbyte – an open-source data integration platform that offers a fully managed cloud-based solution called Airbyte Cloud. Another key example is dbt, which offers dbt Core (open-source) and dbt Cloud. In the orchestration block, Dagster also has a cloud-based platform, Dagster Cloud.

You will also come across the term **managed open-source software**. This has become a popular business model. Many data teams don't have the expertise or resources to self-host and maintain open-source solutions, turning to the managed version instead. Therefore, managed software democratizes access to functionality once restricted to highly software engineering technical teams.

The combination of managed and modular applications adds an essential layer of flexibility to organizations. By simplifying data ingestion, storage, transformation, and serving, while using modular functionality, companies can increase agility and adapt to changes in business requirements.

Now that you understand the definition, tools, and building blocks, it is time to discuss the Modern Data Stack's advantages and disadvantages.

Discussing the advantages and disadvantages of the MDS

Although the MDS simplifies the data life cycle significantly, it is important to highlight and discuss its pitfalls.

The advantages can be summarized as follows:

- **Speed of delivery**: Setting up an MDS can take as little as a few hours to a couple of days, depending on the specific use case. Additionally, its self-service characteristic brings data products and solutions closer to where the business questions arise.

- **Cost**: As the MDS is cloud-based and uses out-of-the-box tools, costs are cut down significantly due to reduced complexity in architecture and hardware. In addition, cloud-native data warehouses provide cheaper data processing and storage when compared to on-premises systems.

- **Democratization**: Here, we see two dimensions of democratization – lowered technical barriers and the dissemination of information across an organization. The combination of managed ingestion and SQL-first tools lowers the technical barrier for data professionals. Therefore, the introduction of this stack shifted the required skill set, also making it easier to hire qualified talent. Also, the self-service block democratizes access to data across an organization, enabling business users to make data-informed decisions without relying solely on data analysts to provide information.

Yet, implementing a Modern Data Stack can have some disadvantages. It is important to be aware of the following:

- **Tool proliferation**: With so many tools available, it might be difficult for companies and data professionals to keep track of the latest developments and decide which set of tools and technologies to use. Moreover, since different tools serve different purposes, organizations might end up with 4-8 different products, adding complexity in managing licenses, vendors, and contracts.

- **Siloed information**: This fragmented approach can lead to knowledge silos, where different teams or individuals focus on a set of tools and technologies, not sharing knowledge across an organization and reducing efficiency.

An important point to highlight is that most MDS companies are startups or scale-ups backed by **VC (venture capital)** investors. In this business model, product pricing changes can happen abruptly, and there is a certain risk associated with the company's continuity of activities. Organizations that adopt these products should be aware of this and make architecture decisions where replacing a tool – or going for an open-source variant if there is one – is feasible and won't drastically impact key business decisions.

Many argue that the simplicity and speed of configuration of the MDS have led data teams to shift their focus to delivering quick insights, rather than emphasizing best practices. It is important to be aware that the MDS does not substitute the need for proper software engineering, data modeling, and architecture principles. This is why analytics engineering continues to be essential in this scenario.

Summary

In this chapter, you learned what the Modern Data Stack is and how it can transform the work of data teams by lowering technical barriers, improving the speed of information delivery, and bringing modular and managed solutions. With its combination of a SQL-first approach, cloud-based systems, and managed and modular tools, the MDS brings improvements compared to legacy, on-premises, and monolithic stacks. Still, it is important to be aware of its pitfalls, such as the large number of tools and considerations about siloed information.

With the MDS, analytics engineers can leverage managed ingestion and data transformation tools to deliver end-to-end analytics.

In the following chapter, you will get the opportunity to deepen your knowledge of one of the MDS's components – data ingestion. You will learn common approaches to it and what the steps are to set up an efficient and performant ingestion pipeline.

Part 2: Building Data Pipelines

This section is arguably the book's core. In these chapters, you will gain hands-on skills in managing data and constructing platforms effectively. Each chapter addresses essential aspects of an analytics engineer's role. Whether you focus on data ingestion, warehousing, modeling, transformation, or serving data, this section aims to provide a holistic understanding, recognizing the interdependence of each step in the pipeline.

This section has the following chapters:

- *Chapter 3, Data Ingestion*
- *Chapter 4, Data Warehousing*
- *Chapter 5, Data Modeling*
- *Chapter 6, Transforming Data*
- *Chapter 7, Serving Data*

3
Data Ingestion

A data platform is useless without any actual data in it. To access your data, combine it with other sources, enrich it, or share it across an organization, you will first need to get that data into your data platform. This is the process we call **data ingestion**. Data ingestion comes in all sorts and forms. Everyone is familiar with the age-old process of emailing Excel sheets back and forth, but luckily, there are more advanced and consistent ways of adding data to your platform.

Whether clicking your way through a managed ingestion tool such as Fivetran, Stitch, or Airbyte, or writing scripts to handle the parallel processing of multiple real-time data streams in a distributed system such as Spark, learning the steps of a **data ingestion pipeline** will help you build robust solutions. Building such a solution will help you guarantee the quality of your data, keep your stakeholders happy, and allow you to spend less time debugging and fixing broken code and more time adding new data to your organization's data analytics platform.

In this chapter, we're going to cover the following main topics:

- Digging into the problem of moving data between two systems
- Understanding the eight essential steps of a data ingestion pipeline
- Managing the quality and scalability of your data ingestion pipeline – the three key topics
- Working with data ingestion – an example pipeline

Digging into the problem of moving data between two systems

We have talked, in *Chapter 1*, *What Is Analytics Engineering?*, about the changing process of **extracting, transforming, and loading** (ETL) data, but understanding these steps is only part of ingesting data. Whenever you add new data to your data platform, whether that is sales data, currency exchange data, web analytics data, or video footage, you will have to make certain choices around the frequency, quality, reliability, and retention of that data and many other choices. If you do not think ahead at the beginning, reality will catch up with you when your data provider makes a change, a pipeline accidentally runs twice, or the requirements from the business change. But why do we need to move data from one system to the other in the first place?

You might consider it a given that you have to manipulate data a bit to make it fit your purpose. Maybe you're used to pivoting tables in an Excel sheet, adjusting formulas where needed, or you have written your fair share of SQL queries to load and transform data for a dashboard or report, but it is a strange thing. Why is it that we need data engineers, analytics engineers, analysts, and who knows how many people, to move data that already exists from one place to another?

It is easy to say, "*Well, it's in the wrong format in the wrong place, so I'll just move it and leave it at that.*"

But understanding why it is in the wrong format – because it likely is – and why it is in the wrong place – because again, it likely is – will help you build better data ingestion pipelines. Understanding the key differences between the requirements for the data at the source compared to the requirements at the destination will allow you to make sure your pipelines fulfill their purpose. Let's understand what these differences are.

The source of all problems

The reason a data ingestion pipeline even needs to exist starts with the way source data is collected. Let's for a moment consider ourselves an analyst in need of source data. What type of data do you need? Sales data, web analytics data, genetic data, IoT-device data, CRM data? Many organizations will use similar types of data for analysis. And what kind of questions do you want to answer about this data? Maybe compare time periods, or calculate a sum, an average, or a ratio between two metrics? Maybe you want to understand trends or anomalies. In any case, it is unlikely that you care about one single observation. It is more likely that you care about combinations or aggregations of observations.

Now, put yourselves in the shoes of the developer or product owner who is responsible for the application that generates the source data. You might be working on a web shop, a CRM system, a web application, or a DNA system. What is the most important thing to you? It is making sure that nothing gets lost: no transaction dropped, no relation missed, and no incomplete sequence? As a generator of source data, you care about the reliability and quality of your application for the users of that application. On the other hand, as an analyst, you care about answering questions from business stakeholders about the usage of that application.

In other words, the stakeholders of the source system care about writing data reliably and fast, while the stakeholders of the destination system care about reading data in high volumes with acceptable latency. This discrepancy is what causes a distinct difference in design between source and destination systems. Let's look at some common differences, as listed in the following table:

Topic	Source	Destination
Primary mode	Write/Update	Read
Data model	Normalized/snowflake: using separate tables for each entity and fact allows for faster writing	Denormalized/star: using minimal distinction between facts and dimensions allows for faster reading
Main database type	Row-based or document store	Column-based
File formats	JSON, XML, CSV	Parquet
Common databases	MySQL, Postgres, MongoDB, SQL Server	Snowflake, BigQuery, RedShift, Vertica, ClickHouse

Table 3.1 – Common differences between data in source and destination systems

On top of these differences, there is of course also a substantial difference in permissions. Usually, a source system cares strongly about who is allowed to write to and read from specific tables and rows. And rightly so, because you would not want to just share your bank transactions or sales data with anyone in the company. But often, that is at odds with analysts looking to find answers to business questions about usage, transactions, volumes, and other scenarios of investigation that might go right against some of the governance principles of the source system.

Understanding the eight essential steps of a data ingestion pipeline

It goes without saying that every data ingestion pipeline is a unique snowflake that is special to your organization and requirements. Nevertheless, every pipeline shares a few common characteristics that are essential to setting up a long-term process of moving data from source to destination. We have shown in *Chapter 1* how essential the process of ELT is to analytics engineering. The data ingestion pipeline is where that process takes place so that afterward, it can be used in the data platform.

When talking about ETL, it is easy to say that data ingestion is just those three steps. But behind the acronym is a way more complex process. Yes, sometimes that process can be as simple as a few clicks in a nice interface, but other times, especially when the origin of the data is unique to your organization, you will have to create a custom pipeline or integration, and the additional complexity that comes with it. Even with the so-called *happy flow* of adding a new source through a user interface, you will have to think about most of the steps in some way or another. So, let us look at an example of that "happy flow" first to get an understanding of the steps.

Marketing campaign data is a common use case for an off-the-shelf managed ingestion tool such as Fivetran, Stitch, or Airbyte. And it makes sense because many companies using Facebook, Google, X (previously Twitter), or similar platforms want the same data about their campaign performance in the same way.

Usually, the process involves steps similar to the following:

1. You select the platform (Google, Facebook, or a similar one) you want to connect to and authorize with the platform using a service account, so the tool can fetch the campaign performance details from the respective API.

2. You set up a schedule or interval at which to get new data from your campaigns.

3. You select the level of granularity you want (campaigns, ad groups, or specific ads) and the respective tables you want to fetch.

4. You select a destination, that is, the database, where you want to store the data coming in.

5. You click on the **Start** button and the tool will start collecting data from the source and load it into the destination on your desired schedule.

6. If you are lucky, the tool will also handle any errors along the way, have some sort of health or quality indication of the pipeline, and even do some light transformations.

Ideally, this works for you, and you have just outsourced your job to a tool that can do it better and is more reliable, so you can sit back and enjoy your coffee. However, in practice, there may be many reasons why this does not fit your use case. For example, you might want the last 10 years of sales data from an old SQL Server database, and in those 10 years, three other companies have been acquired and their sales data migrated into the SQL Server database with varying schemas.

Take a look at *Figure 3.1*, which depicts a data ingestion pipeline:

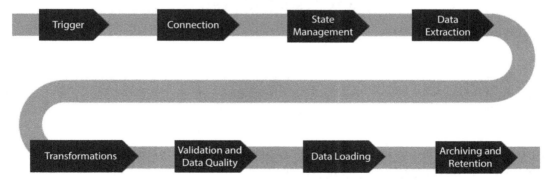

Figure 3.1 – A data ingestion pipeline

To build a robust data ingestion pipeline, we define eight steps and related questions you will need to answer. These eight steps and related questions are listed as follows:

1. **Trigger**: How and when does the pipeline start?

2. **Connection**: What are the requirements for connecting the source system or database to the target or destination?

3. **State management**: How do you keep track of what has and has not changed since your last ingestion? How do you handle changes to the data over time?

4. **Data extraction**: What is the actual process of extracting data? Do you query a database, access an API, or just read files?

5. **Transformations**: Is there any filtering, cleaning, reshaping, deduplication, or similar process that you need to apply to be able to move your data from the source to the destination?

6. **Validation and data quality**: How sure do you want to be that the data is correct? What kind of guarantees do you want to enforce and what kind of anomalies are you willing to accept?

7. **Loading**: Where do you store the data that you captured? How do you handle connecting and adjusting to your destination system?

8. **Archiving and retention**: How long should you store or keep the data you just captured? How do you handle expired data?

In addition to these steps, there are three big overarching topics that are relevant to the entire pipeline:

- **Scalability and resilience**: As the data grows over time, are you still able to handle the additional load? What is the fault tolerance of the entire pipeline and how often does it retry before giving up?

- **Monitoring, logging, and alerting**: How do you make sure you are aware and able to debug when there is an issue anywhere in the ingestion process?

- **Governance**: What kind of agreements do you have with both the source data provider as well as the destination owner? Are there any legal requirements you need to consider when handling this data?

Next, we will look at the details of these steps and key topics.

Trigger

The first step in any pipeline is to decide when your pipeline should run, or rather make sure that the pipeline runs based on the time or event that you have decided on. Even though this might seem simple, there are many distinct types of **triggers**. Very often, a schedule is the simplest way of triggering a pipeline. It can be as simple as running a job every day at midnight, or every hour of the day. Usually, these types of schedules are expressed and implemented as so-called **cron jobs**, named after the `cron` command line utility found in Unix systems. A `cron` expression allows you to specify a schedule with syntax in the form of minute, hour, day (of the month), month, and day of the week.

This allows you to write a daily midnight job as 0 0 * * *, meaning the job runs on minute 0 of hour 0 on every day of the month, in every month of the year, from Sunday to Saturday. Similarly, but adding in some more complexity, we can also write a job that runs every 13th minute of every third hour during business hours from Monday to Friday: 13 9-17/3 * * 1-5.

For all its simplicity, the cron job can get overly complex when you have many different jobs running at the same or similar times, especially when these jobs have dependencies on each other and the duration of the job might vary depending on the underlying data it is processing. There are many times when staggering cron jobs works fine, but sometimes you will need to handle the dependencies between two systems and only start the next job when the first one has finished. A good, open-source, and very often-used scheduling tool that can handle this type of dependency is **Apache Airflow**. It allows you to trigger jobs on a schedule or when another job has finished, as well as handle additional complexity such as dynamically generating jobs from lists of data including, for example, a list of tables in a database. However, what a tool such as Airflow does differently from a simple schedule is run jobs based on events.

An **event trigger** is a simple message that starts a job. It can be a message that a previous job has finished, but there are many other relevant messages out there that can be used as triggers. Some commonly used events are the following:

- A new file that has been added to a folder
- A new table that has been added to a database
- An HTTP request to an endpoint (webhook)
- Specific log or audit events, such as access or permissions for users or service accounts
- Billing or consumption thresholds that have been reached
- A queue with more than a specified number of items in it
- A change to a branch from your version control system

These types of events are often push-based, meaning that there will be a push from another system signaling a change in that system. However, not all systems have these capabilities. If a system does not have this capability, you can also implement a pull functionality. This is basically a sensor in your scheduling tool that checks whether an event such as the adding of rows to a table has occurred and acts as a trigger if the event took place.

If all of this sounds still too complex for your job, you can of course always run your pipeline manually. This is generally a good practice to do as during development, or after certain failures or unforeseen circumstances, you might be asked to run or re-run a pipeline job manually for a specific date or time.

Connection

In its simplest form, a **connection for a data ingestion pipeline** is nothing more than retrieving a publicly available file or URL. In some cases, that might be enough – for example, when you are copying the latest currency exchange rates from the **European Central Bank (ECB)**. But unless you are copying publicly available data, transferring data from one system to another usually means you will need to authenticate in some way or another. This allows the source system to check the permissions and access level of the retrieving party.

Authentication is often the first hurdle in connecting to any source system and a common failure point of any pipeline. It could be that, for example, permissions were wrongfully revoked, a personal user account was used and that user left the company, or even an additional step such as **multi-factor authentication (MFA)** was added to the source system. With hacks and security failures being near-daily news, it is understandable that owners of source systems are careful with permissions and access to those source systems, but unfortunately, that does mean more complexity for our pipeline.

Some of the point-and-click managed ingestion tools make it easy to authenticate a user to, let's say, a Meta, X (previously Twitter), or Google Business account, but if you want to prevent the preceding scenario where a user leaves the company and your pipeline fails, it is usually a better practice to use a service account. This is usually an account similar to a normal user account but intended solely for service-to-service communication without the intervention (and potential security and business risks) of an individual user.

Of course, even a service account still requires some sort of credential to authenticate, and that credential will have to be stored in a certain place. That place will most certainly *not* be your source code, because a key that gives access to a treasure trove of data is always a valuable item that should be treated with care. Preferably, this credential is then stored either in a credential manager from your favorite cloud provider or otherwise in environment variables that are specific to the server or environment that is retrieving the data from the source system.

With the credentials accessible to your code through a credential manager or environment variable, you should now be able to connect to the source system. Some systems provide higher-level libraries for languages such as Python, C, or Java to make connecting a bit more convenient, but under the hood, there are usually remarkably similar patterns across source systems. We will not go into the details of distinct types of connections between systems, but here are a few common patterns:

- HTTP GET or POST requests with the authentication token in the header that allow you to retrieve a response with a data object based on the filters or queries you provided in the request.

- An **ODBC** connection allows for a standardized connection specifically for databases, which is why ODBC stands for **Open Database Connectivity**. With ODBC, you can query almost any database in an equivalent way to, for example, execute a SQL query.

- A **gRPC** connection allows you to execute functions (**remote procedure calls**) on the source system and return their results. gRPC is a structured, high-performance, open-source communication protocol designed by Google to pack up data very efficiently using something called **Protocol Buffers**. It works well to connect distributed or smaller independent services together.

State management

Once a connection has been made to the source system, the next step is **state management**. Managing state means keeping track of what is and what is not. State is literally the status or data of operating our pipeline. Most of the functions you use or program yourself will be stateless; they do not require the presence of globally available data but can compute an output based purely on an input. However, a program itself must often be stateful. In the case of our on-premise database, we do not want to start over from zero every time, but we want to be able to continue where we left off whenever there is an error or a timeout. That requirement will be even more important when we make our program distributed – for example, when we have multiple machines querying different tables of the database at the same time. These machines need information in some way to be able to operate independently and make sure they are not doing the same task at the same time.

State management does not have to be complex, although it can and must be in some situations. Most of the time, a plain text file or even a global variable in your program is enough, and if you need a little bit more of a lightweight (open-source) database, SQLite or DuckDB can usually do the trick. Implementing some kind of state management in your program allows you to really improve your data ingestion pipeline in terms of both performance as well as data quality. Some common examples of keeping state are as follows:

- Keeping track of the status of a data extraction. This allows you to understand which extractions can be started and which have already completed.

- Keeping track of extractions that have timed out or have errors so that you can retry them or even send an alert.

- Keeping track of batches of data that are being extracted so that you can remove or adjust the entire batch whenever you find an error in a single item in the batch.

- Keeping track of the start and end dates and times so that you can understand how long a certain extraction is taking or how the extraction duration is increasing or decreasing over time.

- Keeping track of what has been added to or removed from the source system so that you can monitor changes in the source system over time. This could be for auditing purposes or for keeping a history of a source system over which you have no or little control.

Data extraction

With all the complexity of triggering your pipeline, authenticating the connection, and managing state, you might almost forget the most important part: **extracting data**. This is both the simplest and hardest part. It is simple because it is often nothing more than retrieving a set of rows or a data object, but it is complex because retrieving the correct data can require a deep understanding of the source system.

If you remember that the purpose of a source system is often wildly different than that of the analytical function that a data ingestion pipeline is trying to fulfill, you can start to see that using source data for analyses will always to some extent require an understanding of the source system. If that is too abstract, think of a situation where a marketing manager wants the results of a specific Christmas advertising campaign: What did it cost? How many impressions and how many clicks did we get? It seems easy enough, but now let us imagine that the source system keeps track of cost at the account level, and clicks and impressions are tracked at the individual ad level; the campaign name has changed over time and this change has been stored in the campaign table. Suddenly, for one simple question, you must extract tables with account details, budget details, spend details, campaign history, ad history, campaign results, and ad results.

This is why a simple business question can turn into a complex pipeline, and that pipeline gets more complex when you do not understand the intricacies of the source system. However, when you finally do understand the data you need to gather – and you have of course documented this properly for your successor – you will find that there are many ways of extracting the data. We will skip over the more exotic types of data extraction, but more than 90% of all data ingestion pipelines extract data in batches or even micro batches where data is processed, for example, processed in batches every minute, to get near real-time insights without the complexity of a real-time pipeline. This is especially true when the analysis of that data usually does not happen in under 15 minutes, and for most organizations, it does not even happen daily. In essence, that means that most of your data extraction will be done by calling an API, reading a file, or querying a database. The result of that will then usually be stored either in memory or as a file. For example, a data object can easily be stored as a JSON file and an array of (rows of) data could be stored as a Parquet file.

Extracting data from a file or database in itself is easy, but of course, everything becomes more complex when working with a distributed system. Sometimes, multiple machines need to extract data at the same time – for example, because a data object is too big for one machine. However, if they also write to the same file or folder, you want to prevent write clashes. At the same time, you also do not want to create bottlenecks in your distributed system by preventing those simultaneous writes. In other words, the required concurrency of distributed systems and parallel processing brings a whole new set of problems to your ingestion process. Luckily, with modern-day machines and readily available cloud computing instances going up to 24 terabytes of memory and over 400 processor cores, there is little that a single machine cannot handle. So, if you have the choice, keep your extraction simple – there is plenty of complexity to go around for everyone already.

Transformations

Over the last few years, there has been a big discussion about the order of steps in a data ingestion pipeline. Should it be ETL or **extract, load, transform (ELT)**? As you can see, the T step is the contentious part. So, what is the right order? As any good consultant will tell you, the answer is, "It *depends*." Another way of thinking about this is that it is not one or the other, but both at the same time: **ETLT**. The question you should ask yourself, though, is what type of transformation you want to do and in which step.

Historically, the goal of an ETL process or data ingestion pipeline was not just to get the data into a data warehouse, but also to minimize the load on the data warehouse by doing some transformations in the process itself. This would make it easier to handle "big data" in a normal data warehouse. However, with the onset of columnar distributed databases and data lakes such as BigQuery, Snowflake, Databricks, and Redshift, the need for this type of preprocessing became less prevalent while the need to access raw data became more prevalent. As we discussed in the previous chapters, this correlates with the rise of the analytics engineer, as some of the transformational parts of a data ingestion pipeline that were traditionally in the hands of data engineers shifted to the more technical analysts – that is, analytics engineers.

That is not to say there is no longer a need for **transformations** within the data ingestion pipeline, though. There are a few common use cases where in-flight transformations make a lot of sense. However, the days of big transformations and data modeling inside the ingestion pipeline for cost or storage reasons have indeed passed. We will go through some of the most common transformations for data ingestion pipelines, but in general, you should be aware that the mantra is always "*It depends*." If some transformation makes sense for your specific use case or organization, you do not have to listen to an ELT absolutist.

Here are some transformations your data would frequently need:

- **Filtering**: Even though you could store all data in your data lake, it does not mean you have to. Data still does add up and performance can decrease when reading massive amounts of files. If you know there is data that you will never need – for example, because it is from a different department or business unit, or it is from a time period that does not make sense to analyze – it makes a lot of sense to filter out this data.

- **Cleaning**: You will likely not want to do too much cleaning, or at least not in a way where any business logic is applied, but in general, it does make sense to clean up fields or data that can cause confusion or breakage later. This could be as simple as making sure that a field named `date` is not actually a timestamp, or that a string is not escaped multiple times. Basically, it is anything to make sure that the data and data types match the expectations of the receiver.

- **Joining**: Whenever a source system is heavily normalized – that is, when everything is split up into many different tables for dimensions and facts – it might make sense to join these tables in your ingestion pipeline. This could be denormalization for performance reasons, or just for the convenience of having one table downstream that is a single source of truth.

- **Enriching**: You can argue that all kinds of joins between different systems should be done as late as possible so that information is always up to date, but for some information, you just know that it is never going to change. Some enrichments or lookups can save you a lot of time downstream while simultaneously increasing performance. Just think of enhancements such as looking up a geolocation based on an IP address, adding in the weather for the day and location, or splitting up a string based on a separator.

- **Reshape**: Sometimes, data is not in the shape that you would want it to be. This is especially the case when you are trying to go from a data object to a set of rows. For example, it usually does not make sense to have a table with just one column that then contains a (JSON) data object. Instead, you would usually want to flatten this object's keys into separate columns in your table. Other times, you may just want to make sure that you get the data from a specific set of keys in the data object and populate the values in the corresponding columns.

- **Deduplication**: Making sure there are no duplicates in your data, either through quirks in the source system or because of processing steps in the ingestion pipeline, can save a lot of headaches later. Commonly, this is done either by using a unique identifier for a row, file, or object, or by calculating a hash to determine whether two items are in fact the same item. Sometimes, this hash is also stored with the item to allow deduplication later or to prevent processing something again that already exists.

Validation and data quality

We have already discussed the importance of understanding the source system as well as performing cleaning and deduplication on incoming data. These are important steps to eventually give a certain guarantee on the quality of the provided data in the data warehouse, but even more important is to make sure the data conforms to a specific schema. A **schema** is nothing more than a definition of which field should contain which type of data (string, number, date, and other types). Simple, however, does not mean it cannot get complex very quickly when you have nested fields of objects or arrays of objects. Nonetheless, a schema can help you both in validating the data coming in as well as in documenting the data going out, so an analyst knows what to expect in the data warehouse.

Data quality is more than just checking incoming values against a schema, though. If you care about data quality for your pipeline, one of the first steps you can add, before going all in on a data observability tool, is checking for some common issues or values that you are not expecting. This is usually as simple as checking either the uniqueness of a row or object – which should be easy with the unique identifier or hash key that we generated in the previous step – or the existence of null values where they are not expected. If you want to go one step further, you can start with some simple anomaly detection or profiling of your data. For example, what was the average number of rows you imported over the last few days, and what was the variance? Now you can ask yourself: *"How much deviation from this average am I willing to allow before I send out an alert?"*

Loading

With a clean and validated dataset, we can finally proceed to load the data into our data warehouse. There are many ways to do this, but one important thing to note is that a modern-day data warehouse doesn't need everything to be stored in the actual warehouse. We mentioned before that often, data objects are already stored as files in an intermediate step. These files can be loaded into the data warehouse as most of the data warehouse solutions will allow you to easily import Parquet, JSON, Avro, or CSV files for example, but you can also decide to go for what is often called a data lake. Essentially, a data lake is nothing more than a semi-structured collection of files in some sort of cloud storage such as **Amazon Web Services (AWS)** S3, Google Cloud Storage, or Cloudflare R2.

Most data warehouses can access a data lake, or rather a collection of files, through something called an external table. An external table is a way of storing the actual data in its original location and only keeping a catalog with metadata in the actual data warehouse. If you think about it, it is not hugely different from an actual data warehouse. You could think of a table in your data warehouse as if it were based on files in folders. If you apply partitioning to a column – for example, a column with dates – each date will be a separate folder. If you also apply clustering – for example, on country – there could be another set of subfolders for different countries. Depending on the size of your table, you could split the data in the folder into one or more files that can then be processed independently when you execute a query. For example, looking up the sum of a metric, let's say sales, for a specific country in a specific date range means you can now just grab all the files from the relevant folders, calculate the sum per file independently, and then add the results together to get the final sum of sales.

Archiving and retention

It is easy to think that when the data is loaded into the data warehouse, your job is done. However, the truth is that you will need to take care of your data after it has been loaded. You will need to consider whether you want your data to persist for an infinite amount of time or whether you want to set the **retention** to a certain threshold. Especially when it comes to user or medical data, there may be limits to how long data is allowed to be stored. On top of that, it could be the case that a user will file a request for their data to be deleted. You will need a strategy to handle that deletion request as well. Finally, you will have to consider how "active" you want your data to be. Some data is only relevant as a backup, and even though storage has become cheaper and cheaper, as the amount of data grows, it might still be worth it to move archives and backups to a cheaper, so-called *cold* storage solution.

Let us now talk about how to ensure quality and scale your data ingestion pipelines.

Managing the quality and scalability of data ingestion pipelines – the three key topics

Apart from going through the steps of setting up a data ingestion pipeline, there are also three important topics that are relevant to each step of the entire pipeline.

Scalability and resilience

As the load on your pipeline increases over time, there is more and more pressure on your pipeline to keep up in terms of performance. Even though you might start with a sequential, single-thread program as is common, for example, when writing in Python, over time, you might want to consider turning parts of your pipeline into loosely coupled functions that can scale independently. For example, the extraction might happen on a single machine that you might have to increase in size over time, while the transformations and loading scales dynamically with serverless functions depending on the load.

In any case, you will have to implement some sort of error or exception handling to be able to handle common exceptions such as timeouts, expired credentials for authentication, scheduled maintenance, or hitting rate limits. Your program should have some form of triaging for these types of exceptions to determine which ones it can handle and for which ones it should fail or alert. If it is able to handle the exception, you might want to retry the extraction process. However, you also don't want your program to get stuck in an infinite loop of retries. Often, this is mitigated by specifying a maximum amount of retries. To also make sure you do not waste all your *retries* immediately on a service that is just down for a few minutes, there is often a process called **exponential backoffs**. This means that the time between retries scales exponentially – for example, by going from 1 minute to 4 minutes to 16 minutes.

Monitoring, logging, and alerting

Despite the fact that you have checked everything twice, errors will still happen. Setting an alert will help you get notified about any issues with your pipeline in the channel of your choice. However, there is a delicate balance between making sure you do not get alert fatigue due to an overload of false positives and making sure you do not miss an alert when there is an actual issue.

Monitoring allows you to understand the health of parts of your pipeline or multiple pipelines. Where alerting is pushing information, monitoring is pulling information. Sometimes, especially when you have multiple pipelines, it can be worth monitoring those pipelines on different metrics such as the number of rows ingested or the last ingestion time.

Finally, **logging** will allow you to debug your pipeline when something goes wrong and identify the root cause.

Governance

A cornerstone of any pipeline is building trust. You can have as many alerts or monitors as you like to set up, but if you alert on the wrong issues or monitor irrelevant metrics, the trust in your data will eventually erode. Governance starts with setting the right expectations among stakeholders to build and keep that trust. You can formalize that trust with a **service level agreement** (**SLA**) that determines, among other things, the required quality, interval, and uptime of your data pipeline, as well as what happens when these standards are not met. More recently, data contracts have become popular as they serve a similar purpose but are more oriented toward data consumers instead of services.

While contracts and agreements are often internal to an organization, there are also external factors such as privacy, security, and legislation that need to be taken into account when thinking about data governance. The requirements may vary for your organization, country, or type of data, but common sense goes a long way here. So, start with simple measures such as limiting access and permissions to your data and pipeline infrastructure, as well as making sure proper authorization is in place for every part of your pipeline so only specific roles or users can read, write, or delete data. This will help you prevent data breaches and compliance issues.

Let's see a data ingestion pipeline in practice.

Working with data ingestion – an example pipeline

Let's look at our data ingestion steps in practice. Assume that we do analytics for a factory specializing in Dutch delicacies: Stroopwafels. The CEO of this patisserie paradise has requested better insights into the effectiveness of providing Stroopwafel samples to potential customers. To answer their questions, we need to do the following:

1. Understand which potential customers (leads) have received samples. This data is available in a CRM tool where data from offline events and online requests is captured.

2. Understand whether these potential customers have purchased more than once. This data is only available in our highly secure, on-premise **enterprise resource planning** (ERP) tool.

We will go through the steps to get data from both systems.

Trigger

We have discussed with the CEO that daily updates are enough for the insights. We already have a scheduling tool such as Airflow available and will use that to trigger our data ingestion functions at midnight.

Connection

The connection for our CRM tool is simple. The tool itself provides daily exports as Parquet files to a storage bucket in our cloud provider. We make sure that the specific storage bucket we use only serves this tool to avoid any cross-contamination in terms of security, and for authentication, the tool provides a service account to which we can give access.

For our ERP system, things are a bit more complex. We need to create a separate user in the system that only has view permissions, and the serverless function that we use first needs to connect to the on-premise server via a VPN as it cannot be reached from the outside. We store the credential for the user we created in the credential manager of our cloud provider. That way, we never have to reference a credential in our code.

State management

With our CRM tool, there is not much we have to do in terms of state management. The tool itself will do a full export every day. For our ERP system, we need to be more careful, however. Since the system is on-premises, resources are limited and we cannot just export everything. Our function will write to a manifest if the extraction for a specific date was successful. We can then use this manifest to retrieve the latest date, and in our ERP system, only select data from after that date. This way, we will limit the amount of data the system has to process.

Data extraction

As we've already established, our CRM tool will provide us with Parquet files. We can then write a SQL statement in our data warehouse to use this storage bucket as a so-called external table. We refresh this table daily, which allows us to query the Parquet files directly with SQL. This way, we can easily model the data and apply our business transformations while keeping the source data intact.

For our ERP system, the extraction is a little bit harder.

First, we set up what is called **peering** to connect the on-premise VPN to our private cloud environment. This allows us to connect cloud providers such as AWS, Azure, or GCP to the on-premise server. We can then use a Python library such as `pyodbc` to connect to the Microsoft SQL Server that the ERP system uses. We use a separate storage bucket for our manifest file to keep track of the last successful extractions and retrieve that to determine the start date in our SQL query.

Besides the manifest file, we keep another file, this time in our version-controlled code. This file contains all the databases, tables, and columns that we want to extract as YAML code. This way, we will not have any trouble with newly added or changed columns that we do not need, while still being able to extract what we want in a controlled manner, tracking changes over time. As an added benefit, we can use this to create tables to load our data into our data warehouse as well as validate the data we ingest.

Validation and data quality

For our CRM tool, we have the benefit of Parquet files having an embedded schema. That means we do not have to check individual values; however, we do need to check whether the schema of the latest Parquet file matches the schema of earlier Parquet files. Since this source is very reliable, we have decided to only monitor for errors when the files are processed in our data warehouse.

For our ERP tool, we can use the defined YAML schema and load it into a widely used Python library called Pydantic to validate our data and apply necessary transformations.

Transformations

Since our CRM tool is easy to load into our data warehouse, we will apply all transformations there. For our ERP system, the requirement is to not make any sensitive customer data available in our analytics system. Therefore, we will use the Pydantic implementation to apply a hashing function to any fields marked as *sensitive* in our YAML schema file.

Loading

Loading data is easy for our CRM tool. By using the concept of external tables, our data warehouse can connect to a storage bucket and read Parquet files directly. This way, we do not need to explicitly load data into our data warehouse. For our ERP system, it is a little bit harder. First of all, we need to use our schema file to make sure that tables and columns already exist in our data warehouse. If they do not, we'll have to create them. Then, we need to decide whether we want to load rows one by one, in a batch, or through a file. Since this is not transactional data such as a sales transaction and our columnar data warehouse is not made for performance on transactions, it makes sense to use batch loading. Since we also want to minimize the load on our ERP system, we will first store our extracted rows as Parquet files in a storage bucket. In this case, if anything happens during the loading phase, we do not have to go back to our ERP system but can leverage the stored Parquet files.

Archiving and retention

For both our CRM system and our ERP system, we care mostly about the analysis and insights we can get from the data, not the actual data itself, with all the potentially sensitive information such as email addresses or invoices. Therefore, we decide to let our raw data expire after 30 days. This way, we can still reuse the raw data whenever there is an error during the loading, but we do not carry as much sensitive information and can also guarantee that, for example, any data deletion request from a customer is completed within 30 days.

Summary

In this chapter, we looked at why we need to ingest data in the first place and the different steps needed to create a data ingestion pipeline that is robust and reliable. We learned that there are eight essential steps to ingesting data, which can be covered both by off-the-shelf ETL tools as well as by custom scripts, depending on the specific needs of your data ingestion step. We also learned that to guarantee the long-term quality of your data ingestion pipeline, you need to consider the three key topics of scalability and resilience, monitoring, logging, and alerting, and finally, governance.

With this knowledge, you should be able to capture the data you need from a source system. In the next chapter, we will look at how to load and use this data in your data warehouse and how to pick one for your needs.

4

Data Warehousing

Data warehouses are essential for **business intelligence** (**BI**) and data-informed decisions. Organizations can effectively use vast amounts of information by consolidating and combining multiple data sources. Dating back to the 1980s, warehouse technology and setups have advanced considerably with the rise of big data and cloud computing.

In this chapter, we will delve into data warehouses and industry trends. We will cover the following topics:

- Uncovering the evolution of data warehousing
- Moving to the cloud
- The building blocks of a cloud data warehouse
- Knowing the market leaders in cloud data warehousing

Uncovering the evolution of data warehousing

Data comes in many forms, from text and numbers to images and sound clips. Data is stored across diverse platforms, from basic spreadsheets to data warehouses. For example, a spreadsheet that tracks your monthly expenses is a simple form of a database. Yet, spreadsheets cannot protect sensitive data, such as a company's financials or customer information. They are not secure enough, don't offer an easy way to retrieve data, and can't handle large volumes of information (Excel has a limitation of 1 million records). Database systems are designed to tackle these issues. They offer a way to organize, safeguard, and efficiently manage data while supporting various applications. We'll focus on two of them.

Transactional databases are fine-tuned to handle numerous transaction updates, new entries, and removals while maintaining data integrity and quickly processing each record. They are the go-to for everyday business tasks, from processing orders and managing inventory to handling finances, where consistent and reliable data is essential. Designed for high availability, they deliver precise, up-to-the-minute data, which is perfect for situations that need instant responses, such as online shopping and checkout systems.

As an organization's data pool expands, so does the appetite for more in-depth insights. To get these, there's a need to connect various business systems, each supporting its own business function. Consider different systems such as CRM, ERP suites, financial tracking tools, and supply chain management software. Each collects data for its own area, but the true insight comes from cross-analyzing it together. A data warehouse pulls data from these varied systems, making broad analysis and insight discovery possible across the business.

Data warehouses are specialized databases that are set up for analyzing data. Rather than focusing on a single application or process, they gather data from many places within an organization to create a unified, centralized place for all that information.

Now, you might be wondering, why not just pile all that data into a regular transactional database and analyze it there? Do we need a separate data warehouse? Usually, yes. Having just a transactional database is a common starting point for some companies, but as the organization and its data expand, this approach often brings trouble.

The problem with transactional databases

Popular transactional database systems such as Microsoft's SQL Server, Oracle's Database, and PostgreSQL are optimized for **online transaction processing (OLTP)**. They can handle a vast array of transactions quickly and reliably. These platforms are engineered to process a high volume of simple read-and-write operations efficiently, ensuring data integrity and swift transaction completion for daily business functions.

However, their performance can take a hit when they're asked to do heavy-duty analytical work. For example, if an analyst runs a complex query on an operational database at an e-commerce site to analyze sales data, it could slow down primary operations, such as processing current customer orders. This might cause transaction delays or affect the user experience negatively, leading to customer dissatisfaction and lost sales.

The root of this inefficiency is the row-based storage used by these databases, which is great for transactional data but not mass data analysis. In comparison, data warehouses use columnar storage, which is more efficient for analysis. This is because it's similar to selecting only the relevant columns in a spreadsheet, bypassing the unnecessary data in other columns.

This distinction is critical for businesses that depend on **real-time transaction processing**. While transactional databases never miss a beat in recording every detail of a transaction, their performance can suffer when burdened with analytical queries. Data warehouses, on the other hand, are built for **online analytical processing (OLAP)**. They handle the demands of data analysis seamlessly, ensuring that the transactional databases continue to run smoothly and the customer's experience remains uninterrupted.

Data warehouses were designed from the ground for analytical workloads, using OLAP instead of OLTP. They are meant to handle the unpredictability of ad hoc queries from analysts. While a company might use a transactional database for its analytical workloads without issues, these databases were not designed for analysis. A data warehouse will naturally have more features to support analysts and their workloads. These features include built-in tooling for cleaning and transforming data, user-friendly interfaces for analysis, and the ability to share data more easily with BI tools.

To better understand the evolution of data warehouses, let's trace their history, from their modest inception to their impressive current capabilities.

The history of data warehouses

The exponential data growth of the last few decades has brought new requirements for storage systems. Cloud providers offer a wide range of products and functionality to store large amounts of information in the most scalable, cost-effective, and secure way. With such advanced technology, it is hard to imagine that a couple of decades ago, a floppy disk could only store 80 KB of data.

The 1920s – 1970s – the early days of data storage

"Do not fold, spindle, or mutilate." These were the instructions for handling a punch card – a piece of stiff paper with holes representing digital information. Dating back to the late eighteenth century, initially as a form to give instructions to textile machinery, it was not until 1928, when IBM introduced its version of the card, that it became widely used as a data input and storage medium.

With 12 rows and 80 columns, the *IBM* card (`https://www.ibm.com/ibm/history/ibm100/us/en/icons/punchcard/`), as it was widely known, turned out to be one of the most important innovations from the company at the time. The product was the most used medium for storing and sorting data for over 40 years.

In the 1960s, magnetic tapes slowly emerged as a more advanced alternative to punch cards. Data was encoded on the tape as a series of magnetic particles arranged in patterns. As a result, more data could be stored and retrieved faster.

Additionally, the 1970s and 1980s brought another revolution in this field: the democratization of disk storage. IBM's introduction of the floppy disk in 1971 was a significant breakthrough. A single 20 cm floppy disk could store the same data as 3,000 punch cards (80 KB). These devices enabled people to share digital information, such as computer programs and documents, as never before.

Other innovations followed in the 1980s and 1990s, such as CDs and hard disks. Still, the most significant breakthrough for what we know today as data warehouses was the development of **relational databases**, as will be discussed in the following subsection.

The 1980s – relational and object-oriented databases

The first computerized databases date back to the 1960s. They had a pointer navigational system that required the user to have extensive knowledge about the overall structure of the information stored. Two database models were popular during this time: the CODASYL, or network model; and the hierarchical model, called IMS.

In 1970, an IBM San Jose Lab researcher developed an alternative to this limitation. In the paper *A Relational Model of Data for Large Shared Data Banks (Codd, E. F. (1970)* – https://dl.acm.org/doi/abs/10.1145/362384.362685), Edgar F. Codd introduced the foundation for **relational database management systems** (**RDBMSs**). His idea was to enable a user to access information in a database without knowing how the information was structured. This was possible due to the level of data independence, or relationships, between data points. Using a primary or foreign key made it possible to join different tables to retrieve aggregated information.

However, it was in the 1980s that relational databases became widely used. With the introduction of **Database 2** (**DB2**, a relational database by IBM) in 1983 and with SQL becoming the industry-standard language for working with it, many businesses decided to adopt this innovation. DB2 was one of IBM's most successful products. Still, companies faced difficulties when dealing with this level of complexity, which led to another critical innovation: **parallel processing**.

The 1990s – parallel processing

With the democratization of the internet, the amount of data that was processed grew significantly compared to the previous decade. As a consequence, the data warehouse architecture that was developed until this point became insufficient. Monolithic systems with an individual server started to diminish in performance and increase in costs. This limitation triggered the emergence of parallel processing.

In parallel processing, a large workload can be divided into smaller parts and processed in parallel across multiple servers. This approach significantly improves the speed and efficiency of data processing and analysis, enabling large amounts of data to be processed more quickly and accurately.

A notable milestone in this era was Teradata's achievement in 1992. They built the first data warehouse system exceeding one terabyte for Walmart. This system utilized the **massive parallel processing** (**MPP**) model, a testament to the power and scalability of parallel processing in managing extensive datasets in a commercial environment. Teradata's success with Walmart underscored the growing importance and potential of MPP architectures in data warehousing.

The 2000s – the rise of NoSQL and cloud computing

In the 2000s, data storage costs decreased significantly. As a result, new web applications emerged, such as social media platforms, that required more significant amounts of information to be stored and queried. Moreover, data came in all forms, including structured, semi-structured, and unstructured, making it unfeasible to rely solely on the rigid schema of relational databases.

NoSQL, or **not only SQL**, allowed for better flexibility. NoSQL databases are non-relational, meaning there is no need to predefine schemas and relationships like in RDBMSs. With that, storing unstructured and semi-structured data in distinct formats such as XML and JSON is possible. NoSQL systems also bring parallel processing capabilities, improving speed and scalability. Despite the speed, scalability, and processing improvements compared to RDBMS, NoSQL systems performed poorly when compared to RDBMS when using standard SQL. Therefore, the choice for one or another depended on the use case a company needed.

The 2000s also saw pivotal innovations in the NoSQL space with the advent of technologies such as HBase, Hadoop, and Bigtable. Hadoop, an open-source framework, allowed for distributed storage and processing of big data across clusters of computers. HBase, a part of the Hadoop ecosystem, provided a scalable and flexible database solution, while Google's Bigtable influenced many NoSQL technologies with its wide-column store design. These technologies were crucial in managing large-scale, diverse datasets that traditional databases could not handle effectively.

The mid-2000s marked a significant turning point for the industry with the advent of **cloud computing**. Amazon, a leading name in e-commerce, seized the opportunity to revolutionize data handling and launched some of the most famous components of **Amazon Web Services (AWS)** in 2006.

AWS, the *first public cloud*, provided fully managed computing infrastructure accessible to anyone with a credit card. In contrast to the traditional on-premises model, customers could create and access servers within minutes through a browser. AWS fully managed the underlying hardware in their data centers.

The 2010s – the birth of cloud data warehouses

The data warehousing landscape underwent a revolution in 2012 with the launch of *Amazon Redshift*, introducing the first **cloud-native data warehouse** solution. Redshift, addressing the need for affordable and scalable data services, allowed organizations to pay only for the resources they used. Setup times were reduced from months to hours, simplifying SQL query execution.

That same year, Google entered the arena with BigQuery, a **serverless data warehouse** that automatically managed resource allocation, contrasting with Redshift's cluster-based approach. BigQuery's pricing was based on data processed, offering flexibility but potentially higher costs depending on usage.

The subsequent influx of new entrants such as Snowflake, Synapse, and Databricks added diverse capabilities to the market. Snowflake's architecture, launched in 2014, enabled separate scaling of storage and compute resources and supported semi-structured data, providing more flexibility. Microsoft's Synapse Analytics, debuting in 2015, combined big data and data warehousing, integrating seamlessly with other Azure services.

Databricks, founded by Apache Spark's creators, initially offered a unified platform for data processing and machine learning. It pivoted in 2019 with Delta Lake pioneering the lakehouse architecture, which blends data lake storage with database functionalities:

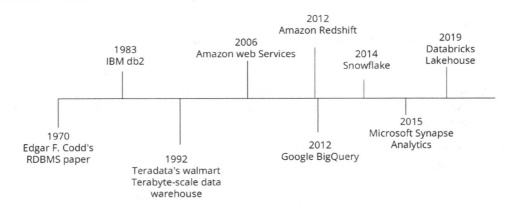

Figure 4.1 – Data warehousing history timeline

Figure 4.1 depicts the evolution of data warehouses. The post-2012 era saw a rapid evolution in cloud data warehousing, driven by new players offering unique innovations that continue to shape this dynamic field. Looking ahead, the trend is expected to lean toward even more automated, intelligent, and flexible data platforms that seamlessly integrate with a wide array of data sources and tools.

We will dive deeper into the cloud data warehouses in the following sections.

Moving to the cloud

In the last decade, the adoption of the cloud by vendors and businesses alike has created a new market in data warehousing. Cloud vendors shook the data warehousing status quo due to their massive infrastructure and market advantage. It looks like the **cloud data warehouse (CDWH)** is here to stay.

This section aims to enhance your understanding of CDWHs. By the end of this discussion, you should understand why companies choose CDWHs over on-premises solutions, which components the CDWH consists of, and the different kinds of cloud data warehouse users.

Over the past few years, many organizations with a data warehouse have migrated to the cloud. One of the biggest reasons is cost. Traditionally, a company wanting a data warehouse would need to host it itself. This meant buying and maintaining expensive hardware, as well as paying a vendor for an annual software license. Migrations between data warehouses were difficult and preferably avoided. If the company did not have the skills in-house to maintain the warehouse, it would have to rely on expensive consultants. Annual fees of over $100,000 for data warehousing licenses and maintenance were not uncommon for large corporations.

The **pay-as-you-go model** of many cloud providers carried on to their data warehouse offerings, which radically cut costs. Many organizations saw the chance to migrate to a CDWH that did not require up-front costs for hardware or its maintenance, or any expensive licensing model. Everything, including the software of the data warehouse, was handled by the cloud provider and already included in the cost.

Benefits of cloud versus on-premises data warehouses

When evaluating data storage solutions, it's crucial to understand various features and how they differ between cloud data warehouses and on-premises data warehouses:

- **Scalability**: Scalability determines a data warehouse's ability to adapt to increasing data and user demands. CDWHs shine in this regard, with their virtually unlimited scalability, allowing resource adjustments on the fly. However, this flexibility can lead to complexities in resource management and cost inefficiencies. In contrast, on-premises data warehouses offer stable physical infrastructure scaling but face inherent limitations in physical capacity, demanding substantial investments for expansion.

- **Performance and speed**: Performance and speed are at the heart of efficient data processing. Cloud solutions excel here, leveraging the latest technologies for high performance, though they may face latency issues during extensive data transfers. On-premises solutions offer direct control over performance, but boosting their capabilities often means costly hardware upgrades.

- **Accessibility and collaboration**: In today's distributed work environment, accessibility and collaboration are vital. Cloud-based warehouses provide effortless internet access, fostering team collaboration, albeit reliant on stable internet connectivity. On-premises warehouses, while offering high security, often require additional infrastructure for remote access, adding complexity to IT operations.

- **Security and compliance**: Security and compliance are paramount in protecting sensitive data. Cloud providers bring robust security features and manage compliance, but shared resources can raise concerns. On-premises warehouses allow tailored security measures but demand significant resource allocation for managing these aspects.

- **Innovation and features**: Staying ahead with technology is another crucial factor. Cloud providers continuously introduce cutting-edge features and analytics tools, albeit with a risk of dependency on their technologies. On-premises systems allow custom solutions but lag in adopting new technologies due to manual update processes.

- **Disaster recovery**: Effective disaster recovery strategies are essential for business continuity. Cloud services excel with their comprehensive, multi-region backup solutions but depend on the provider's capabilities. On-premises systems offer physical control over backups but are more vulnerable to localized disasters and require heavy investment in backup infrastructure.

- **Cost predictability**: Cost predictability is crucial for budget management. The cloud's pay-as-you-go model suits variable workloads but can lead to unpredictable costs. On-premises solutions, while demanding high initial and maintenance costs, provide more predictable financial planning due to their fixed infrastructure investments.

Each feature plays a critical role in the decision-making process for choosing the right data warehouse solution. While CDWHs offer significant advantages in scalability, performance, and innovation, they also bring challenges in cost predictability and data sovereignty.

Cloud data warehouse users – no one-size fits all

Data warehouses serve a broad range of users. Let's explore these user groups, their interaction with the CDWH, and their requirements.

Data analysts

Data analysts dive into data to find patterns, make comparisons, and extract meaningful insights that inform business decisions. They take on the following activities:

- Creating dashboards to visualize sales performance
- Running SQL queries to answer business questions
- Developing reports to track marketing campaign effectiveness
- Analyzing customer feedback to identify areas of improvement
- Comparing historical and current data to spot trends

The skill set required for this role has the following requirements:

- Efficient querying capabilities
- Support for various data visualization tools
- Ability to handle large datasets seamlessly

Data analysts seek data warehouses that are capable of rapidly and precisely analyzing large volumes of data. They prioritize robust querying features, which are typically found in most CDWHs. These professionals often prefer a unified interface, remaining within the data warehouse's **user interface** (**UI**) rather than toggling between various BI tools. Recognizing this trend, modern data warehouse providers are increasingly integrating functionalities traditionally reserved for BI tools, such as data visualization, directly into their platforms.

Data engineers

Data engineers build and maintain the data pipelines. They ensure data flows smoothly from the source to the warehouse and is stored in a clean, usable format. They take on the following activities:

- Designing and building data ingestion pipelines
- Ensuring data quality and integrity as it is collected and stored
- Optimizing data storage for efficient retrieval

- Implementing data transformations to ensure consistency
- Managing and monitoring data ingestion and storage systems

The skillset requirements are as follows:

- Robust and flexible data ingestion and storage solutions
- Tools for monitoring and managing data quality
- Capabilities for data transformation and optimization

Data engineers lean on a data warehouse's ability to integrate, manage, and maintain high-quality data efficiently. They will most likely be working with it day in day out, so they want something that offers state-of-the-art features and can scale well.

Analytics engineers

Analytics engineers bridge the gap between data engineering and analysis. They are instrumental in creating common datasets, documenting and testing data processes, and focusing on data quality to ensure its reliability and utility across all user groups. Their day-to-day activities include the following:

- Developing and maintaining accessible and understandable data models for analysis
- Facilitating collaboration between analysts, scientists, and engineers for insightful data usage
- Enhancing data quality through testing and validation of data
- Working together with data engineers to optimize data warehouse performance

The role requires the following skills:

- Support for collaborative development with analysts and data engineers
- Data governance capabilities to enforce policies and ensure data access for the right users
- Integrations with data modeling and ELT tooling

Modern CDWHs are expected to be more than just data storage solutions. Analytics engineers lead the charge in transforming raw data into strategic assets, thus fueling data-driven decision-making and innovation within organizations.

Data scientists

Data scientists use statistical, mathematical, and computational methods to generate insights. They undertake the following activities on a typical workday:

- Develop machine learning models to predict future sales
- Run complex statistical analysis to identify market trends

- Create algorithms to enhance customer recommendations
- Analyze large datasets to derive actionable insights
- Experiment with different modeling techniques to improve prediction accuracy

The job role requires the following:

- Support for advanced analytics and machine learning frameworks
- High-performance computing resources for running complex models
- Scalable storage to handle growing datasets

For data scientists, a data warehouse must provide robust computational power and advanced analytics capabilities to handle complex, large-scale data analysis. CDWHs are beginning to offer an increasing number of machine learning capabilities and integrations, which data scientists will want to follow closely.

Business users

Business users seek insights that help them make informed decisions. They rely on views and reports generated from the data stored in the CDWH. A business user performs the following activities:

- Reviews monthly sales reports to track performance
- Accesses dashboards to get a snapshot of customer satisfaction
- Analyzes market trends reports to plan future strategies
- Compares current performance metrics with past data
- Reviews financial reports to make budgetary decisions

Here are the requirements for this role:

- Intuitive and user-friendly interfaces
- Access to simplified views and easy-to-understand reports
- Reliable data quality to ensure accurate insights

Business users need a data warehouse that offers intuitive access to data, simplifying complex information. It differs per company if the business analysts work directly in the data warehouse or use BI tools as an interface.

Platform administrators

Platform administrators ensure the system runs smoothly, securely, and is up to date. They undertake the following activities in this role:

- Manage user access and permissions
- Monitor system performance and address issues
- Ensure data security and compliance with regulations
- Implement updates and patches to the CDWH software
- Coordinate with other IT teams for system integrations

The requirements for this role are as follows:

- Comprehensive administrative tools for managing users and security
- Monitoring and alerting capabilities to track system health
- Support for integration with other IT systems and platforms

For platform administrators, the data warehouse must be cost-efficient, provide robust security, and integrate with other systems they manage. They will most likely not be hands-on with many of the system's analytical capabilities but want to keep it running smoothly and cheaply.

BI tools/applications

BI tools and applications serve as the bridge between the technical data environment of the CDWH and the end users who need to interact with the data. Prominent BI tools include Tableau for advanced data visualization, Microsoft Power BI for analytics integrated with Microsoft services, and Looker for intricate data modeling. Custom data applications are also potential users of the CDWH. Applications built for specific purposes, such as tracking sales, managing stock, or logistical planning, can extract and leverage data from the data warehouse, providing businesses with the flexibility and specificity needed for unique organizational requirements. The following activities usually take place in the realm of BI tools:

- Developing interactive dashboards for business users
- Creating automated reports for regular performance tracking
- Building data visualizations to illustrate trends and patterns
- Integrating with other systems to pull in additional data
- Providing training and support to end users on how to use the tools

These BI tools require the following:

- Robust APIs for data retrieval and integration.

- Support for a variety of BI tools and applications

- Consistent and reliable documentation that describes the connectivity support

Connectivity and documentation are key factors when hooking up BI tools and applications to the data warehouse. Ideally, a data warehouse provides a well-documented API and plug-and-play connectivity to popular BI tools, which an application developer can set up once they receive the required credentials from IT:

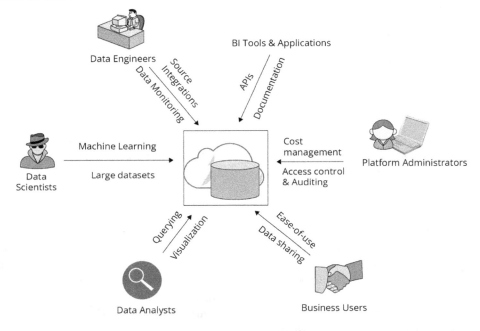

Figure 4.2 – Different cloud data warehouse users

As you can see, the CDWH has different users, all with their expectations. It is essential to involve them in discussing a new data warehouse architecture, especially when moving from an on-premises architecture toward the cloud. Some features might work slightly differently, while others might be missing or replaced by a different workflow altogether. The best bet is to create an inventory of requirements and default workflows from the different users and compare how CDWHs can fulfill them.

The next section will discuss various considerations when picking a cloud data warehouse.

Building blocks of a cloud data warehouse

Fundamentally, cloud data warehouses consist of hardware managed by the cloud provider, operating on proprietary software, and connected to the internet over a network with many complex parts hidden away for the querying analyst. We will not discuss all this in depth. Instead, we will delve into the primary abstractions that are important to understand for a user.

Compute

Compute is the term that's used for the processing power required to perform calculations, handle data operations, and execute queries in a computing environment, such as a CDWH. This involves using **central processing units (CPUs)**, memory, and other computational resources to manage and analyze data efficiently. Some of the key improvements that CDWHs offer in terms of computing are as follows:

- **MPP**: For CDWHs, a huge improvement in computing came through the adoption of distributed computing and, in particular, leveraging MPP. This involves connecting multiple machines, or nodes, together over the network into a cluster spanning many geographical regions. These nodes work collectively, executing database operations like a single machine. This collaborative approach is a significant departure from the traditional model of relying on a single machine that requires substantial hardware upgrades to enhance performance.

- **Fault tolerance**: The advantage of distributed computing in CDWHs extends beyond just adding computational power. It also introduces enhanced fault tolerance and data redundancy, ensuring the system remains operational, even if individual nodes fail. This setup is crucial for businesses that rely on continuous data availability and integrity.

- **Autoscaling resources**: From a practical standpoint, this evolution means businesses can now handle larger and more complex datasets more efficiently, with significant cost savings. The flexibility to scale resources as needed, either manually or through auto-scaling features, allows for efficient use of resources tailored to the current demand. Auto-scaling is a term for dynamically adjusting the number of nodes in the cluster based on the workload, ensuring optimal performance without the unnecessary cost of idle resources.

For data analysts and professionals, this shift translates into a user-friendly experience. Modern CDWHs allow users to select the size and scale of their data warehouse and have options to scale up and down automatically. More advanced users (often, data engineers) will be able to fine-tune the system to meet specific requirements.

Query engine

Although the **query engine** could be considered part of the computing resources of the data warehouse, it is a critical enough component to warrant its own section. It is responsible for interpreting, planning, and executing the SQL queries analysts and applications execute. The engine is pivotal to determining the efficiency and speed with which data can be accessed, analyzed, and turned into actionable insights. Some key features of a query engine are as follows:

- **SQL query processing**: At its core, the query engine processes SQL queries. This involves parsing the query to understand its structure, planning the best execution strategy (such as which indices to use and in what order to join tables), and executing the plan to retrieve or manipulate the data.

- **Optimized for distributed systems**: Modern query engines in CDWHs are optimized for distributed computing environments. They break down complex queries into smaller tasks that can be executed in parallel across multiple nodes in the data warehouse cluster. This parallel processing enables handling large datasets and complex analytical queries more efficiently than traditional single-node databases.

- **Smart caching and indexing**: Advanced query engines employ intelligent caching mechanisms and indexing strategies to speed up query processing. By storing frequently accessed data in faster storage mediums and maintaining efficient indices, query engines can significantly reduce the time it takes to fetch and analyze data.

- **Cost-based query optimization**: Cost-based optimization is a feature where the query engine estimates the resources needed for different query execution plans and chooses the most efficient one. This optimization considers factors such as data distribution, available indices, and the current system load, aiming to minimize the time and computational resources required for executing a query.

- **Support for complex analytics**: The query engine is designed to support various analytical functions, including aggregations, joins, window functions, and machine learning algorithms. This capability lets users perform sophisticated data analysis directly within the data warehouse.

The query engine is a sophisticated component that enhances the capabilities of CDWHs, making it possible to handle complex queries on large datasets efficiently and cost-effectively. Its integration with distributed computing and advanced data processing techniques is key to delivering the speed and flexibility that modern data analytics require.

Storage

In CDWHs, **storage** is a dynamic and crucial aspect that greatly impacts both performance and cost efficiency. Moving away from the simple tabular view akin to a spreadsheet, CDWHs employ sophisticated storage techniques to manage vast and varied data volumes. CDWHs offer a variety of storage options for different kinds of data:

- **Columnar storage**: A significant advancement in storage was the shift from traditional row-oriented to columnar storage. Traditional transactional databases store all the data for a single row together, leading to inefficiencies during analytics queries of only specific columns. In contrast, columnar storage organizes data by columns. This method improves data compression due to the repetitive nature of column values. For example, in a financial dataset, querying only the *transaction date* and *amount* columns becomes more efficient. However, it is good to keep in mind that columnar storage can be less efficient for transactional operations such as updates and inserts, where row-oriented storage may perform better. A data warehouse is meant for ingesting and analyzing data, not necessarily for running applications.

- **Object storage**: Another critical aspect of CDWH storage is the adoption of object storage, exemplified by *Amazon's S3 service*. S3's introduction revolutionized data storage by treating each data item as an individual object with a unique identifier. For instance, a piece of data in object storage could be an individual log file from a web server, stored independently from other files. This structure allows for easy distribution of data across multiple servers and geographic locations. As data volumes grow, adding more storage capacity in a distributed manner is simpler without reorganizing existing data. This flexibility and lack of physical and structural constraints make it much easier to scale up in response to increasing data storage needs, especially for storing vast amounts of unstructured data such as images, videos, or sensor data.

- **Handling structured and unstructured data**: CDWHs are designed to handle both structured and unstructured data. **Structured data**, which adheres to a defined format such as database tables, is seamlessly stored and queried. On the other hand, **unstructured data**, such as free-form text or multimedia files, requires more sophisticated processing for effective analysis. The versatility of CDWHs enables users to store and analyze these diverse data types under a single platform.

We'll talk about the UI next.

The UI

The **UI** is a vital component of CDWHs, serving as the primary interaction point for analysts to harness the system's computing and storage capabilities. Beyond basic functionalities such as schema display and query execution, modern UIs in CDWHs are evolving to become more powerful and user-friendly. Let's look at some UI features CDWHs offer:

- **Advanced features**: Contemporary UIs offer a range of features that significantly enhance the data analysis process. This includes auto-completion, error-checking, and query performance analysis tools. Moreover, many UIs now incorporate sophisticated data visualization capabilities, allowing analysts to create interactive charts and graphs directly within the platform.

- **User experience**: A key focus in UI design is the user experience. Modern UIs are designed for ease of use, with intuitive navigation and customizable interfaces to accommodate different user preferences. This focus on user experience is crucial in minimizing the learning curve and enhancing productivity, especially for new users.

- **Security and access control**: The UI is also a critical factor in managing security and access control. Features such as **role-based access control** (**RBAC**), audit logs, and data encryption settings are accessible via the UI, ensuring that sensitive data is adequately protected while maintaining user accessibility.

- **Evolution and future trends**: As CDWHs continue to advance, we can expect UIs to incorporate more cutting-edge technologies. Trends such as the integration of artificial intelligence for predictive analysis, natural language processing for simplified querying, and enhanced real-time collaboration features are set to redefine how analysts interact with data warehouses.

The UI in CDWHs is not just a gateway to data; it's an evolving platform that blends functionality, user experience, and innovation to empower analysts in their data-driven endeavors.

Access management

Effective **access management** is crucial in CDWHs as it dictates who can access what data and what actions they can perform:

- **RBAC, ABAC, and ACLs**: RBAC is commonly employed. Roles with specific permissions are defined, and users are then assigned to those roles. This approach simplifies management compared to tracking permissions at an individual level. In addition to RBAC, CDWHs may also leverage other access control models such as **attribute-based access control** (**ABAC**), which allows for permissions based on various attributes (for example, user roles and data sensitivity), and **access control lists** (**ACLs**) for more granular control.

- **Dynamic access control**: Modern CDWHs often support dynamic access control, which adjusts access rights based on factors such as user location, time, or data sensitivity. This adaptability is key in managing the diverse and evolving access requirements of a large organization.

- **Integrations**: Integration with enterprise identity management systems, such as LDAP or Active Directory, is common, allowing for a unified approach to user and role management across the organization. This integration is crucial for maintaining consistent security policies and streamlining administrative processes.

- **Auditing**: Furthermore, robust access management plays a vital role in compliance with data protection regulations. Maintaining audit trails to monitor data access and modifications is essential for regulatory compliance and identifying potential security breaches.

However, managing access in CDWHs can be challenging. It requires a balance between ensuring data security and providing ease of access. Best practices include regular access rights reviews, employing the least privilege principle, and continuous monitoring for anomalous access patterns. These practices help maintain a secure yet functional data access environment within the CDWH.

Security

Security is a cornerstone in the effectiveness of CDWHs. This includes a range of measures designed to safeguard access and protect stored data.

- **Access control**: Comprehensive access control is essential. This involves not only **single sign-on (SSO)** capabilities, which integrate an organization's existing account management systems with the cloud platform, but also the implementation of robust network security settings. These settings can restrict access to authorized networks, such as a company's internal network, enhancing the security perimeter.

- **Encryption**: Data encryption is pivotal in securing data, both at rest and during transit. Advanced encryption standards such as AES are typically employed, with cloud vendors offering managed and client-managed encryption key options. The choice between these options affects how encryption keys are controlled and can affect security and compliance.

- **Compliance and regulations**: CDWHs must adhere to industry-specific regulations and standards, such as GDPR for data privacy in the EU or HIPAA for healthcare data in the USA. Compliance is supported through various security features and regular audits. It is critical to check with your company's regulatory guidelines to see what boxes the CDWH needs to tick.

- **Zero-trust architecture**: Adopting a zero-trust architecture is becoming a norm in cloud data warehousing. This security model operates on the principle of "never trust, always verify," ensuring continuous validation of all users and devices accessing the data warehouse. At its core, zero-trust architecture operates under the assumption that no user or device, whether inside or outside the network, should be automatically trusted. Central to zero trust is the concept of least privilege access. Users are granted the minimum level of access necessary to perform their tasks to limit potential damage from a breach.

Establishing robust security in CDWHs is challenging. Organizations need to balance security measures with usability and performance. Best practices include regular security audits, consistent application of security policies, and continuous monitoring for potential threats. Adhering to these practices helps ensure a secure yet efficient data warehousing environment in the cloud.

Pricing

Understanding the pricing structure is critical when selecting a cloud data warehousing solution. The cost implications vary significantly across different models, and choosing the right one depends on your specific data usage patterns and business needs. Here is an overview of common pricing models:

- **On-demand pricing**: This model is similar to paying utility bills. You pay only for the resources you consume, such as compute power and storage, without any long-term commitments. It's ideal for businesses with fluctuating or unpredictable data warehousing needs since it offers maximum flexibility.

- **Reserved instance pricing**: Suitable for predictable workloads, this model involves committing to a fixed period (usually one to three years) for resource usage. In exchange, you receive a significant discount compared to on-demand rates. It is a cost-effective option for stable, long-term projects.

- **Credits or units-based pricing**: You purchase credits or units upfront, which are then consumed as you use various resources. This model can offer cost savings and budget predictability but requires a good understanding of your resource needs to avoid over or under-purchasing. Not all CDWHs provide this option.

- **Query-based pricing**: This model charges based on the amount of data processed by queries, such as in Google BigQuery. It is particularly suited for businesses whose primary cost driver is the frequency and complexity of data queries rather than storage or compute capacity. This model encourages efficient query design and can be cost-effective for organizations with heavy data analysis needs but moderate storage requirements.

- **Hybrid pricing model**: Combining the aforementioned models, the hybrid pricing approach allows businesses to tailor their payment structure to their specific needs. It can include a mix of on-demand and reserved instance pricing for compute and storage-based fees, as well as query-based charges. This model offers the flexibility to optimize costs based on varying usage patterns, making it ideal for businesses with dynamic data warehousing requirements for compute intensity, storage volume, and query complexity.

When evaluating the total cost of cloud data warehousing, several key factors extend beyond basic compute and storage pricing models:

- **Varied storage costs**: Storage expenses are predominantly based on data volume. However, costs can differ significantly depending on storage types, such as hot or cold storage (frequently accessed data versus rarely accessed), and redundancy options. It is crucial to consider not only the storage of raw data but also derived datasets, backups, and snapshots, as these can considerably increase the overall storage footprint.

- **Data transfer fees**: While importing data (ingress) into a CDWH is usually free, transferring data out (egress) can incur costs. These fees can add up, particularly for businesses that frequently move large data volumes to external services or the internet. Understanding and managing these egress costs is vital for cost-effective cloud data warehousing.

- **Performance tier implications**: Different performance tiers offer varying levels of query speed and data processing capabilities. Choosing the right tier involves balancing the need for performance with budget limitations. Higher tiers provide enhanced performance but at a higher cost, which may only be justified for some workloads.

- **Additional service costs**: Additional expenses can arise from services such as advanced data integration tools, enhanced security features, and specialized analytics services. Each of these services adds value but also contributes to the overall cost. It's important to assess which services are essential based on specific business needs and use cases.

- **Cost management and predictability tools**: Many cloud providers offer tools to help manage and predict costs. These tools can be instrumental in monitoring spending, forecasting future expenses, and optimizing resource utilization for cost efficiency.

- **Impact of scaling**: Scaling decisions, whether scaling up for more power or scaling down to save costs, directly affect overall expenses. This includes both compute resources and storage needs, and it's important to understand how scaling affects the total cost concerning performance and storage requirements.

Each pricing model has its advantages and trade-offs. It's advisable to analyze your data usage patterns, predict future needs, and consider potential growth to make an informed decision. It is also key to consider personnel costs since sometimes, you might prefer a managed solution that doesn't require a worker on your end, and other times, you might favor a more DIY approach if you have the staff to tend to your CDWH. Some cloud data warehousing providers offer cost estimation tools to help you simulate different scenarios and choose the most cost-effective model for your needs.

Support for multi-cloud

Another important consideration is the support for **multi-cloud workflows**. The term **multi-cloud** refers to the use of multiple cloud computing and storage services in a single network architecture. For instance, an organization could leverage both Amazon's AWS and Google's GCP cloud services for parts of their organization's software services. A multi-cloud setup could occur for different reasons – for instance, due to freedom of choice of technology by different teams, or a deliberate strategy by the central IT team. Whatever the case may be, multi-cloud architecture is quite common in large organizations, and it's important to keep in mind when choosing a CDWH.

Advantages of multi-cloud solutions

Multi-cloud solutions provide notable benefits. The primary advantage is flexibility, allowing organizations to leverage the best features and services of each cloud service provider. This adaptability is crucial in a rapidly evolving digital landscape. Another significant advantage is risk mitigation. By reducing dependence on a single provider, businesses can alleviate risks associated with service outages, data loss, or vendor lock-in. This diversified approach can ensure business continuity and data accessibility under various scenarios.

Challenges of multi-cloud solutions

However, adopting a multi-cloud strategy also comes with its challenges. Managing multiple cloud services can be complex and often demands specialized skills and sophisticated management tools. This complexity can lead to an increased overhead in governance, security, and cost management. Ensuring consistent security policies and compliance across different platforms and maintaining cost efficiency while managing multiple providers can be daunting tasks.

Now that we have explored various considerations for a CDWH, let's shift our focus to the current market leaders in the cloud data warehousing landscape.

Knowing the market leaders in cloud data warehousing

This section provides a high-level overview of the leading providers in cloud data warehousing, focusing on how they incorporate the components. This is not an exhaustive review, but it should offer a sense of their similarities and differences at the time of writing.

As of 2023, a select group of CDWHs has risen to prominence within the analytics and engineering sectors. Cloud vendors Amazon, Google, and Microsoft, with their substantial capital and robust platforms, are key players in this field. Their ability to leverage existing infrastructure and continuously deliver new features guarantees their market dominance in the foreseeable future.

Amazon Redshift

Amazon Redshift (`https://aws.amazon.com/redshift/features/`) is a powerful, fully managed data warehouse service that excels in handling large-scale data workloads and complex queries thanks to its MPP architecture. Its integration with the AWS ecosystem makes it a strong contender for businesses already reliant on Amazon's cloud services.

However, this strength can also be a limitation. For organizations not deeply integrated with AWS, the learning curve can be steep, and the full benefits of Redshift might not be realized. Furthermore, Redshift offers significant scalability and performance, but it can be overkill for smaller datasets or businesses with modest data warehousing needs. Its pricing model, although flexible, can become costly as demands increase, necessitating careful management and optimization to control expenses. *Table 4.3* elaborates on several features, strengths, and weaknesses of Amazon RedShift.

Features	Description	Advantage	Disadvantage
Compute	MPP architecture, supports query optimization	Ideal for complex queries over large datasets, flexible compute power	May be complex for small-scale or simpler operations
Storage	Columnar format, optimized for aggregations, integrates with Amazon S3	Efficient for read-heavy workloads and aggregations	Less optimal for unstructured data handling
UI	Redshift dashboard in the AWS Management Console	Unified AWS experience, intuitive for AWS users	Requires familiarity with the AWS ecosystem
Access Management	Utilizes AWS IAM for user and role management	Advanced and integrated with AWS, suitable for complex IAM setups	Can be complex for users not familiar with AWS IAM

Features	Description	Advantage	Disadvantage
Security	Network isolation with Amazon VPC, comprehensive data encryption	Top-tier network security, ideal for high-security requirements	Might be overkill for small or less sensitive datasets
Unique Feature	Redshift Spectrum for SQL on unstructured data in Amazon S3	Allows unstructured data to be queried without preloading	Useful primarily for AWS-centric data ecosystems

Table 4.3 – AWS Redshift's features

Google BigQuery is another popular cloud datawarehouse that we will discuss next.

Google BigQuery

Google BigQuery (https://cloud.google.com/bigquery/docs/introduction) is a serverless, highly scalable, and cost-effective multi-cloud data warehouse. It automatically manages and scales resources to meet the demand of data queries without the need for infrastructure management. BigQuery is part of **Google Cloud Platform** (**GCP**) and integrates easily with other services.

It stands out for its serverless architecture, which allows for impressive scalability and ease of management, making it ideal for handling fluctuating workloads without the hassle of infrastructure management. This serverless model, however, means less control over the compute resources, which might not fit organizations that prefer more hands-on control. Additionally, while BigQuery is excellent for large-scale data processing, its pricing model, which is based on the amount of data processed, can become expensive for heavy querying, demanding careful query optimization and management. BigQuery fits seamlessly into the Google Cloud ecosystem but might present integration challenges for businesses not already using Google Cloud services.

Table 4.4 provides an overview of BigQuery's features:

Feature	Description	Advantage	Disadvantage
Compute	Serverless, fully managed, auto-scaling based on query load	Hassle-free setup, automatic scalability, great for varying workloads	Less control over compute resources
Storage	Columnar storage for petabytes of data, uses Google Cloud Storage	Handles large datasets efficiently, high performance	Cost may escalate with extensive data storage

Feature	Description	Advantage	Disadvantage
UI	Google Cloud Console with GUI interface, includes a query editor	User-friendly, powerful query editing tools	May require learning for those new to Google Cloud
Access Management	Uses Google Cloud IAM for granular control at the dataset, table, and column levels	Detailed access control for data security	Can be complex for beginners
Security	Data encryption, IAM, and VPC service controls, complies with major standards	Strong compliance with privacy and security standards	Setup and maintenance of security features can be involved
Unique Features	Direct querying from external sources such as Google Cloud Storage and Google Sheets	Flexible data querying without data movement	Primarily advantageous within the Google Cloud ecosystem

Table 4.4 – Google BigQuery's features

Snowflake CDWH has most recently gained significant traction. Let's take a look.

Snowflake

Among the new entrants, Snowflake (`https://docs.snowflake.com/en/user-guide/warehouses-overview`) stands out. Originating from a team of former Oracle database experts, Snowflake has a growing customer base and a suite of innovative features. These include data warehousing, machine learning capabilities, and secure data sharing, setting it apart from established industry giants. Its support for multi-cloud environments is a significant advantage for companies seeking to avoid vendor lock-in.

However, Snowflake's pricing structure, which charges separately for compute and storage, can be complex and may lead to unexpected costs if not carefully monitored. Additionally, while Snowflake is user-friendly and easy to set up, it might not offer the same depth of integration with specific cloud ecosystems compared to vendor-native services such as AWS Redshift, Google's BigQuery, or Microsoft's Synapse Analytics, potentially making it less appealing for businesses looking for deep cloud integration.

Let's explore Snowflake's features, which are shown in *Table 4.5*:

Features	Description	Advantage	Disadvantage
Compute	Separates compute from storage, enables automatic scaling	Flexibility in managing compute and storage, scalable performance	Cost management can be challenging with scaling
Storage	Columnar storage, supports structured and semi-structured data	Efficient for various data formats, integrates with cloud storage	Storage costs can accumulate
UI	Web UI for managing and interacting with accounts, supports SQL queries	Straightforward for data operations	Less comprehensive than some competitors
Access Management	RBAC, supports federated authentication and SSO	Strong role-based security, external authentication support	Setup may require detailed role configuration
Security	Always-on encryption, multi-factor authentication, private data exchanges	High standard of data security and privacy	Implementation of security measures can be complex
Unique Feature	Multi-cloud platform availability, minimal vendor lock-in	Flexibility in cloud provider choice, reduces lock-in	Beneficial mainly for multi-cloud strategies

Table 4.5 – Snowflake's features

Next, we will discuss another new entrant to the cloud data warehousing scene: Databricks.

Databricks

Databricks (`https://docs.databricks.com/getting-started/concepts.html`) was initially developed as a commercial offering of the open-source distributed computing framework Apache Spark, Databricks now presents itself as a *data lakehouse* – a hybrid platform that effectively merges the strengths of data lakes and data warehouses. The data lakehouse model merges these two worlds. It retains the data lake's ability to handle massive, diverse datasets while adding the data management and optimized query capabilities of a data warehouse. This integration is powered by the *Delta Lake* framework, which applies a structured schema to the raw data in data lakes and adds metadata. This approach enables functionalities typically associated with databases, such as conducting transactions and accessing historical data (often referred to as "time traveling"), within a data lake environment.

Databricks' strength in advanced analytics and machine learning also positions it as a specialized tool, which might be more than what is needed for straightforward data warehousing tasks. Additionally, its pricing model, based on Databricks Units, can be opaque and potentially expensive, particularly for large-scale data processing tasks. While it supports multiple cloud environments, fully utilizing its capabilities often requires a deep understanding of Spark and big data technologies, which might present a steep learning curve for teams without this expertise. Let's examine the various features of Databricks, all of which are shown in *Table 4.6*:

Feature	Description	Advantage	Disadvantage
Compute	Runs on Apache Spark, supports serverless and managed workflows	Fast, in-memory processing ideal for analytics and ML workloads	Best for those with Spark expertise
Storage	Leverages cloud-native object storage, integrated with Delta Lake	Enhanced data reliability and performance in big data scenarios	Delta Lake integration complexity
UI	Notebook-based environment, supports multiple languages	A flexible, collaborative environment for diverse programming needs	Requires adaptation for those used to traditional UIs
Access Management	Fine-grained access control on notebooks, clusters, jobs, and data	Detailed control over various data assets and processing units	Can be intricate for simpler access management needs
Security	Complies with major regulations such as GDPR and HIPAA	High compliance with regulatory standards	Setup and maintenance of compliance features can be extensive
Unique Feature	Delta Lake for ACID transactions and data consistency	Ensures data integrity and consistency in big data operations	Most beneficial for large-scale data environments

Table 4.6 – Databricks features

In addition to these main providers, Microsoft Synapse Analytics (https://azure.microsoft.com/en-us/products/synapse-analytics#Features) is an ambitious attempt by Microsoft to provide a comprehensive analytics solution within the Azure ecosystem. For organizations already invested in Azure, Synapse offers a familiar environment tightly integrated with other Azure services. However, Synapse's ambition to be a one-stop solution for a wide range of data tasks can also be its shortcoming. The platform tries to cover a broad spectrum of data needs – from data warehousing to big data analytics and artificial intelligence – which can lead to a complex and sometimes overwhelming user experience.

In 2023 Microsoft released Microsoft Fabric (`https://www.microsoft.com/en-us/microsoft-fabric`) which combines existing Azure services for data engineering, data science, and analytics in a single interface. Among other features, Fabric offers a unified storage abstraction called OneLake that serves as a central lakehouse within Azure. OneLake stores a single copy of the data for re-use among services, which makes the copying of data in-and-out of Azure services obsolete.

The landscape of cloud data warehousing is rapidly evolving and is led by key players offering unique strengths to suit various business needs. These platforms have significantly advanced in computing power, storage efficiency, UIs, access management, security, and pricing flexibility, making them adaptable to numerous data challenges. Staying updated with the rapid developments in this sector is crucial for businesses looking to effectively leverage their data.

Remember, no one platform is objectively the best; the right choice depends on your organization's specific needs, scale, and goals. Take your time, trial each platform if possible, and select based on your findings and requirements. To better illustrate this, we will look at contrasting use cases.

Use case – choosing the right cloud data warehouse

Consider two very different companies: the first one is a small e-commerce start-up, *EcoGoods*, while the second is a large multinational corporation, *GlobalTech*. We will focus on the distinct requirements and constraints of a small company versus a large enterprise. Through this comparison, we aim to provide practical insights into how factors such as company size, technical expertise, budget constraints, and data complexity shape the decision-making process for selecting the most suitable data warehouse.

EcoGoods – embracing simplicity and cost-effectiveness

EcoGoods, an eco-friendly consumer goods retailer, is growing and wants to modernize its data stack. With a lean team of 50 employees and no prior experience with cloud services, EcoGoods seeks a solution that is both affordable and simple to operate. The company has been utilizing Google Analytics for its web shop, which is managed by two business analysts. EcoGoods is in the early stages of considering bringing a data engineer on board to further strengthen its data capabilities.

Given the situation, *Google BigQuery* seems like an excellent choice for EcoGoods due to the following reasons:

- **Seamless integration with Google Analytics**: EcoGoods already utilizes Google Analytics for website analytics. BigQuery offers an export integration with Google Analytics, enabling the company to combine, analyze, and visualize its web data alongside other business data. This integration significantly reduces the setup complexity and time required to begin creating insights.

- **User-friendly and cost-effective**: For a team with limited exposure to cloud technologies, BigQuery's intuitive interface is a major advantage. Its pay-as-you-go model is particularly attractive for EcoGoods, aligning with their need for a cost-effective solution that doesn't sacrifice functionality. This model ensures spending aligns with actual usage, allowing analysts to explore BigQuery's features without the pressure of escalating costs.

- **No need for a complex cloud environment**: EcoGoods is just starting in cloud computing and does not have strong engineering talent in-house. BigQuery, being a fully managed service, does not require complex cloud environment setup or ongoing maintenance. This factor significantly lowers the entry barrier for EcoGoods, allowing them to focus more on their core business rather than on managing IT infrastructure.

Next, we'll look at another scenario for a company called GlobalTech and discuss which is the right CDWH for this company.

GlobalTech – catering to complexity and scalability

GlobalTech is a multinational electronics manufacturer with thousands of employees spread across multiple countries. GlobalTech's central IT office is eager to unify its data management and is on the hunt for a state-of-the-art data warehouse. The company's data needs are intricate and varied, spanning from real-time analytics to the depth of data engineering and science. GlobalTech's cloud services are spread over all three major vendors: Amazon's AWS, Azure, and GCP. They require a data warehouse that's not just versatile but also highly capable of integrating with this multi-cloud setup.

In this context, Snowflake and Databricks Lakehouse stand out as the leading choices, offering the scalability and flexibility needed for GlobalTech's ambitious data strategy.

Snowflake offers the following advantages:

- **Multi-cloud compatibility**: Snowflake's ability to function across AWS, Azure, and GCP aligns perfectly with GlobalTech's diverse cloud services, offering a unified data warehousing solution without vendor lock-in.

- **External table support**: Snowflake's support for external tables allows GlobalTech to efficiently manage and query data stored in various cloud storage solutions such as Amazon S3, Azure Blob Storage, and Google Cloud Storage.

- **Data governance and compliance**: Snowflake's strong data governance capabilities are crucial for GlobalTech, ensuring compliance with various international regulations.

- **Scalability and performance**: Given GlobalTech's large-scale operations, Snowflake's architecture, which decouples storage and compute, offers the scalability and performance necessary for handling vast datasets and complex queries.

The Databricks Lakehouse has the following offerings:

- **Integration with multiple clouds**: Databricks Lakehouse, aligning with GlobalTech's diverse cloud environment, stands out as an optimal choice due to its multi-cloud support. It seamlessly reads data across the storage systems of all three major cloud providers, enabling GlobalTech to access source data directly from its original cloud location within Databricks.

- **Advanced analytics and machine learning**: Databricks, built on Apache Spark, offers a compelling solution for GlobalTech's sophisticated analytics and machine learning initiatives. Its architecture is uniquely suited to handle both data warehousing and data science tasks, providing a unified platform for processing, exploring, and modeling large datasets. This capability is particularly beneficial for GlobalTech as it allows them to leverage their data for predictive analytics and AI-driven insights, which are crucial in a technology-driven industry.

- **Data lake and warehouse hybrid**: The innovative lakehouse architecture of Databricks merges the flexibility of data lakes with the structured environment of data warehouses. This hybrid model is particularly advantageous for GlobalTech, which deals with a range of data types-from structured transactional data to unstructured sensor data from manufacturing equipment. The lakehouse model enables efficient storage, management, and querying of diverse data formats, facilitating more comprehensive and accurate data analysis across the company's global operations.

- **Granular resource configuration**: Databricks offers granular control over compute resources. This means GlobalTech's engineers can tailor specific clusters to their needs, ensuring optimal use of resources for different tasks. Compute resources in Databricks (**clusters**) can be configured as needed, maximizing efficiency and cost-effectiveness. Furthermore, Databricks' serverless SQL Warehouse adds another layer of flexibility. This feature enables GlobalTech to run analytics without the overhead of managing infrastructure, making it easier to scale operations up or down based on their current needs.

By exploring EcoGoods and GlobalTech in selecting their data warehousing solutions, it's clear that each organization's specific needs and existing infrastructure play crucial roles in guiding their choices. EcoGoods found a fitting solution in Google BigQuery, while GlobalTech navigated toward Snowflake and Databricks Lakehouse due to their large-scale and complex requirements.

Remember, in the ever-evolving world of cloud data warehousing, staying informed and open to the diverse range of available platforms is key. Each comes with its own set of strengths and considerations, and the most suitable choice will depend on your organization's unique blend of needs, scale, technical expertise, and long-term data strategy.

Next, we will talk about how managed and self-hosted data warehouses to help you pick the one best suited for your specific requirements.

Managed versus self-hosted data warehouses

Finally, after discussing the different **managed cloud data warehouses** offered by vendors, you should be aware of the option of self-hosting one.

In a **self-hosted environment**, organizations take on the responsibility of installing, configuring, and managing their data warehouse software. By combining compute and storage services offered by most cloud vendors with open-source software, it's possible to create a *DIY* data warehouse. Open-source systems such as PostgreSQL, ClickHouse, and Apache Doris are popular choices for self-hosting due to their flexibility and lack of licensing costs. PostgreSQL, traditionally known for its robust relational database capabilities, has been increasingly adopted in data warehousing for smaller-scale projects. ClickHouse stands out for its impressive performance in OLAP tasks, making it a suitable choice for real-time analytics. Apache Doris, another powerful option, offers a distributed analytics engine optimized for high-performance queries on large datasets.

While the prospect of a self-hosted data warehouse might be appealing due to its customizability and avoidance of vendor lock-in, it's important to consider the drawbacks. The most significant of these is the requirement for in-house expertise. Successfully deploying and maintaining a self-hosted data warehouse demands a deep understanding of both the chosen technology and the underlying cloud infrastructure. This can be an unrealistic expectation, especially for smaller organizations or those without dedicated data engineers.

Moreover, self-hosting means taking on all aspects of data warehouse management, including security, scalability, and performance optimization. This is a non-trivial commitment as ensuring the security and efficient operation of a data warehouse in a constantly evolving cloud environment can be both challenging and time-consuming.

While self-hosting a data warehouse can offer greater control and customization, it also requires significant technical expertise and resources. Organizations must weigh the benefits of a tailored solution against the costs and complexities involved in self-managing their data warehouse infrastructure. For many, particularly those without the necessary technical skills or resources, a managed cloud data warehousing solution might be a more practical and efficient choice.

Summary

In this chapter, we delved into data warehousing, tracing its evolution and spotlighting the leading players shaping the current market landscape.

You learned about the fundamental aspects of a modern CDWH, including critical features such as scalability, the strategic separation of computing and storage functions, access management, and security. These insights have provided a solid foundation for understanding how contemporary data warehouses operate and what makes them integral to data management strategies.

In the last part of this chapter, we shone a spotlight on the industry's heavyweights – Amazon Redshift, Google BigQuery, Snowflake, and the Databricks Lakehouse platform. You now have a clearer understanding of the distinctive advantages each of these platforms offers, and how choosing the right one largely depends on factors such as your specific requirements, existing technological infrastructure, budget constraints, and the technical proficiency of your team.

The next chapter will guide you through the intricacies of data modeling. We will cover the methodologies and best practices for structuring and organizing data – an important step in exploiting the full potential of your data warehouse.

5

Data Modeling

Data modeling is a proactive design process that establishes relationships between data within information systems. A well-designed data model can lower costs, contribute to data democratization, and adapt easily to changing needs.

This chapter explores the various data modeling techniques and what to consider when building a data model. In particular, it focuses on the following:

- The importance of data models
- Designing your data model
- Data modeling techniques
- Choosing a data model

The importance of data models

The primary objective of an effective data model is to translate business requirements into data structures that facilitate the understanding of the current status, identify new opportunities, and drive initiatives based on insights gained from data analysis.

For analytics engineers, it is crucial to build data systems with long-term planning in mind, ensuring seamless integration between business requirements and the data procured in the system. As a result, data modeling is one of the most vital tools to prevent future issues and maintain optimal system performance as complexity increases.

In traditional data warehouses, data models were essential to manage storage and computational costs. However, as seen in *Chapter 4*, the shift to cloud computing presents another set of challenges.

With the increasing adoption of cloud computing, many of the problems data modeling solves can now be overcome by harnessing the increased computational power of cloud-based data warehouses. These challenges have now shifted from performance issues to cost concerns. This goes to the extent that some data professionals suggest modeling may be a waste of time and effort.

However, even when there is no conscious effort to build a data model, whenever data is stored in an information system, it adopts a specific form or structure. This structure forms an inherent data model that governs many of the system's data usage, retrieval, and transformation constraints.

Consequently, designing the right model for the intended usage can significantly improve data accessibility, reducing costs and time to value.

There is no one-size-fits-all solution; modelers must devise multiple candidate models, drawing upon experience, analysis, heuristics, abstraction, and creativity.

A data model should address completeness, non-redundancy, adherence to business rules, reusability, stability, elegance, integration, and effective communication for the specific use case of the data. We will now delve into these concepts.

Completeness

Completeness addresses the question, do we have all the data we need? In other words, we assess whether the data supports a system design that fulfills all business requirements. Now, we do not need all the data that source systems offer, but we must consider what is relevant to the business use cases. As modelers, we should strive to accommodate the data model's current and future uses. Since predicting long-term usage can be challenging when designing a new model, it is crucial to evaluate the need for additional data in the future and the likelihood of adding new elements to the data model. Based on this assessment, the model can be designed to be more adaptable to such changes.

As an example, consider a data application that stores customer information. After some time, the business decides that storing the marital status would be beneficial. Therefore, the modeler adds a column with this information. While this change might seem trivial to implement in the database, it could significantly impact the downstream services, users, and systems that utilize this table.

First, we must decide what to do with the records we already have in the database. Do we leave them with a null value, or do we grab the information from somewhere else and run a backfill of the data?

Modifying all downstream dependencies to accommodate this change can be costly. Therefore, a data model that is complete or flexible enough to incorporate such changes can easily reduce the need for future adjustments.

Enforcement of business rules

Let's start with an example: when building a new house, you must comply with local rules, laws, and policies. These rules address different aspects, and some might impact the project's cost. Knowing these rules in advance helps to scope the project and avoid fines.

Similarly, a data model must comply with the business rules set for the data it holds. As mentioned in the introduction of this chapter, a data model represents the data and its relationships within an information system and the business it serves.

Some business rules are implemented to enhance or simplify operations, while others are required by law and regulations in specific regions. Consequently, the data model can be a powerful tool to enforce these business requirements, promoting best practices and improving data quality.

Consider, for example, a factory where **invoices** must have a **unique identifier**. Enforcing this in the data model helps implement this in operations. However, rectifying it later can be challenging if the modeler needs to be more accurate in representing a business rule or if the rule changes over time.

Involving business stakeholders in the model's design and documenting and enforcing business rules ensures a clear and common understanding of those rules, helps anticipate potential changes, and raises awareness about the importance of these business rules.

Minimizing redundancy

To ensure completeness, we need to make sure that we have all the parts we need, but we also want to achieve this with the minimum number of resources.

In a small house, for instance, we would want each room to fulfill a specific need, and it would make no sense to have two bathrooms and no living room. Every structure that performs the same function as another takes up space affects user experience and increases the cost of building that house.

Similarly, when consolidating data from multiple systems into a data warehouse to establish a single source of truth for business users, it is common to find different tables storing the same data, albeit in varying forms or captured in different locations.

Imagine we have a data information system with the following tables:

customers		invoices		customer_reviews	
PK	customers id	PK	invoice id	PK	reviews id
	full_name		invoice_date		customer_first_name
	first_name		customer_name		customer_last_name
	last_name		total_amount		review

Figure 5.1 – Tables storing the same data

The columns `full_name`, `customer_name`, and `customer_first_name` seem to capture similar data in different formats. Besides the cost of repeatedly storing this data being unnecessary, it creates ambiguity that can affect usability.

A high-quality data model should define a database where data are complete and stored only once, avoiding repetition and allowing information to be derived from it.

Data reusability

Just like the living room of a house that can be used to eat, watch movies, have a party, or simply relax and read a book, we can see how one space can have multiple uses. Data is typically captured for a specific purpose; however, other uses can be derived from it.

If the data capture and storage method is designed exclusively for the initial purpose, it could render the data unusable for other users. Therefore, data should be organized and stored independently from any specific application.

It is always preferable to store non-aggregated data and only perform calculations as needed. That way, future users may reuse the original metric for their calculations. This helps with reusability but also with non-redundancy, as there is no need to save the original metric multiple times for different calculations.

Stability and flexibility

Imagine hosting a party in the yard of a house. If it is a one-off occurrence, then a rental tent might be enough; if you host this type of event constantly, you could build a more permanent structure.

Business requirements frequently change as the business itself evolves. The data model must be adaptable to accommodate changes that are hard to anticipate.

Let us revisit the invoice example from earlier. In the model, if we enforce that the invoice should have a unique identifier, and then a new invoicing system is introduced in a different region, there might be a possibility that two different invoices share the same unique identifier. In this case, making changes to the model might require significant structural adjustments, impacting various parts of the system. On the other hand, if we had specified a source system column from the beginning, we could have included the new system without making any changes to the existing model.

Elegance

Elegant models are simple, consistent, and succinct, making them robust and easy to use. Achieving elegance demands a thorough understanding of the business processes and use cases.

As a business changes and grows, its data model can become complex. Keeping an eye on how the data model evolves over time is important to avoid higher development costs and diminished usability in the future.

Communication

A data model should also serve as a communication tool to convey the nature of available data. To do so, the model's elements must represent business concepts that users are familiar with. The informed feedback from business users interacting with the model will determine how well it represents business concepts.

Typical communication issues arise from excessive complexity, the introduction of novel concepts, and the employment of unknown or ambiguous terms.

Maintaining guidelines and documenting definitions and business rules help minimize these problems in the long run.

Integration

Before the emergence of data warehouses, users had to query data directly from source systems. This raw data was typically stored in **relational databases**, each with its own model.

In the contemporary "everything-as-a-service" landscape, many of these source systems are third-party applications or **application programming interfaces** (**APIs**) where control over the data model is limited.

A data model consolidates data from these various sources into a single data-driven decision support system.

When building new structures, it is essential to understand how they interact with and affect existing ones. The data model must fit and coexist with the different components of the information system.

To do so, the modeler must gather an understanding of the overall data architecture and flows and develop the data model according to existing standards and compatibility constraints.

Potential trade-offs

Adhering to the preceding principles comes with trade-offs. For example, enforcing too many business rules may compromise the stability of the model. On the other hand, a model that uses too many well-established definitions might be easy to understand by the final users but challenging to reuse or connect with other systems.

As data model designers, we aim to create a model that best balances conflicting objectives. This is an iterative process; some solutions may only become apparent once a first iteration is made. Therefore, like other design disciplines, this process is a series of propositions and evaluations that seek feedback from business stakeholders to better represent the business through data.

The elephant in the room – performance

In the past, the major modeling techniques focused heavily on performance since this was one of the main constraints of a data system when they started to be used widely at the beginning of the 1980s.

So far, we have discussed designing a data model without addressing performance. This is because the execution performance depends on the platform and infrastructure it runs on. Systems have varying constraints, and a high-performing model on one platform might not be performant on another. For example, some cloud platforms calculate costs based on data usage. Designing or migrating a model to reduce costs on such a platform might represent structural changes to the original model.

As modelers, it is easy to fall into the trap of trying to **optimize for performance** too early in the design process. Doing so can drastically affect the quality of the model, which has little value in terms of performance. Instead, we should first focus on creating a sound data model and then consult with the database manager to determine if it can be improved for performance.

Now that we understand the benefits and principles of data modeling, let us explore the techniques at our disposal in the next section.

Designing your data model

The design process of a data model progresses from generic to specific. The first step is the conceptual diagram, which provides a high-level, generic view of how the data will be stored and connected within the information system and its relationship with business activities. It is usually technology-agnostic. With this initial diagram, the modeler seeks informed feedback from business specialists, data owners, and end users to ensure that the model accurately represents the business and that the main data relationships are represented.

Figure 5.2 shows an example of a conceptual diagram for a simple management system. This diagram contains the basic building blocks of the data model to start the modeling process. We can see how the elements are related. For example, one order item represents a product and is part of an order; the customer places an order, and the model generates an invoice with invoice items; each invoice item represents a product:

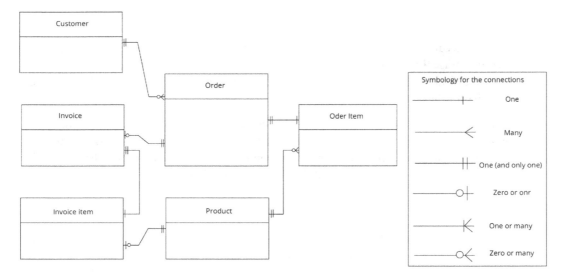

Figure 5.2 – Conceptual diagram for a simple order management system

Based on the conceptual diagram, we can create a logical diagram, as shown in *Figure 5.3*. The logical diagram can be designed using the chosen database management system. This usually entails representing tables and columns, as they are the fundamental components of relational databases. A distinct diagram may be required for other database types, employing object-oriented approaches and notation:

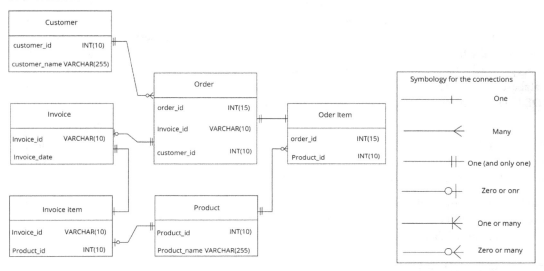

Figure 5.3 – Logical diagram for a simple order management system

Lastly, the physical data model considers platform and infrastructure constraints. It is represented by tables and columns, including specifications for storage, access mechanisms, and other considerations necessary to achieve the desired performance.

Typically, these diagrams are represented using **entity relationship diagrams** (**ERD**) or can be depicted using the **unified modeling language** (**UML**) notation.

Three-schema architecture

In the mid-1970s, the three-schema architecture was officially established as a standard by ANSI/SPARC and was commonly used in database design. This architecture comprises the **conceptual** schema, which outlines data organization in tables and columns and serves as the shared data view. This schema is built upon the **internal** schema, detailing data storage and access methods. Additionally, the **external** schema accesses the conceptual schema, which defines various views, allowing users to perceive data differently.

Within the internal schema, the database management system can be tailored to store data in a specific manner. This includes decisions on partitioning, clustering, utilizing table types, or storing data in separate locations through external tables.

The primary function of the three-schema architecture is to shield end-users from potentially irrelevant changes. By separating the conceptual and internal schemas, users are protected from alterations in the physical organization of data. Similarly, the distinction between the external and conceptual schemas prevents users from modifying tables and columns that may not concern them.

While the formal terminology for **internal**, **conceptual**, and **external** schemas may not be widespread, most database designers and administrators recognize the comprehensive database design process involving these three schemas. This process is often referred to as database design or **physical design**. The external schema is commonly known as **marts**, views, or the views it contains. Meanwhile, the conceptual schema is typically called the **logical database design**. As for the internal schema, most database designers and administrators understand that it consists of the **data definition language** (**DDL**) employed in each database management system.

It is crucial to highlight that any modifications in the conceptual schema should result directly from the data modeling process, as it represents a negotiated and approved deliverable between stakeholders and the modeler. This approach prevents other individuals involved in database management from altering tables or columns without the data modeler's involvement.

Having covered the various design principles of data modeling, the primary focus of an analytics engineer now shifts to the physical implementation of data systems. The next section will explore how we can model data warehouses.

Data modeling techniques

During the 1990s, as data warehouses rapidly integrated into numerous enterprises and businesses, Bill Inmon, Ralph Kimball, and Daniel Linstedt developed methodologies with architectures for constructing data warehouses.

Each of these methods has its own associated data model. While other methods or possible combinations exist, the three main forms discussed in the following subsections are the most common.

Bill Inmon and relational modeling

In 1992, William (Bill) Inmon published *Building the Data Warehouse* (https://www.wiley.com/en-us/Building+the+Data+Warehouse,+4th+Edition-p-9780764599446). For this work, he is recognized as one of the fathers of the data warehouse.

Inmon's methodology for data warehouse architecture highlights the importance of a unified data storage system structured according to the **third normal form** (**3NF**), which will be described in depth in the next section. He asserts that robust relational modeling contributes to consistency across the entire company, thereby simplifying the creation of tailored data marts for different departments.

Bill Inmon's top-down design for enterprise data warehouses entails initially constructing a normalized data model. Subsequently, **dimensional data marts** are created, which house the data necessary for distinct business operations or departments.

Inmon characterizes the data warehouse using the following principles:

- **Subject-oriented**: The warehouse's data organization ensures that all data elements associated with the same real-world event or object are interconnected.

- **Time-variant**: Modifications to the data in the database are tracked and recorded, allowing for the generation of reports that depict changes over a specified timeline.

- **Non-volatile**: Data within the data warehouse remain unchanged and are never removed. Once committed, the data transforms into a static, read-only state, preserved for future reporting purposes.

- **Integrated**: The database incorporates data from a majority (if not all) of an organization's operational applications, guaranteeing the consistency of this data.

The data model that follows Inmon's data warehouse design adheres to the third normal form. As normalized models expand in size, their complexity increases accordingly. Comprehending the relationships between entities when dealing with a hundred or more tables can be as challenging as finding one's way around a large city map.

Bill Inmon's approach is also known as the **corporate information factory** (**CIF**). It features a three-layered data warehouse design. The first layer, data acquisition, utilizes an ETL tool to extract information from the source system and assists with data enrichment, cleaning, and normalization. The data then arrives at the enterprise data warehouse, the second layer, where it is modeled in the 3NF. In this stage, the data is represented in its most atomic form, meaning the lowest granularity or highest level of detail, and is available for user queries. Finally, the data delivery layer consists of data marts designed for specific use cases, often catering to individual departments within the organization.

Inmon envisioned a data warehouse as a unified storage system for the whole organization. Such a warehouse maintains the most detailed **atomic data** at the finest level of granularity. Dimensional data marts are constructed once the extensive data warehouse is established. As a result, the data warehouse operates as the core element of the CIF, providing a coherent structure for delivering business intelligence.

The main characteristic of the CIF is that the information is normalized.

Normalization

Normalization encompasses a set of steps to arrange data within tables, aiming to eliminate redundancy and incompleteness, thus minimizing complexity or anomalies during updates. The process starts with a single source, which the modeler then separates into tables according to the dependencies of the data items. Although the process can be seen as mechanical, the initial data will invariably include business assumptions that could influence the results. It is the responsibility of the data modeler to confirm and, if necessary, question these assumptions and the business rules depicted by data dependencies.

Normalization depends on the accurate identification of determinants and keys. The most common way to normalize is the 3NF. A table adheres to the 3NF if each determinant of a non-key element is a candidate key. Nevertheless, a table in the 3NF might only be partially normalized.

Figure 5.4 shows how an unnormalized table goes through different stages before ending in its 3NF:

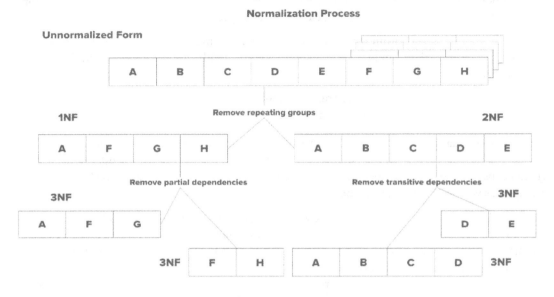

Figure 5.4 – Normalization process

In practice, normalization is primarily used to verify the correctness of a model developed through a top-down approach.

Normalization, rooted in a mathematical approach, can be executed systematically and is arguably the most extensively researched area of data modeling. In a simplified form, it can be described as a two-step process. First, the available data are organized into tables, eliminating repeating groups. Next, duplicated data are removed and placed into separate tables. A crucial aspect of these two steps is identifying a unique key or primary key that effectively distinguishes a single record within the table.

We will now discuss the normalization steps in detail.

Steps to normalization

Normalization operates on specific assumptions. Before initiating the normalization process, it is crucial to validate the accuracy of these assumptions.

First, ensure that there is only one fact per column. For instance, a `full_name` column where users can input both first and last names contains multiple strings that could constitute separate facts. As this information could be used separately in different parts of the business process, it is preferable to split it into separate columns.

Second, check that no data were lost during the transition to tabular form, especially in the case of unstructured data, such as text.

Third, remove data that can be derived, deduced, or calculated from other fields unless needed for performance reasons.

Lastly, each table must have a primary key. A **primary key** is defined as the minimal set of columns that contain a unique combination of values for each row in the table, allowing for the distinct identification of each record. After the modeler has established a primary key, it is essential to consult with the business expert to confirm that this combination of values is unique.

First normal form and repeating groups

Let us consider a curriculum vitae paper form that we want to store in tabular form, with fields to capture **certifications**. For each candidate, the record may have zero to many certifications. If we add columns to the table to store this information, the main challenge is limiting the maximum number of occurrences, as our table would need the same number of columns. This would require defining the number of columns according to the highest possible occurrence in practice.

Let's look at *Figure 5.5*, where we can see the CV paper form:

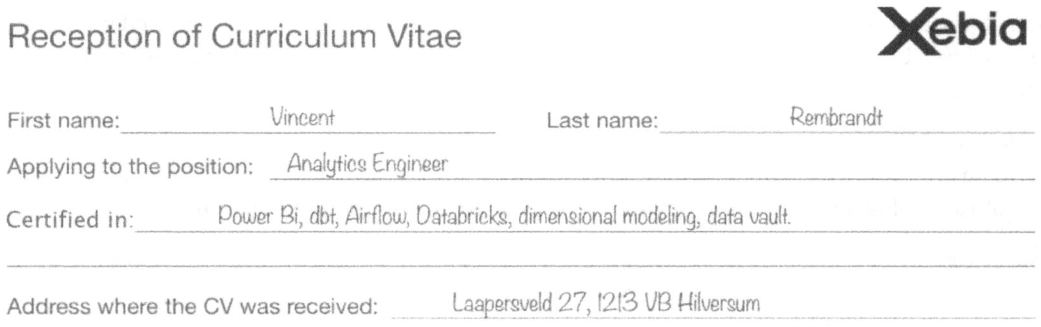
Reception of Curriculum Vitae

Xebia

First name: Vincent Last name: Rembrandt

Applying to the position: Analytics Engineer

Certified in: Power Bi, dbt, Airflow, Databricks, dimensional modeling, data vault.

Address where the CV was received: Laapersveld 27, 1213 VB Hilversum

Figure 5.5 – Paper form for curriculum vitae

This CV on paper can be translated to a tabular form using its fields as the starting point, as depicted in *Figure 5.6*:

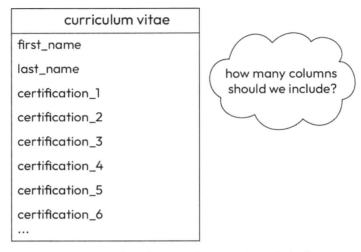

Figure 5.6 – Paper form for curriculum vitae in a tabular format

Moving to tabular form introduces a problem—not all rows in our table will have data in all columns for certifications. This results in empty values and increased complexity for the system handling this data. Moreover, reusability is affected since it might be necessary to perform complex program logic to handle these data.

Upon closer examination of this form, it becomes evident that we have a set of repeated columns: certification_1, certification_2, and so on. This repeating group introduces inflexibility, complexity, and poor data reusability to our data model.

A general and flexible solution to this issue is part of the first step of normalization: putting data into table form and identifying and removing repeating groups. This can be done by splitting the original table into several tables—one for the primary data and one for each repeating group.

First, we remove each distinct set of repeating group columns and relocate them to a new table. It is essential to include the primary key of the core table in each new table, serving as a cross-reference. In the repeating group tables, this is referred to as a **foreign key** since it is the primary key of a foreign table. It is crucial to determine if the sequence of the repeated groups holds business value and to add a sequence column accordingly.

In *Figure 5.7*, we remove the repeating group and create a second table to hold this information:

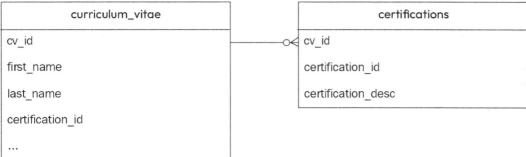

Figure 5.7 – Removing repeating groups

After defining the new tables, we assign relevant names to them and identify the new primary key for each table. Identifying this new key may be the most challenging aspect of the normalization process. If we cannot find a new set of columns uniquely identifying each record, we can create a new unique key.

Following this first step, our tables are technically in the first form of normalization, also known as the **first normal form**; this means that all data of the same kind are held in the same place, and the repeating groups are now only limited by the maximum number of possible rows in their own table.

Second normal form

Although we eliminated repeating groups in the first step, let's consider our CV example, where we also captured the address of the office where the candidate submitted their CV. This address is not a repeating group; it is just one address but is represented by multiple columns such as street, number, postal code, or others.

In this example, it is evident that each row created to record a CV in the table will repeatedly contain the office address or location information since it remains unchanged. We can eliminate this redundancy by extracting the location information into a separate table and using a unique identifier for each distinct location. This approach not only allows us to store the location information just once but also allows us to add a new location to the system, even if there are no records in the `curriculum_vitae` core table referencing this location.

Identifying determinants

Upon further examination of our data, we may discover that the content of one column influences other columns in the table, meaning they are determinants of the other columns. In our previous example, `location_name` determines the address columns, as they cannot differ for the same location. In other words, they share the same context.

Determinants are not necessarily single columns; they can also be a combination of columns. For instance, the `first_name` and `last_name` columns can determine the `birth_date`, `gender`, and all personally identifiable information columns in a table. In the second step, we need to identify any determinants besides the primary key and the columns they influence. Next, establish a new table for each determinant and its associated columns. Assign a suitable name for the new table and use the determinant column as the new primary key. In the original table, eliminate the determined columns, retaining only the determinants to act as a foreign key used as a reference between tables.

To easily identify determinants, looking for columns that appear to be identifiers (via their names) or seem to describe something different from the table's subject is helpful. Sometimes, feedback from a business specialist may be required to confirm if a set of columns determines others.

This process is iterative, as creating new tables may reveal issues in the data or expose repeating groups, making it necessary to revisit previous normalization steps.

In *Figure 5.8*, we can see how we can eliminate redundancy by creating new tables to hold this information, using foreign keys to connect all tables to our main table. After doing this, our model goes through the 2NF:

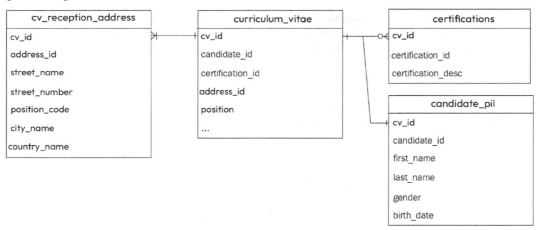

Figure 5.8 – Eliminating redundancy and moving out determinants

Once all determinants have been moved to new tables, our model is in its 3NF.

Third normal form (3NF)

Many texts recommend beginning by identifying the determinants that are part of the table's primary key. Once these determinants are moved to new tables, the table reaches its **second normal form (2NF)**. However, the 2NF is merely a stage in the process, as we also need to relocate all determinants that are not part of the primary key. After addressing all determinants, our tables will be in their 3NF.

In more complex scenarios, where every column in the table is part of the primary key or where tables contain time-dependent data, other normalization forms are used. However, the 3NF is usually enough to achieve a robust data model.

You might assume that the normalization process, which creates more tables, would negatively impact system performance. However, advances in database management systems technology and computational power have made the number of tables less likely to affect performance. It is important to note that performance is not a primary concern at this stage of the modeling process.

To provide a formal definition of a model's 3NF, it is crucial to acknowledge that sometimes a table may have more than one potential primary key. These alternative columns are referred to as candidate keys. With this new term in mind, we can assert that a table is in 3NF if the only determinants of non-key columns are candidate keys.

Verifying table normalization and identifying redundancies

Upon achieving the 3NF for our tables, we can verify the success of the process by examining all foreign keys and ensuring that every column name appears once in the overall model, indicating that the data are not stored in multiple locations.

If redundancies are left, verify that you removed the columns from the original table after transferring them to a new table, used distinct column names, and marked the foreign keys correctly.

Throughout normalization, we divided our data into relevant tables to store information significant to the business. To restore the original state of our data, we must recombine all the tables using the foreign keys and primary keys of the tables we created. The primary check we need to perform on a normalized model is ensuring all references in the core table have a corresponding record in one of the foreign tables. This is known as cardinality. Most database management systems offer a referential integrity feature to automatically ensure that each foreign key corresponds to a matching primary key value.

Once the normalization process is completed successfully, we should be able to reconstruct our initial dataset without losing any data in the process.

The main benefits of using normalization

Normalization concentrates on several fundamental data modeling goals, including eliminating redundancy, enhancing data reusability, reducing complexity, verifying completeness, and improving communication effectiveness. Choosing suitable names for tables and columns is crucial when converting data from its original form to the normal form. Establishing consistent naming conventions throughout the model can assist us in this process and serve as an effective tool for identifying duplicate data across various model sections.

Normalization is crucial in minimizing update anomalies, which can occur during data manipulation operations such as insertion, modification, and deletion. When a data model is not normalized, these operations may lead to potential issues in the tables and columns of the model.

Figure 5.9 illustrates the differences between the stages of normalization:

Normalization   COMPARISON CHART

CONSTRAINTS	UNF	1NF	2NF	3NF
Unique rows with no duplicate records	✓	✓	✓	✓
Columns cannot contain composite values or relations		✓	✓	✓
Every non-prime attribute has a full functional dependency on a candidate key			✓	✓
Every non-trivial functional dependency either begins with a superkey or ends with a prime attribute (attributes depend only on candidate keys)				✓

UNF: Unnormalized form
1NF: First normal form
2NF: Second normal form
3NF: Third normal form

Figure 5.9 – Comparison chart of normalization stages

By employing normalization, update anomalies can be effectively mitigated during data insertion, modification, and deletion. Consider an initial dataset where all the information is consolidated into a single, large table. In such a scenario, any modification must apply changes to the entire table. Conversely, in a normalized model, these alterations are localized and executed in just one location, subsequently affecting the entire model without causing inconsistencies. This streamlined approach enhances data integrity and simplifies the overall data management process.

As a general guideline, normalization techniques are suitable for transactional systems that capture large volumes of events. The strength of the third normal form is that the updates and inserts of these transactions impact the database in only one place. Queries are simplified as they look up information stored in a single field. However, to analyze normalized data, one may have to perform lots of joins.

Ralph Kimball and dimensional modeling

Contrary to popular belief, Ralph Kimball did not coin the terms **fact** and **dimension**. The source of these terms can be linked to a collaborative research project between General Mills and Dartmouth University in the 1960s. It is safe to say that no single individual is responsible for creating the dimensional approach. However, Ralph Kimball structured it as one of the main techniques used for data warehouse modeling.

Dimensional modeling has long been a reliable method for simplifying databases. For over 50 years, the simple form of the dimensional model has been the choice of many organizations and data professionals. Simplicity is great for the modeler to understand how the data is structured with low effort and allows the software and hardware tools to navigate the model to deliver value faster.

Besides, the dimensional model or star schema allows data storage in a business-oriented form. Therefore, it is suitable for analytical purposes, such as drilling down on data, generating reports, and performing aggregations or calculations. This modeling technique is quite popular and well-integrated into some business intelligence tools.

At first glance, when analyzing the business in a cubic form, in the familiar 2D graph with the X and Y axes, we can align the market and product and add a third dimension to see these relationships over time. Using this analogy, the points inside the cube represent a metric such as sales, quantities, or profits, as you can see in the following *Figure 5.10*:

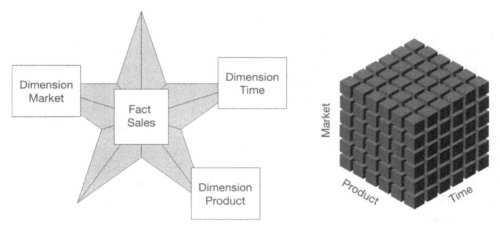

Figure 5.10 – Star schema versus OLAP cube

Employing normalized modeling in the data warehouse's presentation area complicates data retrieval. Thankfully, dimensional modeling tackles this problem by avoiding overly intricate schemas in the presentation area.

Dimensional models employed within the traditional **relational database management systems (RDBMSs)** are usually depicted with a star that describes the internal relationships between the dimensions and facts. For this reason, they are usually called star schemas.

During the early 2000s, handling large amounts of data was challenging and costly, making computations on the star schema inefficient. Another type of system called **online analytical processing (OLAP)** cubes, solved this problem. OLAP cubes consist of pre-computed sets of tables. When retrieving a metric, you just look for the pre-computed value inside the cube. However, everything must be computed in advance, meaning that the smallest change requires recalculating the cube, which can be inconvenient.

Designing a dimensional model in four steps

Designing a dimensional model involves the following decisions:

- Choosing the business process
- Defining the grain
- Determining the dimensions
- Identifying the facts

This is done iteratively. A team is assembled once the modeler chooses the business process that will be modeled. This team defines the grain to represent the data in each row of the tables in the model and then the context relevant for each measure; this will determine the dimensions. The naming of the tables and columns should be familiar to the business users; there will be cases where a specific term needs a clear definition from the business to avoid confusion. Finally, the modeling team decides on the sample domain values and business rules.

Next, we will describe how the team can define the business process to be modeled.

Defining business processes to model

We can describe the daily operations performed by an organization as business processes. The performance of these operations influences the business's direction; therefore, having clear performance metrics is paramount. The dimensional model strives to describe these business processes one at a time with a set of fact and dimension tables. Selecting one business process helps to delimit a specific design objective and makes choosing a level of grain easier.

Generally, most fact tables focus on the results of a singular business process. Understanding the selected process allows the modeler to customize the model to address the organization's unique needs. This way, the dimensional model should reflect the desired performance metrics and the relationship between dimensions that emerge as part of the modeling process of the whole business.

The next step is to decide at what level we will describe the metrics in the data model. This level of detail is known as grain, and it is one of the most important parts of a dimensional model.

Finding the grain

Declaring the **grain** is the same as defining the meaning of each row of one table. It acts as a binding agreement on the design, ensuring consistency and clarity, making it an essential step in the dimensional design process. The grain must be declared before selecting dimensions or facts, as every potential table needs to be in line with the grain.

Starting with **atomic-grained data** is highly recommended, taking the data to the finest level possible at which the chosen business process captures data. It offers greater flexibility and adaptability to accommodate the unpredictability of user queries.

For example, imagine that the supplier of a certain product handles and delivers canned goods to sell at a supermarket. From the supplier's perspective, the grain for these packages can be a pallet, a batch, or a six-pack. However, if we want to be able to support all of these aggregations, we should use the atomic unit, that is, one can.

By focusing on atomic-grained data, the modeler can ensure that the resulting design can be aggregated and analyzed at various levels, allowing users to explore and understand the data from multiple perspectives without changing the underlying model. This approach ultimately leads to a more versatile and valuable dimensional model that addresses diverse analytical needs and supports informed decision-making across the organization.

With these topics covered, we can step back and have an overview of the whole process. Developing a dimensional model is a continuous effort. Just as the business evolves, the model should adapt to these changes.

Determining dimensions

We saw that fact tables are meant to hold business events in the form of transactions or occurrences, but we need a way to store the textual context of a business process measurement event, describing **who**, **what**, **where**, **when**, **how**, and **why**. For this purpose, we use **dimension tables**.

The dimension tables complement the transactions recorded in the fact table, giving us the context to understand the metric fully. Dimension tables use columns or attributes; it is not unusual for a dimension table to have 50 to 100 attributes.

In contrast to fact tables, dimension tables generally contain fewer rows. Each dimension is identified by a unique primary key, which forms the foundation for referential integrity with any connected fact table.

When it is difficult to determine whether a particular field should be part of a fact or dimension table or when both are technically correct, the modeler should consider how this field will be used.

When designing a query to retrieve information from the database, the analyst can use the attributes stored in the dimension table as the primary source for constraints, groups, and labels for reporting tools. It is recommended for these attributes to be meaningful words rather than codes or cryptic abbreviations. When designing the model, it is best to reduce the use of codes unless they are used by the business to drive value; the codes should be replaced by text that is easy to understand by the analysts querying the model.

If the business needs to use specific codes, then the modeler should add new attributes that map the code or its parts with a human-readable explanation of its meaning. This allows analysts to use these new attributes as labels in reports.

The codes should be displayed as distinct dimension attributes alongside the corresponding user-friendly textual descriptors.

Dimension tables often hold hierarchical relationships, such as those between a federal entity and a country or between a manager and an employee. This creates repetitions, as a single country has multiple federal entities. We saw in the normalization section of this chapter that we can remove this repeating group by creating a new table that is used as a lookup table and replacing the country with a foreign key. However, when using the star schema, the modeler should resist the urge to normalize data by storing only the code in the dimension and creating a separate dimension table. Indeed, dimension tables are usually denormalized using many-to-one relationships. If we added subtables, the star shape would transform into a snowflake.

Identifying facts

In a dimensional model, the fact table holds the performance metrics from an organization's business process events. As measurement data are typically the most extensive dataset, it is better not to duplicate the same data in multiple locations for different organizational functions across the enterprise.

We use the term **fact** to denote a business metric. When we think about what is important for the business to measure, we see the real transactions as the facts of main importance. In a fact table, each row aims to reflect a direct measurement, instance, or occurrence of these business events that drive value. The level of detail or aggregation of each row is called the grain.

One of the main principles of designing a good dimensional model is that all rows in a fact table must maintain the same level of aggregation or grain. Creating fact tables with a singular level of detail helps avoid the inaccurate double-counting of measurements.

The most valuable facts are numeric and additive. The fundamental principle of dimensional modeling is that a measurement event in the physical world corresponds to a single row in the related fact table.

Additivity is crucial because, for analytical applications, the analyst rarely wants to retrieve a single row of the table. Instead, they access hundreds, thousands, or even millions of rows at once, which they aggregate to extract insight. Facts can occasionally be **semi-additive** or **non-additive**. In these instances, the analysts must employ counts and averages or display the fact rows individually.

Facts are often characterized as continuously valued to distinguish them from dimension attributes, meaning they can assume virtually any value within a wide range.

In theory, facts can be in textual form, but this is rare since free-form text comments and the unpredictable content of text strings render them nearly impossible to analyze. In this case, the modeler must try to move the textual information within the dimensions where it can be more efficiently associated with other textual dimension attributes. Usually, the textual information captured is used to give context to facts; therefore, its natural place is inside a dimension.

Fact tables are usually long and narrow, with many rows but few columns.

The grain of a fact table can be classified into three categories: **transaction**, **accumulating snapshot**, and **periodic snapshot**. Transaction is the most common of the three. Fact tables must contain at least two foreign keys that serve as a bridge when connecting with the primary keys of the dimension tables.

As a rule of thumb, fact tables typically feature a primary key comprising a subset of foreign keys, commonly referred to as a **composite key**. Any table containing a composite key is considered a fact table. The modeler can use this characteristic to distinguish if a table should hold facts or dimensions. Fact tables embody many-to-many relationships, whereas all other tables are deemed dimension tables.

The star schema

Having grasped the concepts of fact and dimension tables, the modeler can now merge these components to conform to a dimensional model. This means that each business process is represented by a metric stored in a fact table as numeric values, and we can surround it with many dimension tables providing the context of this business metric.

Its simple shape resembles a star with the fact in the center and the dimensions in the point ends. This star-like configuration seen in *Figure 5.11* is frequently called a **star join**, a term that emerged in the early stages of relational databases:

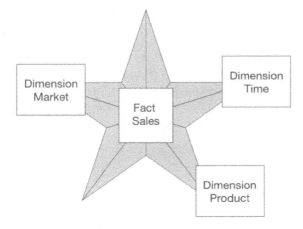

Figure 5.11 – Star schema

The first characteristic to observe in the dimensional model is its simplicity and symmetry. The design's attractiveness stems from its strong familiarity with business users. Additionally, the simplicity of a dimensional model provides performance benefits. For example, the database optimizer can leverage this method to evaluate all potential joins to a fact table in a single pass through the table's index.

Finally, dimensional models are readily expandable to accommodate changes. The modeler will find that the most detailed or atomic data is the most useful when displaying the highest dimensionality. Unaggregated atomic data is the most expressive and must be used as the basis for the grain of the fact tables. Doing this ensures that many different aggregations and calculations can be done with the original data; if the business needs a new metric, it can be obtained easily from the atomic data.

The flexibility of the dimensional model resides in the ability to add any dimension needed to the schema. The only requisite is that a unique value for that dimension is stored in each fact table row to draw a relationship between them.

Similarly, new facts can be introduced to the model as long as their granularity is consistent with the rest of the fact tables in the existing model.

If the modeler finds a complex system that is related not only to one business or that is interconnected to many different subsystems, a different type of model might be more flexible, as we will see in the next section.

Daniel Linstedt and Data Vault

Some systems require greater flexibility due to the volume of data and its evolution over time. In the early 1990s, the US Department of Defense tasked Daniel Linstedt with developing a scalable data warehouse capable of handling vast datasets. This system needed to accommodate high-frequency data inputs and incorporate various structures and subsystems.

Daniel Linstedt named his innovative approach **common foundational warehouse architecture**. This methodology tackles big data, NoSQL, performance, team agility, and complexity by establishing standards and best practices centered around three primary pillars: modeling, implementation, and the methodology and architecture of the enterprise data warehouse.

The methodology subsequently evolved and was registered as a Data Vault open standard. With advancements in technology and the need to manage streaming real-time data, version 2.0 was released. Data Vault 2.0 comprises four primary components: the model paradigm, a methodology adhering to Scrum and Agile best practices, and an architecture.

Daniel Linstedt added other well-known management techniques to the Data Vault 2.0 standard, using the principles from Agile planning, Six Sigma for error handling, or the software development life cycle.

Data Vault model

For this chapter, we will focus on the Data Vault modeling technique. For a more comprehensive understanding of the Data Vault open standard, we recommend referring to Daniel Linstedt and Michael Olschimke's book, *Building a Scalable Data Warehouse with Data Vault 2.0* (https://www.oreilly.com/library/view/building-a-scalable/9780128026489/).

The Data Vault data model relies on modular fundamental structures. These structures interconnect to form a network resembling the human brain's neural network, which consists of nodes (or vertices) linked by connections (or edges).

To convert this network into a data model, **Data Vault** represents the business process by defining **business entities** and assigning **business keys**. The model illustrates how businesses integrate, access, process, and connect information within their systems while mirroring the connections of the business entities in their daily operations.

The Data Vault model, aiming to represent and support a business as accurately as possible, is designed to facilitate rapid adaptation to changing business requirements, the integration of diverse information systems and sources, the navigation of complex business environments and organizational structures, the flexibility to seize new market opportunities, transparency and accountability, the creation of customized and highly specialized reports, and scalability to accommodate business growth.

Therefore, highly complex systems with multiple sources, frequent changes, auditability and traceability requirements, real- or near-real-time data, and rapidly growing datasets can benefit from the Data Vault model. However, understanding and managing a Data Vault model demands much expertise, and there may not be clear added value for using it to model simple systems.

The Data Vault model employs three basic entity types to accomplish these objectives: hubs, links, and satellites. Each entity type serves a specific role within the model. **Hubs** store business keys for individual business entities; **links** store the relationships between business keys (and thus, between hubs); **satellites** store context as attributes for each business key or relationships between business keys.

Hubs

Business entities, such as employees, warehouses, products, and so on, manage every aspect of the business process. Each can be distinctly identified, and their interactions can be mapped to one or a combination of these business entities.

To define business entities, the modeler must consult with the owner of the business process, comprehend the process's execution, and determine how these entities are identified to monitor the business flow.

Identifying business entities requires a unique identifier. This could be a specific system identifier, such as an employee ID, barcode, part number, or a combination of attributes that make the business entity unique, such as its name or a combination of name and location. This unique identifier is known as the **business key**.

In the Data Vault model, the modeler creates a table to hold the business keys and some other information called metadata for each type of business entity; the main benefit of having this unique table for the business keys is that it can integrate various sources and information systems that hold keys for these entities, also standardizing the way they are stored.

It is crucial to establish hubs with business keys that share the same semantic meaning, ensuring they maintain consistent granularity. This implies that a hub containing business keys for customers as individuals should be distinct from a hub containing business keys for customers as corporations.

A **hub table** monitors the business keys added to the data warehouse; for this, it uses metadata fields, such as `source_system`, which helps identify where the data is coming from, or `load_date`, which helps to understand when the business key was added. A **hash key** is generated for each business key as a unique ID. This key will be used to reference the business entity in other components of the Data Vault model, such as links and satellites. The hash key is introduced to enhance performance when joining tables within the model and to enable a reproducible, unique, anonymized key with the same value across different information systems. This approach also allows parallel loading in various structures within the data warehouse.

Links

The link entity maps transactions, hierarchies, the definitions of business terms, and the associations between business entities. If the model accurately reflects the business process, no business entity should be entirely disconnected from the others, as business operations connect them.

The modeler must document all relationships between entities over time at the finest granularity possible. However, the timeline or temporality of these relationships is not stored in the link tables, as the context determines whether the relationship is active is not part of the link table. As mentioned earlier, the context is stored in satellite entities.

Link tables store many relationships. This helps the data model absorb changes in business rules without having to re-engineer the link tables. The granularity is expressed using the number of hubs or business keys being referenced.

Link entities within the Data Vault model offer significant flexibility. When adding new business entities, the modeler should create a new hub and update or add the new relationship to existing links. If a fresh relationship between business entities arises due to different business opportunities or activities, the modeler only needs to introduce a new link that captures this fresh relationship.

Link tables capture the relationships between business entities across multiple systems that employ the Data Vault modeling technique. Since relationships are documented in a standardized way, queries executed on different systems can use the same structure to find data within the data warehouse.

Columns in link tables consist of the hash keys of the business keys referenced in various hubs, which is a newly generated hash key representing the combination of both business keys (indicating their relationship), the load date and time, and the source system.

Satellites

In the Data Vault model, **satellite entities** are specifically designed to capture the contextual information of the described business entity. They document the entity's attributes and offer context about the time when these attributes were valid. As a result, satellites contribute context to hubs and links at a specific time frame. It is essential to avoid adding this type of information or metadata to links and hubs.

Most data captured in satellites is descriptive and changes as the business evolves. The role of satellites is to document these changes as well. This is possible since satellites are connected to only one hub or link, allowing them to be identified by the parent hash key and the timestamp of the captured change.

Satellites can only be dependent on one **parent entity**, meaning one hub or one link, and they also cannot be parent tables to any other entity, so they do not inherit their hash keys.

Another feature of the Data Vault model is that it allows the modeler the freedom and creativity to separate contextual and descriptive information. As a result, a business entity represented in a hub or link can have multiple satellites, which aids in organizing data based on various criteria, such as slowly changing versus fast-changing data, personally identifiable information, or data requiring different access clearances for viewing or modification. If the contextual data comes from various source systems, storing all data from a single source system in the same satellite is recommended, which results in multiple satellites for multiple source systems.

Distributing data across multiple satellites enables the modeler to add new sources without modifying existing satellite entities and eliminates the need to adjust new data to fit existing structures. This feature allows the Data Vault model to capture the history of all changes for each source system. It also enhances parallelism when loading data into the data warehouse. New systems can leverage this capability to load multiple sources simultaneously without competing for read or write access to the same table. Furthermore, it facilitates the integration of real-time or streaming data without mixing it with batch-loaded data.

Satellites are designed to preserve the entire history within a data warehouse. Modifying the structure of a satellite is only permitted if the historical data are fully retained. This ensures that the data warehouse remains the sole repository where the data and their attributes are recorded and preserved at any given time, making it the system of record. Users are not allowed to update or alter the information within a satellite, except for updating the end date of a previous version of the record, thereby closing a time frame and validity for that record while retaining it in the data warehouse.

In addition, satellites contain metadata fields that aid in managing the data warehouse. Typically, a satellite table includes a load date, source system, parent hash key, load end date, and, if applicable, an extract date and hash difference or checksum columns:

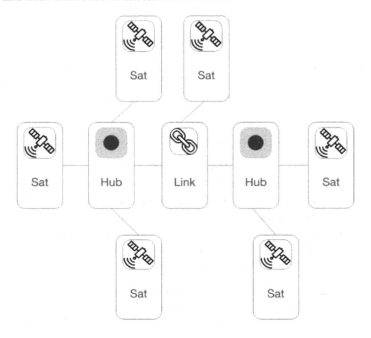

Figure 5.12 – Example schema of a Data Vault model

Figure 5.12 illustrates the structure of a Data Vault model. The hubs are towards the center of the model; the link table relates these hubs, and the satellites extend to the outside with contextual information.

Comparison of the different data models

Now that we have looked into these three modeling techniques, we can compare them using the chart presented in *Figure 5.13*. By using the criteria listed in the first column, the data models are evaluated with a 1 to 5-star rating:

Data models   COMPARISON CHART

CRITERIA	INMON (3NF)	KIMBALL (STAR SCHEMA)	LINSTEDT (DATA VAULT)
Flexibility regarding changes on the source data	★	★★★	★★★★★
Flexibility for new analysis requirements	★★★	★	★★★★★
Making changes to the model	★	★★★	★★★★★
Audit and traceability	★★★	★★★★★	★★★★★
Query performance	★	★★★★	★★★
Mainteinance effort	★★★	★★★★★	★

Figure 5.13 – Data models comparison chart

We will now discuss these ratings for each of the data models.

Bill Inmon's 3NF review

Let us explain these scores for the 3NF data model from Bill Inmon's corporate information factory. When we have changes in the data source, we need to change the tables directly, creating a cascade effect that impacts all the downstream elements that are linked to this table.

When there is a new requirement for a new analysis, the data model changes only if the data is not already in the system, making it easy to cover the new requirement.

If there is a need to change the model, a migration of historical data to a different table or system might be needed for the fully normalized model.

For auditing and traceability, the 3NF model stores historical data by writing a new row for each new event and not deleting anything on the tables that needs to be audited. This can lead to very big tables.

The query performance on a fully normalized model gets impacted as the model grows since the 3NF requires multiple tables, and the number of joins and tables needed to get the information required by an analysis grows as the system grows.

Maintaining a normalized model can be challenging if the platform where it is running has low computing performance; in the cloud data warehouse, this is more of a cost problem since most vendors offer options to increase computing capacity.

Ralph Kimball's dimensional model review

For the dimensional model, the star schema helps reduce the number of tables in the system, de-normalizing the data when possible, but it still gets impacted when there are changes in the source data. Every change in the tables must also be replicated in all downstream tables.

The star schema is designed with the help of a business specialist to reflect the actual operation of the business. This means that any new requirement impacts the data model and needs to be adjusted accordingly.

Dimensional modeling introduces the idea of storing history for audit and traceability as **slowly changing dimension** tables, reducing the number of rows needed to store changes in the data, and keeping the full history available for audit purposes.

The star schema stands out for its ease of use while querying the data. Since the data are stored with familiar names and follow business logic, it is easier to understand the SQL queries required for a specific metric. Additionally, the number of joins needed between tables gets reduced since the relevant data are stored and grouped together.

Maintaining a star schema data warehouse is relatively easy. It constantly evolves with the business, and its simplicity makes it easy to understand; most vendors support this as the default data model for analytical purposes or business intelligence. Its popularity makes it easier to find someone to maintain the model.

Daniel Linstedt's Data Vault review

Finally, the Data Vault model by Daniel Linstedt is designed to be flexible and integrate different information systems, requiring almost no changes to the data model when the source data changes or a new analysis is required.

Since the Data Vault is designed to have a delivery layer with the data marts needed for consumption, these data marts are usually designed using the star schema. When a new analysis is needed, the changes are made on the data mart layer, and the underlying data model is unaffected.

The Data Vault model was designed for the US government with audibility and traceability in mind. All the satellites in the model are treated as slowly changing dimension type-2 tables, and no data gets deleted from the data system; every time a change is needed, the previous data are archived as a historical satellite, and a new satellite with the new changes is made available.

Querying the Data Vault model is not usually advised. Instead, the queries are carried out on the delivery layer over the data marts modeled using the star schema, so the familiarity to the business users is kept. This gives extra flexibility to adapt the underlying data model but also creates the need to model the data in the Data Vault and the delivery layer.

Finally, the Data Vault model is not as popular as the star schema, and finding data professionals with the proper training and knowledge to maintain it is difficult.

We have now explored various modeling techniques, with the three presented being the most used. Each method has its benefits and drawbacks. Let's now discuss how to choose a data model for your particular use case.

Choosing a data model

Modelers should be familiar with these modeling techniques and apply them when appropriate. In practice, most systems have mixed data models, and finding a pure data model that adheres to all the recommended characteristics explored in this chapter is nearly impossible.

As a general guideline, normalization techniques are suitable for transactional systems focused on capturing events, sometimes involving millions of rows in a short period. The strength of the 3NF is that the updates and inserts of these transactions impact the database in only one place.

The dimensional model or star schema is more suitable for analytical purposes, such as drilling down on data, generating reports, and performing aggregations or calculations. This modeling technique is integrated into some business intelligence tools, making it easier for users to understand and query directly for data extraction and create reports or dashboards.

Highly complex systems with multiple sources, frequent changes, clear auditability and traceability requirements, real-time or near-real-time data, and rapidly growing datasets can benefit from the Data Vault model.

Data practitioners must interact with various systems, some of which may have different data models. Understanding the strengths and weaknesses of these techniques can improve the interaction between the data practitioner and the data warehouse system, enabling them to extract maximum value from the stored data.

Other data models serve different uses. For example, the **one big table** (**OBT**) model is good for some analytics platforms, whereas the **snowflake schema** that is derived from the star schema is used in some business intelligence tools. Ultimately, the data practitioner should look for the model that best fits their needs.

Summary

In this chapter, we have covered the benefits of data modeling, some of the best practices to build a data model, and the principal methodologies used to model a data warehouse. After reviewing their main characteristics, we covered how to choose the best model to fulfill the needs of the business according to the use case.

In the next chapter, we will talk about data transformation and how the evolution of tools has drastically changed the way it is carried out.

6

Transforming Data

In the fast-paced world of data-driven decision-making, the ability to transform raw data into valuable insights is a critical competitive advantage. This is part of the foundation of analytics work: enabling organizations to extract meaningful information from vast and complex datasets.

In *Chapter 5, Data Modeling*, we learned about the benefits and techniques of data modeling. A well-designed data model guides the transformation process that turns raw data into ready-to-use data.

This chapter covers the following topics:

- Transforming data – the foundation of analytics work
- Design choices
- Tools that facilitate data transformations

Transforming data – the foundation of analytics work

Raw data is of little value unless it is transformed into valuable insights. In this section, we look into why transforming data is such a crucial step within the data value chain.

A key step in the data value chain

The digitalization of businesses, rapid advancements in technologies such as the **Internet of Things (IoT)**, and the proliferation of smart devices, social media, and advertising platforms have generated abundant data that companies can leverage to understand their customers better, optimize their operations, and enhance their products and services. These phenomena, together known as **big data**, have revolutionized how organizations operate, make decisions, and generate revenue.

However, collecting data is not enough to create a competitive edge in the market. The zettabytes of data that organizations collect daily must be transformed into actionable insight to be of any value. Quantity does not equal quality, and poor quality input produces worthless output; in other words: garbage in, garbage out.

Before being transformed, raw data is usually inconsistent, imprecise, and repetitive. Typically, raw data fits the needs of source systems and, therefore contains irrelevant information or needs to be more adequately structured. By transforming data, we improve its quality and organize it to be ready for analytics applications that fit business needs.

Preparing these vast amounts of data is a time-consuming and expensive task that has become the bottleneck of the data value chain (see *Chapter 12, Driving Business Adoption*, for more details on the data value chain).

Challenges in transforming data

Transforming data can be expensive and resource-intensive. This high effort-to-value ratio is due to a tension between data collection and analytics applications. For instance, your customer service software may fit the needs of the customer support team but stores data in a format unsuitable for analytics.

This tension materializes during transformation, as illustrated in the following figure:

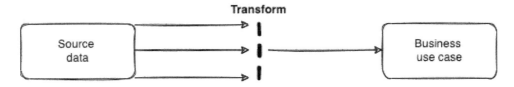

Figure 6.1 – Transforming data can become a bottleneck in your data value chain

Data interpretability

No matter how skilled your data team is or how advanced the tech stack it uses is, the team members will only be successful if they understand the data at hand. Yet, this is a common issue faced by organizations that miss proper data management. Overlooking the reliability and interpretability of source data leads to time-consuming exploration and inadequate transformations, eventually creating frustration for the data teams and a lack of trust for their stakeholders.

To assess the reliability and interpretability of data, consider the following:

- Are data governance and management policies in place? Are they enforced (for example, with data stewards)?
- Are the data owners identified?
- Is the source data accurately documented?

Data discovery is an essential first step in designing transformation pipelines. It is the process of finding and cataloging data sources into a comprehensive inventory. This might include a description of your data, its owner, its lineage, and a glossary.

Data catalogs use metadata to support discovery and governance by enabling, among other things, part or all of the following features:

- **Entity relationship diagrams** (**ERDs**): Help determine the relationships (join keys) and dependencies among data sources to provide an exhaustive view of your data models and inform the development of accurate transformations.

- **Data lineage**: Visually represents end-to-end data flows, from provenance to consumption. It helps identify where transformations are applied and anticipate the downstream impact of changes and issues.

- **Data glossaries**: Provide information on the meaning, context, and usage of data to promote a common language throughout the organization.

Besides getting access to the documentation of the raw data ingested in the data warehouse or lake, it is important to involve data owners and stakeholders during the exploration phases, as they hold precious system and domain knowledge.

Quality of source data

When evaluating the complexity of your transformations, you must consider data quality, structure, and volume. For example, you should investigate the following:

- How reliable is the data collected through the source systems? Are data quality checks and alerts in place? What level of accuracy is expected?

- Are schemas known? How complex are the relationships between data sources? How easily can data sources be combined?

- What volume of data needs to be handled? Will that impact the performance and demand optimization of your transformations?

The first step of an analytics use case exploration should involve data profiling—exploring data to understand its content and structure:

1. The first step is to investigate data types, formats, anomalies, and schemas and to analyze descriptive statistics. This can be as simple as producing summary statistics such as the min, max, mean, standard deviation, count of rows, and distinct values in a table.

2. Observe the structure of the data: How is it organized? Are there any nested fields? Are there any particularly large or wide tables? Do they contain natural keys?

3. Finally, uncover any significant data quality concerns by assessing the accuracy and validity of the data, checking for missing values, duplicates, and outliers, and evaluating the risk of late data.

When data governance is in place, data stewards can help gain visibility and control over your data assets and their usage. This process is sometimes mandatory to comply with data privacy laws.

Business consensus

The end goal must be clear: how will these data be used down the line? This may seem trivial, but it poses a real challenge. The considerations arising from the data transformation process will kick-start discussions among teams around **key performance indicators** (**KPIs**) and business rules. If those are not anticipated, the data team risks rewriting transformation pipelines to accommodate many changes along the way or managing conflicting views on how metrics are defined, resulting in multiple sources of truth.

To assess the level of consensus, consider the following:

- Do stakeholders agree on common business rules? Are these documented?

- How well defined and mature are the use cases?

The process of gathering precise business requirements and scoping use cases is described in *Chapter 12, Driving Business Adoption*.

In the next sections, we will address how to approach data transformations at scale.

Design choices

To implement data transformations that are robust and scalable, we must make some conscious design choices. Agreeing on how and where you will transform your data will allow your team to collaborate more effectively and coherently across pipelines.

Where to apply transformations

As seen in *Chapter 2, The Modern Data Stack*, a high-level architecture of the data stack resembles the following:

Figure 6.2 – High-level architecture example of a data stack (see *Chapter 2*, The Modern Data Stack)

At each of these steps, you might consider applying transformations. For instance, as seen in *Chapter 3, Data Ingestion*, transformations performed during ingestion focus on shaping data into a format and structure that are compatible with the destination system, such as a relational database. This mainly involves parsing and translating source data. Sometimes, however, one might consider cleaning, aggregation, and enrichment during ingestion to simplify downstream operations or for performance reasons.

Figure 6.3 depicts the types of transformations to consider in each step of the data stack:

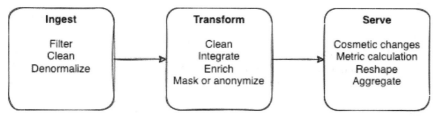

Figure 6.3 – Relevant (non-exhaustive) transformations across the data stack

When deciding where a particular transformation should be applied in your pipelines, consider the following questions:

- Will this transformation remain relevant downstream? Suppose you apply a calculation that must be reverted or add a field that must be removed in your transformation or serving layers. In that case, the transformation should be performed where necessary downstream. Conversely, certain transformations should be applied as early as possible. As a rule of thumb, primary metrics should be calculated in the transformation layer, and secondary metrics should be calculated in the serving layer.

- Does it involve storing data that is not useful at this stage? Filtering data might be relevant at ingestion if the data to be filtered out have no value later. For instance, there is no need to store duplicates if they can be removed at ingestion. Additionally, consider removing any **personal identifiable information** (**PII**) as early as possible in your transformations. If it can be done at ingestion, even better.

- What are the costs of performing this operation at this stage versus before or after? Certain transformations should be performed on aggregated data so that they are only applied where needed. For instance, suppose you have a table of orders containing all orders for your webshop and are building a dashboard of quarterly sales with a year filter. If so, then it is wiser to aggregate the orders table per quarter and create a year field in your BI tool rather than extracting the year from the date in your orders table before aggregating it. The latter would mean performing the operation on more rows and storing an extra, useless field.

- Is it easy to understand and debug? Preparing data in BI tools may be more accessible to business analysts, but these tools frequently lack visibility and transparency, making their transformations hard to debug. For instance, changing a field to uppercase can be done in your BI tool, as it is an easy-to-understand, low-effort transformation that will not need debugging. However, creating new categories can be done earlier as part of the transformation to make the business logic transparent and reusable.

Specify your data model

As we saw in *Chapter 5, Data Modeling*, which is dedicated to data modeling, data models specify the way business rules are enforced as part of transformation pipelines. They help visualize a representation of data that matches business logic. Many techniques and methods exist, the most common being relational and dimensional data models. Choosing which techniques to adopt will depend on your business, the type and volume of data collected, and how it will be used.

In some information systems, it will be necessary to set up more than one data model to fulfill all business needs. The most important aspect of data modeling is to do it proactively to improve the stability and resilience of the system over time.

Layering transformations

As we prepare data for business use, transformations are done in a dedicated transformation layer, which will be the focus of the current section.

Modern tools advertise different frameworks for managing data transformations. For instance, **Databricks** recommends the medallion architecture—**Bronze**, **Silver**, and **Gold**—approach (https://www.databricks.com/glossary/medallion-architecture), while **dbt** advises structuring your project by splitting models into **Staging**, **Intermediate**, and **Marts** layers (https://docs.getdbt.com/best-practices/how-we-structure/1-guide-overview). Regardless, all follow the same paradigm: transforming your data should follow steps that make transformations transparent, reusable, and easy to understand.

Adopting a staged approach to transformation contributes to modular data transformations, improving the scalability of the effort and reducing the time to value when developing new use cases or enhancing existing use cases.

This process typically involves three steps, but it can be split into as many as necessary:

1. **Clean**: Improve data quality and standardize raw data.
2. **Integrate**: Map and model data into a comprehensive set of tables.
3. **Enrich and summarize**: Bring business logic into your data so it is ready to use for analytics.

These steps are illustrated in the following figure:

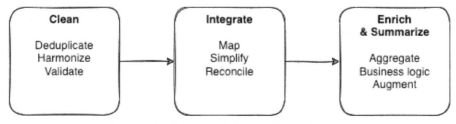

Figure 6.4 – The steps of the transformation layer

In the following subsections, we will describe some of the most common transformation techniques typically involved at each step of the transformation layer. However, you may find these to be useful elsewhere within your pipelines, depending on their purpose. For instance, consider handling categorization as part of normalizing your data in the clean layer but also as part of enriching it at a later stage.

Clean

Data cleaning is the process of identifying and correcting or removing errors, inconsistencies, and inaccuracies. In this step, transformations remain minimal and focus on achieving better data quality without enriching or incorporating business logic.

This step is the foundation of your data transformation pipelines. Data quality issues must be handled as early as possible, as they can ripple throughout your pipelines. Additionally, data collected through various heterogeneous source systems must be harmonized so it can be combined in a later step.

There is much literature on data cleaning, and techniques can be as advanced as natural language processing. At this stage, the main tasks to tackle are the following:

- **Deduplicate**: An essential step in data cleaning is identifying and removing duplicate records. This involves ensuring either a natural key is present or creating a surrogate primary key. De-duplicating early is key to avoiding faulty joins in the integration and enrichment steps. You might even consider performing de-duplication during ingestion.

- **Harmonize**: Harmonizing consists of correcting inconsistencies by resolving discrepancies in data types, units, or categories to maintain consistency across the dataset. This might involve renaming columns, casting data types, converting units, harmonizing time zones, and re-categorizing dimensions. Missing values should also be handled at this step to ensure they are consistently identified and eventually filtered out or interpolated.

- **Validate**: After the first stages of cleaning, data quality checks are implemented to validate data completeness and consistency based on a predefined set of rules.

Next, we discuss how to integrate data from disparate sources for a single comprehensive view.

Integrate

The integration layer provides a comprehensive view of all business activities. Combining data from multiple sources enables valuable analytics use cases that would not otherwise be feasible. For example, an e-commerce business may want to combine data collected via third-party advertising platforms with user behavior on its website to draw the entire user journey from acquisition to conversion.

Building this unified view allows the business to overcome silos at collection and break up the complexity of transformations for better readability and easier debugging of your pipelines.

The following are the critical steps for building an integration layer:

- **Map**: At this step, you will enforce your data model, most likely starting with a certain degree of normalization, depending on the schema of your source data. Normalization is the process of organizing data consistently to ensure its integrity (see *Chapter 5, Data Modeling*). Therefore, you must establish relationships between data elements from different sources to create a unified data model:

  - This involves defining primary and foreign keys and documenting an **entity relationship diagram (ERD)**:

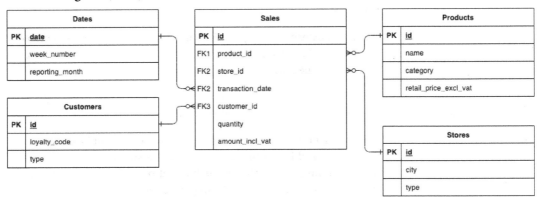

Figure 6.5 – Example of an entity relationship diagram for a sales table and
related dimension tables (dates, customers, products, and stores)

  - As part of creating these entities, consider regraining some tables to a different level of granularity. For instance, you may want to regrain a table containing orders into a table containing product quantities. It may also be relevant to restructure your data, such as unnesting arrays.

  - After normalization, you might consider combining data sources by applying joins and unions. This is particularly relevant when data from multiple sources must be combined and reshaped into a new entity. For instance, if your company gets orders online and in-store, you may want to bring all orders together by stacking the orders coming from different sources into a single transactions table with a common primary key. Alternatively, if product attributes (such as color codes or sizes) are grouped as part of a custom business logic defined in a table outside your operational systems, you may want to join them together in a key such as the product SKU.

- **Simplify**: Calculations that can be reused downstream can be performed at this stage to avoid repeating them later. For instance, if your company reports cost and revenues in euros, you will benefit from performing these conversions early on.

- **Reconcile**: By reconciling different data sources, you can verify the quality and integrity of your data routinely. This might involve implementing data quality monitoring tests and cross-analyzing various data sources for discrepancies.

Enriching data is another important step to consider before we present it to the users. We talk about this next.

Enrich and summarize

This last step consists of preparing data to be exposed and used by business end-users and tools.

Data enrichment enhances data by incorporating additional information or attributes relevant to the business, enabling actionable insight and data-driven decision-making.

The last steps of preparing ready-to-use data involve the following:

- **Aggregate**: In this step, you can summarize or group your data based on specific attributes or dimensions that provide the level of granularity relevant to your business stakeholders. Although aggregating will limit flexibility and the functionalities within your BI tool, it will improve performance depending on the volume of data exposed. Aggregations can be time-based (daily, weekly, or quarterly), location-based (by country or region), or grouped on any kind of dimension relevant to your analysis (product category, marketing channel, and customer type).

- **Apply business rules**: To support decision-making, data exposed in dashboards, analyses, or models should incorporate the following business rules:

  - Filter certain records (for instance, excluding outliers) or irrelevant fields.

  - Incorporate domain-specific constraints and apply custom categorizations.

  - Certain metrics can be calculated and materialized before serving them in your BI tools, such as revenue after taxes.

  - At this stage, consider applying cosmetic renaming, reshaping, such as pivoting, or date formatting. However, be critical about whether these should be materialized or can be done in a BI tool. Avoid creating multiple versions of the same table that will serve a single dashboard each. As much as possible, apply transformations that result in a table that can be reused across many dashboards. For instance, if a stakeholder asks to rename all fields to a different language to accommodate a single user, do so directly in your dashboard.

- **Augment**: Enriching data may also involve denormalization, that is, merging tables. Whether or not you should de-normalize your data depends on the volume of data and how it will be served. If certain analytics applications or services need to be able to retrieve data quickly, you might consider de-normalizing. For instance, if a customer service analyst needs to regularly query data to retrieve customer orders and details, consider bringing together the facts and dimensions. On the other hand, if product information and order quantities are exposed through a BI dashboard, depending on the tool, it may be wiser to keep them normalized and to create relationships within the tool itself. For example, Power BI manages the relationships between tables in the modeling tab of the tool.

- Other enrichment techniques include splitting long fields into multiple columns, such as extracting URL substrings with regular expressions.

Now that we have covered where transformations should occur across your pipelines, let us see how to implement them, from understanding the data at hand to writing production-ready code.

Data transformation best practices

As seen in previous chapters, analytics engineering embraces software engineering best practices to model, transform, test, deploy, and document data in a reusable way.

When it comes to writing transformation pipelines, SQL is the industry standard. Still, you might also want to use other languages, such as Python or Scala, depending on the tools you use for transformation.

The barrier to entry to writing SQL code is quite low. Thanks to its declarative nature, SQL is easy to read. Most data specialists know how to write SQL, making it easier for organizations to hire talent who can work with SQL pipelines, an important factor in democratizing transformation capabilities.

In this section, we will tackle SQL best practices for your transformation pipelines. We will also mention language specific to dbt and Databricks. In dbt, the SQL files in which developers write SELECT statements are called **models**. In Databricks, code is organized within **notebooks**. We assume you are using **Delta Lake** tables, as these are the default in Databricks.

Readability and reusability first, optimization second

Regardless of the language in which you write your pipelines, a couple of principles apply to ensure your code's reusability, readability, and, ultimately, scalability.

Ensuring code **reusability** involves breaking down your code into chunks that can be repurposed when developing your pipelines.

Readability is about ensuring your code is easy to understand, modify, and maintain by your peers. Good transformation pipelines are self-explanatory and easy to follow. Readable code can make the most complex transformations easy to understand.

What about **optimization**? As a rule of thumb, optimization should be performed once your code has been broken down into simple, understandable parts. This allows for the isolation and testing of each piece of logic and the identification of performance issues. Debugging inaccurate, long, and complex queries is like finding a needle in a haystack.

If a step in the transformation process is costly or slow, consider optimizing it. How you will improve query performance will depend on the strategies supported by your data warehouse. Configurations may be platform-specific. Here, we will cover the two main techniques for **incremental strategies**: **partitioning** and **clustering**.

Incremental updates

You should consider incremental strategies for large tables, such as transaction tables that record events. For instance, you can incrementally update an orders table by appending new orders and updating existing orders with their latest status.

In Databricks, Delta Lake tables support the `MERGE INTO` statement (`https://learn.microsoft.com/en-us/azure/databricks/sql/language-manual/delta-merge-into`), which allows merging updates, insertions, and deletions based on a source table into a target table. Note that the syntax and parameters of `MERGE INTO` vary per database—refer to the documentation of the appropriate database.

In dbt, models can be configured to be **incremental** (`https://docs.getdbt.com/docs/build/incremental-models`), allowing you to insert or update records into a table since the last time the model was run. Using incremental models can significantly reduce the build time. These models are built as tables in your data warehouse. Available incremental strategies differ per data warehouse, so the configuration of your incremental model will need to be adapted accordingly (`https://docs.getdbt.com/docs/build/incremental-models#supported-incremental-strategies-by-adapter`).

Partitioning

Partitioning divides large tables into smaller partitions that can be physically stored on multiple disks. This improves query performance by reducing the number of bytes read by a query and allowing parallel access to different partitions.

Configuring partitioning strategies will depend on the database. dbt allows you to configure models accordingly. For instance, in BigQuery, tables can easily be partitioned by column, and dbt lets you add a `partition_by` dictionary to the model configuration, which is compiled as a `PARTITION BY` statement (`https://docs.getdbt.com/reference/resource-configs/bigquery-configs`).

In Databricks, unpartitioned tables are automatically clustered by ingestion time (`https://www.databricks.com/blog/2022/11/18/introducing-ingestion-time-clustering-dbr-112.html`), which optimizes query performance out of the box. You can use `OPTIMIZE` to optimize the layout of Delta Lake tables by producing evenly balanced files in terms of disk size. Additionally, you can reduce the amount of data that needs to be read by collocating column information in the same set of files using the `ZORDER BY` parameter.

Clustering

When a table is clustered, blocks are physically ordered based on column values. In this way, queries that filter or aggregate by the clustered columns only scan the relevant blocks.

In Databricks, you can enable **liquid clustering** (`https://docs.gcp.databricks.com/en/delta/clustering.html`) and let Databricks manage the layout and optimization of your tables instead of partitioning or using `ZORDER` yourself.

Modularity

Making your code reusable translates into **modularization**, which means breaking up the logic of your code into smaller independent pieces, or modules, that other modules can call.

To achieve **modularity**, you can write reusable queries and reusable SQL expressions with two levels of modularity:

- Across queries
- Within the same query

Across queries

Across multiple queries, the following techniques allow you to achieve modularity:

- **Modular data modeling**: The first thing to consider is making your data model modular. This will allow any user of the data model to reuse the foundational work rather than start their data transformation from scratch. Writing a modular data model involves layering your transformation pipelines and creating sound dependencies between transformation jobs.

  - In dbt, models can be referenced by other models using a `ref` function. These dependencies are illustrated by a **directed acrylic graph** (**DAG**) that, if your code is modular, will clearly show the layers of the data modeling logic. dbt allows for enforcing conventions that support modular data modeling, such as organizing SQL files in a structured dbt project to easily navigate the different layers of transformation.

  - In Databricks, you can modularize your code by breaking down workflows into logical chunks. **Jobs** are composed of **tasks** that can, in turn, call smaller "child" jobs. This allows you to reuse logic by creating downstream dependencies and an easily understandable DAG.

- **UDFs**: Defining **user-defined functions** (**UDFs**) outside of queries allows you to reuse their logic throughout, which ensures the consistency of operations and maintainability. In Databricks, you can define functions in files that can be imported and reused in other notebooks using standard Python commands.

- **Macros** (in dbt): In dbt, you can write reusable pieces of code called macros. Macros are written in a templating language called Jinja and are analogous to functions in other languages such as Python.

- **Stored procedures**: Stored procedures can take parameters, contain variables and loops, use data manipulation language, and call other stored procedures. They constitute a powerful way to combine querying data with parameters.

We will now talk about how we can reuse SQL expressions within a query.

Within the same query

Within a SQL query, there are two main ways to ensure code reusability:

- **Common table expressions** (**CTEs**): CTEs are temporary views you can refer to within your query. They allow you to break down your query into simpler and smaller pieces of logic that can be referenced and chained together. Refactoring code with CTEs can easily be done using a `WITH` statement, encapsulating your reusable query. In dbt, CTEs can be materialized as ephemeral models. Ephemeral models are interpolated as CTEs within dependent models but can be reused and tested.

- **Temporary user-defined functions** (**UDFs**): Like views, **UDFs** encapsulate transformation logic, with the main difference being that they take input parameters and return output values or tables. UDFs are commonly used to encapsulate operations, `CASE WHEN` statements, and regular expressions. You might consider UDFs for converting units and categorizing or extracting strings. Temporary functions can be created and reused within a query and are dropped as soon as the query finishes. They allow you to apply the same operations throughout your query without repeating the logic involved.

Other best practices

The following practices can help your team keep their code readable and modular:

- **Don't repeat yourself** (**DRY**) is the principle of moving any piece of logic that is copy-pasted in multiple places into a reusable query (CTE, view, or dbt model) or expression (UDF, stored procedure, or dbt macro). The opposite of DRY is **write everything twice** (**WET**), which means you repeatedly write the same code throughout your pipelines.

- The **single responsibility principle** (**SRP**) states that each module of your code should have a single purpose. This allows us to break down the logic of transformations instead of coupling them and creating complexity.

- **Propagate logic**: To make your model DRY, certain logical transformations should be moved upstream so that they can be reused downstream. For instance, if the quantity of product purchases should always be an integer, you can enforce that transformation in the **clean step** of *Figure 6.4* to avoid having to cast floats in the integration and enrichment layers.

- **Comment on the why, not the how**: Well-written code is self-explanatory. Use aliases for table names and columns, ensuring the naming convention is intuitive and consistent and that column names are explicitly referenced in `SELECT` statements. For instance, if you are selecting from joined tables with wildcards (`*`), make sure to alias and reference the source table of each column chosen so that it is clear where each field is coming from. If your code is easy to read, comments will not be necessary. However, as you incorporate business rules and transform your data for specific purposes, you might need to explain the **why**: why are you filtering on, let's say, this event code?

- **Document**: Most of the time, applied logic should not only be commented on within the code but documented outside of the code. Accurate documentation allows developers and stakeholders to quickly understand what the code does and how to work with it.

Now let's look at an example of how to modularize your code.

An example of writing modular code

Imagine you work for a bakery. The manager wants to analyze the average consumer discount on products over time. The tables at your disposal in the bakery dataset are documented in the ERD of *Figure 6.5*.

If you try to write the SQL in one go to produce a table of daily average discounts per product, you might end up with the following code:

```
SELECT
    D.product_id,
    D.date,
    P.product_name,
    -- Apply VAT to retail price and substract selling price including
VAT to calculate discount amount
    (CASE
        WHEN P.product_category = 1 THEN P.retail_price_excl_vat *
1.09
        WHEN P.product_category = 2 THEN P.retail_price_excl_vat *
1.21
        WHEN P.product_category = 3 THEN P.retail_price_excl_vat
        ELSE P.retail_price_excl_vat * 1.21
    END)- D.avg_selling_price as avg_discount_amount_incl_vat
FROM (
    SELECT
```

```
        date,
        product_id,
        ROUND(AVG(amount/quantity), 2) AS avg_selling_price
    FROM bakery.Sales
    GROUP BY
        date,
        product_id
) AS D
LEFT JOIN bakery.Products as P ON D.product_id = P.id
GROUP BY
    D.product_id,
    D.date
```

The preceding code snippet requires comments. Moreover, it could create repetitions, as it is likely that you will need to repeat the logic to apply VAT in other queries. Finally, the join on a subquery makes it more challenging to understand what the field names in the SELECT statement are referring to, especially since the alias D is not self-explanatory.

> **Note**
>
> This chapter features code snippets designed to showcase best practices. However, executing these snippets may need extra setup, not covered in this book. Readers should view these snippets as illustrative examples and adapt the underlying best practices to their unique scenarios.

To make it more readable and DRY, you could refactor this code as follows.

First, you would create a user-defined function in your data warehouse or a macro in dbt to apply VAT to the retail price, depending on the product category. This UDF or macro is defined outside your query to be reused elsewhere and managed centrally. As a UDF, it could be something like this:

```
CREATE FUNCTION apply_vat(price FLOAT, product_category INT)
RETURNS FLOAT64
AS (
    CASE
        WHEN product_category = 1 THEN price * 1.09
        WHEN product_category = 2 THEN price * 1.21
        WHEN product_category = 3 THEN price
        ELSE price * 1.21
    END
);
```

Alternatively, in dbt, the following could be a macro:

```
{% macro apply_vat(price_column, product_category_column) %}
    CASE
WHEN {{ product_category_column }} = 1 THEN {{ price_column }} *
1.09
WHEN {{ product_category_column }} = 2 THEN {{ price_column }} *
1.21
WHEN {{ product_category_column }} = 3 THEN {{ price_column }}
ELSE {{ price_column }} * 1.21
END
{% endmacro %}
```

Then, within your SQL file, you would write a common table expression to calculate the daily selling prices of the products:

```
WITH daily_selling_prices AS (
    SELECT
        S.date,
        S.product_id,
        ROUND(AVG(S.amount/S.quantity), 2) AS avg_selling_price
    FROM
        bakery.Sales AS S
    GROUP BY
        S.date,
        S.product_id
)
```

In a dbt model, this CTE could be moved to a separate ephemeral model so that it can be reused and tested. The query would be the same except for referencing the sales table using the ref function {{ ref('Sales') }}.

Finally, you would calculate the discount applied every day to products based on the difference between the selling price and retail price, including VAT:

```
SELECT
    S.product_id,
    S.date,
    P.product_name,
    apply_vat(P.retail_price_excl_vat, P.product_category) - S.avg_
selling_price as avg_discount_amount_incl_vat
FROM
    daily_selling_prices as S
LEFT JOIN
    bakery.Products as P ON S.product_id = P.id
GROUP BY
```

```
    S.product_id,
    S.date,
    P.product_name
```

In dbt, the resulting model would be the same as the preceding query, except it would reference the ephemeral model for daily selling prices instead of a CTE:

```
SELECT
    S.product_id,
    S.date,
    P.product_name,
    {{ apply_vat('retail_price_excl_vat', 'product_category') }} -
S.avg_selling_price as avg_discount_amount_incl_vat
FROM {{ ref('daily_selling_prices') }} as S
LEFT JOIN {{ ref('Products') }} as P
ON S.product_id = P.id
GROUP BY
    S.product_id,
    S.date,
    P.product_name
```

The preceding code is modular—it breaks down the logic into small chunks that are easy to reuse, interpret, and debug.

Some tools are dedicated to facilitating best practices in data transformations. The next section gives an overview of the market.

Tools that facilitate data transformations

As data volumes, complexity, and usage continue to grow, tools that facilitate data transformations have emerged to simplify and streamline this process. During the early 2020s, dbt became one of the most prominent and used tools for data transformation.

These tools have revolutionized the way data engineers and analysts work, making it easier and more efficient to transform and analyze data. Previously, data transformations consisted of a series of files containing SQL queries, requiring extensive coding and scripting to ensure they ran in the desired order.

Now, most tools can transform data, sometimes with low or even no code. However, the fact that you **can** doesn't mean that you **should**. Most of the time, the answer to whether you should transform data in a tool is "it depends." The following section explores what to consider when making that decision.

Types of transformation tools

As seen in the *Where to apply transformations* section, they can occur in many of the steps of the data supply chain, from ingesting to serving your data. With the increased interest in easy-to-write and efficient transformations, many tools try to expand their scope by offering data transformation functionalities and features that improve the quality and governance of data throughout transformation pipelines.

Be it at ingestion, with tools such as **Fivetran**, **Stitch**, or **Supermetrics**, or at serving, with BI tools such as **Power BI**, **Tableau**, or **Qlik Sense**, many tools offer possibilities to transform your data.

At the extreme end of this spectrum, self-service analytics tools also provide capabilities to empower business users with limited technical skills to prepare and transform data on their own. They often provide a user-friendly interface and intuitive features for data profiling, cleaning, and enrichment. For instance, business stakeholders might use **Power Query** in **Excel** or transform and visualize data in marketing platforms such as **Salesforce Marketing Cloud or Segment**.

However, these also come with limitations that make it hard for your teams to debug and maintain pipelines or support your stakeholders.

Therefore, you must consider at which stage you should be doing your transformations, regardless of the possibilities at other stages, and as much as possible, favor performing your transformations in the transformation layer.

The industry leader dedicated to data transformations is dbt. It allows users to define data transformations as code, making it easier to version control, test, and collaborate on data pipelines. It also provides features such as data lineage tracking and documentation generation, which support documenting business logic and the overall interpretability of transformation pipelines.

Dataform is also a powerful data modeling and management tool that allows analytics engineers to transform and organize data pipelines in BigQuery. When compared to dbt, Dataform focuses on enforcing robust data models and governance and enabling collaboration.

Finally, tools such as Alteryx allow data teams to transform data without coding skills and offer user-friendly, drag-and-drop interfaces with low or no code.

Considerations

When deciding which tools offer the appropriate features to perform transformations, you should consider the following:

- **Accessibility**: Who needs to prepare data and read and interpret transformations at this stage? What kind of skills do they have? This might raise the question of low/no-code tools.

- **Collaboration**: How many people will need to collaborate on these pipelines? Version control will help track any changes in your pipelines, prevent conflicting changes, and allow you to roll back in case of an issue.

- **Testing and monitoring**: How will you create trust in the data served? Robust pipelines should be thoroughly tested and input and output data quality monitored to anticipate and rapidly solve issues.

- **Data governance**: How do you ensure the transparency and interpretability of your pipelines? Documenting data, transformations, and lineage improves collaboration, reduces data exploration tasks, and contributes to data literacy throughout the organization.

- **Support and community**: The benefit of adopting an established tool is access to an active community of peers who share tips and help each other troubleshoot common issues.

- **Security and compliance**: Will sensitive data be exposed? Does the tool offer appropriate access management? Is it compliant with local regulations?

- **Integrations**: How easily does this tool integrate with your current data stack?

- **Proliferation of tools**: Will the tool you consider replace one or more existing tools in your stack, or are you adding tools to get extra features? If so, what is the value of these features against the cost of maintaining many tools?

- **Scalability**: You may not find it critical to address all the preceding points right now, but what about tomorrow? Investing in future-proof solutions and modernizing your data stack is a strategic choice that will increase your organization's ability to tackle future challenges and pivot when needed.

Summary

In this chapter, we have discussed the importance of data transformation pipelines as a crucial step in the data value chain. We have delved into the practical topics and best practices that developers should consider when designing their transformation pipelines.

Finally, we explored the families of tools that facilitate transformation and how to break down your needs to identify the right tools for your organization in an evolving industry.

In the next chapter, we will delve into the next step of the analytics workflow: Serving data.

7
Serving Data

You have probably heard it said that data is the new oil. What most experts neglect to mention is that data is a costly asset that is only valuable for two things: automating processes and informing your users' decision-making. In other words, data only becomes useful when you serve it.

So far, we have discussed the multiple stages of the data life cycle (e.g., storage and ingestion). However, the truth is that most of your users do not care about any of that. They do not want to hear about data warehouses, Python packages, or Docker images. If anything, they take all the work necessary to create a bar chart for granted.

This part of the process is your users' first and only contact with the data. It is the interface between your work and the rest of your organization. So, you want to make a great impression. If you learn how to do it well, you will become invaluable. Every important person in an organization needs data, so knowing how to serve data well is an easy way to obtain visibility. But for now, remember it is straightforward to deliver incorrect information and hard to get trust back.

Serving data well can be daunting. Besides the challenges specific to serving data, there are many upstream dependencies. Many data problems, often outside your scope, become evident at this point (e.g., data quality, performance, and discoverability). Simply put, a wrong number in a dashboard might not always be your fault. In this chapter, however, we will only address the challenges and considerations specific to this stage of the life cycle. Still, we cannot stress enough the importance of these other problems.

This chapter will focus on how data reaches your users and finally becomes useful, highlighting methods, tools, and considerations to realize the value of your data. Some of the topics we will discuss are the following:

- Exposing data using dashboarding and BI tools

- Data as a product

- Serving data – four key topics

Exposing data using dashboarding and BI tools

We often think of serving data as simply making dashboards. While dashboarding is essential in any data strategy, serving data is a more complex process.

Part of doing this well is fulfilling the needs of all your users. Your more technical users may prefer a programming language to query your data. Others prefer a text message when a certain threshold has been met. Other users might not even be human. You could be serving data to your applications via an API or using it in your warehouse to enrich an application's capabilities.

In this chapter, we are working with a broad definition when we refer to serving data. We will present some of the most common approaches to sharing data and how to make the most of them depending on your organization's needs.

Dashboards

A **dashboard** is a collection of related datasets presented using information design principles to make data more accessible and is often shown as a screen full of graphs, indicators, numbers, and tables. Many data tools center around building dashboards. Some of their most common selling points include empowering users to understand their data by giving a comprehensive dataset overview.

Some might think making data look pretty is superfluous, and there is some truth behind that statement. Some graphs look nice but are hard to understand at a glance. This often applies to visuals such as Sankey charts and pie charts with many categories or 3D visuals.

Perhaps one of the best examples of data visualization as an art is the famous Florence Nightingale's rose diagram (https://commons.wikimedia.org/wiki/File:Nightingale-mortality.jpg). This diagram (*Figure 7.1*) shows the proportions of deaths attributed to different causes. Even in the 1850s, when the diagram was first published, it caused awe and fascination among the viewers. However, it is difficult to process what you see at first glance. Understanding what each color means or that the two radial charts represent two consecutive years takes some time.

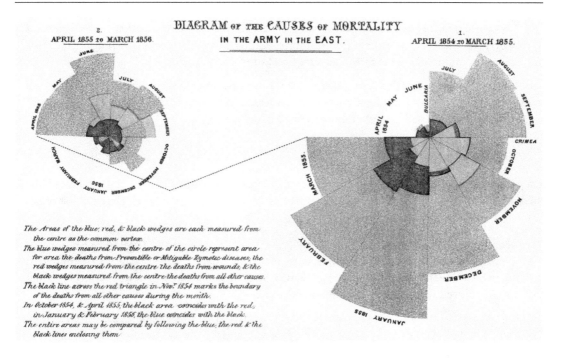

Figure 7.1 – Florence Nightingale's rose diagram

There is nothing wrong with using data visualization as a form of art. However, the true power of information design is how it facilitates comprehension. If done well, it enhances humans' ability to understand data at a glance. For instance, in *Figure 7.2,* it is objectively easier to count occurrences of the number two in the image on the right.

```
545195        545195
   254           254
681136        681136
   218           218
145122        145122
   877           877
```

Figure 7.2 – Data visualization makes data easy to understand

In some cases, static graphs are enough. However, modern BI and dashboarding tools allow users to interact with dashboards. Some examples include the following:

- **Drilling down**: Refers to navigating from a high-level summary to a more detailed view – for example, breaking down the data by year or by month.

- **What-if scenarios**: Involves changing variables or inputs to simulate outcomes. A typical example is "Will we hit our target if we sell three more units per day?"

- **Dynamic window calculations**: Allows users to analyze trends and patterns over time and aggregate data over a specific window of time (e.g., the last 30 days or one year ago). The most common examples are the moving average and running sum.

- **Alerts**: Events or notifications are triggered when certain conditions are met or data hits a specific threshold. Examples are "Send me a message if a client makes a purchase above 10k" or "Email me if a delivery takes more than 10 days."

Spreadsheets

Most people are familiar with them; they are easy to teach and allow users to control their data. While casual users love them, most data professionals frown upon using spreadsheets. Here is a list of the most common complaints:

- **Scalability**: Some spreadsheets have hard limits. As of February 2021, Excel has a row limit of 1,048,576 for all versions from 2007 onward, including Microsoft 365. Columns are limited to 16,384. However, even without the hard limits, large spreadsheets are prone to longer loading times, reduced performance, and unresponsiveness.

- **Compression**: File formats, such as Apache Parquet (`https://parquet.apache.org/`), can be up to 90% more efficient at storing data, keeping the file size smaller.

- **Data integrity**: Anybody can delete a row or even modify a number, maliciously or not.

- **Version control**: It is tough to see a detailed change log (i.e., an exhaustive list of who made which change and when). Newer versions often allow you to view and restore older copies of a spreadsheet using a revision system. However, this is not comparable to the version control capabilities of frameworks such as Git.

- **Security**: Users may leak confidential information via email or allow many others to download the file. Once a spreadsheet has been sent as a file, you have very little control over who sees it or who is currently using your data.

- **Collaboration**: It is hard to merge the work people have carried out in multiple files.

- **Destructive formatting**: By default, columns may be automatically cast into a particular data type without notifying you – for example, when phone numbers get cast as numbers and the leading zeros disappear.

All these concerns make spreadsheets less than ideal. However, as much as we prefer not to work with them, they are ubiquitous. You can help your users mitigate the problems that spreadsheets cause by using the following:

- **Cloud versions**: This prevents users from creating multiple versions of the same sheet and facilitates collaboration. Additionally, you can restrict access and track who has seen a specific sheet.

- **Add-ons or other tools**: A good example is **Power Query**. It is an Excel add-on that helps you track changes users make to data and allows you to revert to previous versions. Additionally, it allows working with data programmatically by using the M language.

- **Protected ranges**: This feature prevents some users from modifying specific columns, rows, or tables in your data.

- **Live connections**: You can ensure that users read data directly from the source (without copying and pasting). Some methods include third-party add-ons, import functions (e.g., IMPORTDATA and IMPORTRANGE), or exposing SQL views to specific users.

Programming environments

Programmers are a small yet vital group of your data users. They need data to power applications or automate processes. While most programmers are skilled enough to access the data without your help, there are some things you can do to enable them:

- **Create a mount point for your data**: You can mount data to different locations such as clusters, **Docker containers**, or **Jupyter notebooks**. This works similarly to seeing a folder when you connect a hard drive to your computer.

- **Help create service accounts**: While most users will use their personal credentials to query data, many programmers will need non-human, privileged accounts to automate processes. These are commonly known as service accounts. It is common for tools such as **Fivetran** or **dbt** to use service accounts to operate.

- **Make a library or package**: Tools such as dbt or programming languages allow you to bundle modules and pieces of pre-written code. Instead of asking every programmer to create the same connectors, you can reduce it to one or two lines of code. In the case of dbt, you can think of macros, such as the ones from the dbt-utils package.

- **Build APIs**: You can create programmatic interfaces to share your data. Most of your applications already communicate with each other using API's. As a result, using a well-known protocol to share your data will make the lives of programmers much more manageable.

Why use service accounts?

The most practical reason to use a **service account** is that it transcends the humans who create an application. You do not want any processes to stop when you deactivate a user's account who moved to another job. Additionally, creating unique service accounts with well-defined security scopes, allows you to monitor applications more efficiently and reduces the damage if the account gets compromised.

Low-code tools

Some tools enable end users to perform heavy-duty data use cases with very little supervision from IT. Some examples include the following:

- **Dataiku** and **DataRobot** for data science
- **Alteryx** and **Matillion** for ETL

While these tools are not exclusively meant to serve data, organizations often use them as a **self-service layer**. Usually, a centralized data team creates data models, exposing them to users of low-code tools for further transformations of use cases.

Low-code tools can be a double-edged sword; they democratize access to data across your organization. Instead of teaching your data team about a particular domain, you teach the domain expert how to work with these tools. However, some challenges exist. Encouraging individuals with limited data literacy to use these tools can lead to data redundancy, unintended errors, or data that doesn't meet the quality requirements.

Another issue is the declarative nature of these tools. Put simply, low-code platforms enable users to specify what needs to occur but offer limited control over the process. An apt analogy would be the distinction between driving and taking the bus. Driving affords greater control over the route but it demands more effort, while taking the bus provides less control yet offers convenience. Both options reach the same destination, but the lack of control inherent in some low-code tools may prove constraining or inefficient for certain use cases.

Despite their limitations, there will always be room for these tools. For example, enabling a financial team to use low-code tools is usually easier than teaching the data team the intricacies of calculating financial indicators.

Reverse ETL

Reverse ETL is a booming industry. Its core idea is to take data from your data warehouse and ingest it back into applications. This way, you can clean and enrich the data in a centralized location, making it available for your applications.

The concept of enriching data is not new. Many systems and applications already have a data enrichment feature. These tools can manually add information, import data from files, or read data directly from your database. The novelty is that these tools standardize the process and reduce the complexity. Reverse ETL reduces the whole process to some clicks or a few lines of code. Analogous to managed ingestion, reverse ETL reduces the entire process to some clicks or a few lines of code.

An everyday use case for reverse ETL involves **customer relationship management (CRM)** systems. In many organizations, salespeople use a CRM system to manage and log customer interactions, generally in the form of meeting notes and client information. Thanks to reverse ETL, you can enrich these systems with data from other systems, such as sales data, web data, or even the output of machine learning models. You can do all this without learning how to use an API or preparing the data in a specific format.

Next, we will discuss the importance of a product mindset when serving data.

Data as a product

Data has a lot of potential, but you need to put in some work before you start unlocking its value. This led to the concept of data as a product. Conceptually, data as a product endorses using a product mindset and a user-centric approach toward data. The term was coined in 2012 by the mathematician DJ Patil. However, **data mesh** has brought the concept to the forefront in recent years.

Data as a product has multiple definitions, but most agree that data should be valuable, usable, and sensible.

Valuable

Your user must want to use your data. Every organization has data products, such as dashboards or SQL views, that have barely been used. To prevent this, data should do the following:

- Make life simpler
- Assist your users
- Be actionable
- This leads to better decisions
- Drive positive outcomes

Usable

Using your data should be frictionless. You should always remove hurdles such as difficult-to-read header names or lack of consistency in naming conventions. Data should be the following:

- Easy to find
- Well-documented
- Pre-joined
- Pre-aggregated
- Pre-filtered
- Easy to understand

Sensible

Creating and maintaining a data product should make business sense for the data team. Some organizations may spend impractical amounts of manpower building dashboards that deliver very little strategic value to the business. Even worse, they might get in trouble for irresponsibly sharing confidential data such as salaries. The data you promise to your users should be as follows:

- Technically possible
- Reasonably priced
- Easy to maintain
- Secure and not a liability
- Legal, compliant, ethical, and responsible

There are infinite ways to serve data. However, regardless of what you do, sticking to the previous principles and treating your data as a product is key for successful adoption. The world is already full of dashboards and tables that nobody uses.

Adopting a product mindset is an excellent start to serving data in your organization. However, serving data well requires careful consideration of various factors and the ability to adapt to changing needs. Generally, the best data teams are the ones who have a strong vision about data-driven organizations.

The next section will delve into four strategic topics around serving data. If you strive to have a mature data team, you should definitely consider these points.

Serving data – four key topics

Serving data well is a balancing act. You should consider what is best for your organization, create a strategy, and constantly see how these principles apply to different features and tools.

In this section, we will discuss four topics that always arise in different data teams:

- Self-serving analytics and report factories
- Interactive and static reports
- Actionable and vanity metrics
- Reusability and bespoke processes

Self-serving analytics and report factories

Data tools were difficult to learn in the past, and analyzing data required technical prowess. The most common setup was to hire data professionals to deploy use cases for the rest of the organization. These teams worked on a request-by-request basis. Having a small team made it easier to reuse assets, ensure one single source of truth, stay compliant, and keep a strict guard on any data process.

For the end users, however, this was less than ideal. They had to submit a ticket to a person who might not have enough domain expertise to understand what they meant. Also, due to limited capacity, requests would take days or even months to be completed. It often happened that, by the time a dashboard was finished, the question it answered was no longer relevant.

This approach is known as traditional BI or *report factory*. It led to the rise of a counter-movement called **self-service analytics**. Contrary to the previous paradigm, the latter approach empowers users to analyze their data. In essence, it turns information and insight into democratic processes.

Self-service analytics is only possible because the tools have become easier to use. With the speed at which we generate data, it makes sense to allow domain experts to analyze what they think is relevant and answer their questions. However, this approach still requires some degree of data literacy from your user. Self-service means constantly teaching your users how to use a tool, placing a higher emphasis on adhering to established best practices and ensuring a certain standard of data quality.

Even though the narrative might place self-service as a superior option, centralized data teams may be the correct approach for some organizations. This is especially true for companies that want to prevent data quality issues, require strict compliance, or cannot afford data misuse.

Both report factories and self-service may lead to negative outcomes. If done wrong, self-service may lead to incorrect numbers and hundreds of unfinished dashboards, ultimately diminishing the users' trust in data. On the other hand, a bad report factory can discourage users from using data or, even worse, make the most skilled users deploy their own shadow IT system.

If you run a centralized data team, we suggest you do the following:

- Find a person responsible for prioritizing. People will pressure you into delivering their use cases. Having a person decide what gets done first can make the work much more pleasant. For example, you could hire a product owner or manager to determine the team's tasks.

- Be proactive when it comes to updates. Dealing with users' expectations can be a time-consuming task. A weekly update or demonstration can save a lot of time, instead of sending individual responses every time you get an inquiry.

- Do not fear sharing bad news. Even if the work is not completed, users still prefer knowing about it to adjust their expectations. By taking a more open approach, your users can empathize and help you.

- Promise a specific number of feedback rounds. Most data work is an iterative process. Users will often request changes or increase the scope. You should strike a balance between embracing feedback and not getting stuck in an endless loop.

- Plan capacity for maintenance and repair. Data products, like everything else, often break. Make some time every week to allow for repairs.

Part 3:
Hands-On Guide to Building a Data Platform

In this section, you will have the opportunity to put the knowledge you've acquired into practice by constructing a basic data platform. We will utilize Airbyte Cloud for managed data ingestion, Google BigQuery for data warehousing, dbt Cloud for data transformations, and Tableau for data visualization.

This section has the following chapter:

- *Chapter 8, Hands-On Analytics Engineering*

On the other hand, if you think self-service analytics is a much better-suited approach for your organization, we recommend you do the following:

- Invest in data discoverability. Having a centralized location that aids your users when looking for data is invaluable. Some data catalogs in the market can help you automate some of the hassle (e.g., profiling, monitoring usage).

- Acquire tools based on their ease of use. You will need tools that are easy to learn, even if they lack some features that you consider vital.

- Find tools with an active community. Your users will have many questions and need to learn and re-learn the basics. Choosing a tool with a vibrant community means it is easy to find tutorials or forums to ask questions. Do not underestimate how much time this can save.

- Force users to productionize. Your users will occasionally create game-changing data products but often lack a real incentive to finish them, share them, or keep them up to date. An extreme example could be to allow users to publish data products to private sandboxes that delete content every 90 days. Try to give users a process to promote content to a more permanent location.

Interactive and static reports

Simple dashboarding tools create static reports. These are fine if you want to print or export them as images. However, interactive reports are often better for analyzing and understanding your data. The catch is that while it is straightforward to make a static graph, interactive graphs require a data engine. In other words, the dashboarding tool must be able to make calculations on its own.

As previously discussed, most modern data tools can make calculations and clean data. It might be tempting for users to do a lot of data transformation inside of their dashboarding since this removes the dependency that they have on the IT team (i.e., I don't need to ask somebody else to modify the database). Unfortunately, using these tools to transform data comes with many issues.

The problem with using these tools to transform data is only evident when numbers do not match. As a developer, it can become a nightmare to check a handful of places and tools to find a potential bug in your code.

There is a good case to stay away from data transformation at the consumption layer if the following statements are true:

- Your formula or query should be reused elsewhere

- You are fixing something that only needs fixing once (e.g., typos, removing trailing spaces, and changing letter cases)

- You risk creating multiple definitions (e.g., two users sharing the same credit card could be interpreted as one or two clients)

However, there are some important exceptions. If you do not know what your user will ask in advance, it is better to let the tool calculate that on the fly. Here is a detailed overview of some of the most common reasons to use formulas in your data-serving tool:

- **Create design assets**: This category is meant for anything that powers any visual element. For example, color according to rules (e.g., red representing a value below a certain threshold) or what happens when they click (e.g., if a user clicks here, show them a map).

- **Define window functions**: Formulas such as running sum or moving average require a predefined window. Instead of pre-calculating the most common windows, you can allow your users to play with different windows (e.g., a 7-day average or 30-day average).

- **Input parameters**: Your tool allows users to input data to calculate what-if scenarios or analytical experiments. This will enable them to answer questions such as, "If we sell 100 units per day for the rest of the year, will we meet our yearly target?"

- **Access control**: While you should manage access centrally, doing it again in your data tool is not a bad idea, just to be sure. For example, you can apply row-level security to your dashboard and limit data access directly in your warehouse.

Actionable and vanity metrics

Unexperienced report builders often make dashboards filled with only superficially important metrics. Putting together a report that has sales, the number of clients, the views on your landing page, and any column that feels relevant in your data warehouse can be a flawed approach, even if your end users are happy and check the dashboard regularly.

Numbers that do not provide insight into business performance, drive actions, or help you find the cause of a problem are known as **vanity metrics,** as opposed to **actionable metrics**, which lead to action and are, by definition, useful.

If you are having trouble putting a monetary value on your data efforts, here are some tips to make your data actionable:

1. **Pick an important decision**: Ask stakeholders about the important decisions in their jobs. They might include difficult, lengthy, costly, or heavily penalized processes when done wrong.

2. **Understand the drivers**: The stakeholder considers some factors before making a decision. This can be data but also a gut feeling or professional judgment.

3. **Figure out the ideal outcomes**: List all the positive and negative outcomes that can arise from this decision.

4. **Choose metrics**: Now that you understand the decision, the drivers, and the outcomes, it is time to find data in your warehouse that could be helpful. It is possible that some of the data you need is missing or that you are working with a proxy (e.g., hours without eating instead of hunger).

5.   **Serve data**: Find the right way to inform your stakeholders' decision-making process. This can be a dashboard, but also something else, such as a text message or a spreadsheet.

6.   **Evaluate**: Make sure that your stakeholders are actually using your solution and that it genuinely drives better outcomes. This is an iterative process; you might need to go back to any of the steps and make changes.

7.   **Automate**: Eventually, once you fully understand the problem, you can work toward automation. While many data professionals would jump directly to automation, making the effort to serve data first is worthwhile. Your stakeholder is still making the decisions, teaching you the process, and guiding your efforts. Automating a process without fully understanding it can be catastrophic.

Now, we will apply the preceding framework to a real-world use case.

A real-world example of actionable metrics

Imagine you work for a supermarket, and your stakeholders are trying to determine how many store employees they need behind the counter at a certain time. If you overestimate this number, you will pay people who are not working. If you underestimate it, clients might not have the patience to wait and will leave. How would you approach this problem?

Based on your initial impressions, you should inspect your organization's current data regarding the problem. You will most likely not have everything you need, but here are some examples of data points that can help you:

* Number of concurrent customers

* Number of active employees

* Size of the waiting lines at the register

* Customer's impressions of the waiting times

For this problem, some example proxies you could consider are the following:

* **The number of transactions with a timestamp**: This could serve as a proxy for people in the store at the same time. It does not tell you how long somebody was in the store, but it is helpful.

* **Parking payments**: Not everybody uses a car, but if your users pay for parking, you could use that data to estimate how long somebody spends doing groceries.

* **People waiting in line (as seen in security footage)**: If you have cameras nearby, you can count the number of people waiting in line. This might not be feasible, either because of privacy concerns or because it is impractical.

* **Employee shifts**: HR may have a system that tells you how many employees showed up to work on a certain day; you do not need to know exactly who did, so the number of employees per hour should be more than enough.

Once you have selected your metrics, it is time to serve your data. You can build a dashboard or use reverse ETL to push this data to a source system. This is a matter of judgment.

Your first attempt will never be perfect. It is possible that you do not fully understand the problem or that the proxies are not enough. However, do not worry; serving data is an iterative process, and you can learn from your failures.

> **Important note**
>
> Every metric can be a vanity metric, and there is nothing inherent about a number that makes it useful or not. It is purely contextual. If the right data is presented to the right audience at the right time (i.e., right before a decision must be taken), it will drive positive outcomes.

Reusability and bespoke processes

Mature data organizations are not generally built around using only one data tool. They create processes that serve data to multiple locations. Every tool causes overhead, so reusability is key. For example, you do not want to check data quality or flag sensitive information in every single product. These are examples of processes you should strive to do only once (and do them well).

Please note that a centralized approach to data quality and security does not mean you will do it well. Still, it mitigates the risk of having KPIs in two systems that do not match or have inconsistent security protocols. However, many tools will nudge you to prepare the data in a bespoke way. In some cases, reusability might prevent you from getting the best out of your tools. The following are just a few examples:

- **Tableau**: This supports querying your warehouse directly by using a live connection. However, performance is often better when you create a Tableau extract. Extracts represent a snapshot of your data enriched with some metadata the developer has added (e.g., renaming fields, adding comments, and changing data types).

- **Power BI**: Power BI models are infinitely easier to build and faster when the data is modeled as a star schema (i.e., the dimension tables are not linked to other dimension tables, and there is only one fact table). These are not hard rules, but ignoring them may lead to a lot of time spent debugging directional cross-filters.

- **Looker**: This uses a declarative approach called LookML as a layer to abstract SQL. You can use it to create aggregates and calculations, define relationships, and create objects (e.g., views and dimensions). You are never fully forced to use LookML. It is possible to do a lot with pure SQL. However, you might need to write LookML to make the best use of some features.

It is imperative to find the right balance between creating reusable data models and getting the best out of the tools. We are not asking you to avoid replication, proprietary formats, remodeling data, or writing logic inside the BI tool. However, it is an important decision that your team should take.

Summary

Serving data requires special attention. It is your users' first point of contact with the data. Often, it is interchangeably used with dashboarding, but as we saw, there are multiple ways of serving data. A non-exhaustive list in this chapter mentioned reverse ETL, low-code tools, and even APIs.

In this chapter, we discussed different approaches to data democratization (i.e., self-service, report factories). We also discuss how interactive charts can be better and how to avoid making a mess by creating slightly different calculations inside every dashboard. We also explained a framework to turn vanity metrics into actionable metrics. Finally, we spoke about finding a balance between reusability and bespoke processes when you want to make the most out of your data tools.

We cannot stress enough the importance of treating data as a product. The only way you can unlock the value of your data is by directing efforts toward building something valuable, usable, and sensible.

In the previous chapters, you learned how analytics engineers are core to creating and maintaining data platforms. We discussed this profession's role during data ingestion, warehousing, data modeling, data transformations, and serving data. In the next chapter, you will practice all these skills by creating your own data platform.

8

Hands-On Analytics Engineering

Now that we've discussed quite a lot of theory in the previous chapters, your hands might be itching to get to work with some technology! In this chapter, you will put theory into practice by helping an old friend gain analytical insights into their fledgling company. Along the way, you will use several tools for the heavy lifting and get acquainted with different parts of the analytical engineering stack. Additionally, you can access the book's GitHub repository, which contains step-by-step instructions for setting up the tooling that will be used in the chapter.

In this chapter, we will discuss the following topics:

- Understanding the Stroopwafelshop use case

- Preparing Google Cloud

- ELT using Airbyte Cloud

- Modeling data using **data build tool** (**dbt**) Cloud

- Visualizing data with Tableau

Technical requirements

For this chapter, you will need the following:

- **Internet connection**: All the tools we'll be using are cloud-based, so a reliable internet connection is essential.

- **Google account**: To use the tooling in this chapter, you will need to create some accounts unless you have them already. To use Google BigQuery (https://cloud.google.com/bigquery/docs/introduction) and Google Sheets (https://www.google.com/sheets/about/), you will need a Google account. You will need **payment information** to make use of BigQuery's full features, but since we will only make use of the free credits, there is no cost to using Google's products.

- **Other accounts**: Similarly, you will need an account for Airbyte Cloud (`https://cloud.airbyte.com/signup`), dbt Cloud (`https://www.getdbt.com/signup`), and Tableau (`https://www.tableau.com/products/trial`). You can leverage your Google account for Airbyte Cloud using SSO, but you will need to create an account for dbt Cloud yourself. Again, there will be no cost, since no payment information is required to set up these services.

- **Basic working knowledge of SQL**: While the tools mentioned previously aim to simplify the data engineering process, a foundational understanding of SQL and basic data manipulation concepts will be incredibly beneficial. In this chapter, we will explain every step we take, but working as an analytics engineer means being able to read and write SQL. If you feel you are not very comfortable yet, visit (`https://www.w3schools.com/sql/sql_intro.asp`) for a quick refresher.

Understanding the Stroopwafelshop use case

A few months ago, your friend Jan founded a business in Amsterdam. He lucked out on a prime location near the center of Amsterdam. There, Jan decided to start selling the Dutch delicacy of Stroopwafels, a cake consisting of two layers of waffles with caramel-like syrup in the middle. Tourists and Dutch residents love these traditional treats. You decide to visit him in the store and try one of his now-famous Stroopwafels over a cup of coffee. Delicious!

While the two of you talk, Jan tells you that they have gained a lot of customers in a short time – so many that they have been feeling overwhelmed lately. As the number of customers grows, so does the information load. Jan would love to get a better insight into the business's performance, but since he is so busy managing the store, he only finds a little time to explore insights. Besides, his data is scattered over multiple systems, and he only has a little experience working with it. Jan pauses for a moment and looks at you, "Weren't you involved in that kind of stuff?" You smile proudly and say you might be able to help him, thinking you can finally apply some of your newfound skills!

Business objectives, metrics, and KPIs

Before diving into the data, you should ask yourself some questions. Your future stakeholders will thank you later. Some of the questions you should ask yourself when beginning such a task are, what exactly does your stakeholder want to achieve? Do they want to gain insights into a particular business process to optimize it? For instance, does Jan want to better understand customer behavior on certain days so he can increase sales? Or is he trying to optimize the stock handling so that no grain of sugar goes unused? These are our **business objectives** and they will drive the analytical efforts that we will set up.

To better understand our business objectives, we will turn them into questions that can be answered with hard numbers. For example, we might want to know which product is the top seller every Wednesday or identify the days when we have too many supplies in stock. The numerical answers to these questions are what we refer to as metrics. We will track them and pass them on to our shopkeeper-friend.

Lastly, consider **Key Performance Indicators**, or **KPIs**. While metrics tell you what is happening, KPIs tell you what to focus on. They tie the metrics directly to the goals that matter for your business. For instance, if you are measuring store sales as a general metric, a related KPI might be the monthly sales growth rate. This not only zeroes in on how many people buy waffles but also shows the increase or decline of this behavior over time, which directly impacts the Stroopwafelshop's bottom line. So, remember, all KPIs are metrics, but not every metric deserves to be a KPI.

Coming up with these indicators can be tough for your stakeholder, depending on their experience and expertise. Sometimes, you will encounter a client or company with crystal clear business objectives, metrics, and KPIs. In other cases, you will have to work hard to help the business define these before you start. It will help you explore the available data to produce the possible metrics and KPIs, although it can also lead to tunnel vision if you limit yourself only to what is currently available.

We will keep it simple for now and circle back to creating the metrics and KPIs later, once we are more familiar with the data. Jan proposes to start with one business objective: *increase in-store sales*. That sounds like a reasonable objective for a fledgling business! You ask him if there is data to support the analysis. He tells you that he has a **Point of Sale** (**POS**) system in the store and that the vendor of the system sends him daily spreadsheets by email. So, you will start from there!

Looking at the data

Before we can continue with the use case, we need to upload the Stroopwafelshop data to Google Sheets. Google Sheets is a popular and free online spreadsheet **Software-as-a-Service** (**SaaS**). We chose it because of the widespread use of spreadsheets in companies, and to demonstrate the capabilities of a tool such as Airbyte, which can extract data from SaaS products without the need for code. Follow this step-by-step guide to upload the Stroopwafelshop data to Google Sheets: `https://github.com/PacktPublishing/Fundamentals-of-Analytics-Engineering/blob/main/chapter_8/guides/upload_data_to_google_sheets.md`.

Next, look at the data provided by Jan to see what we are working with. You advised Jan to ask the vendor for the complete sales history, alongside all other useful information that the POS collects. The vendor creates a manual extract into spreadsheets from their database and emails this to Jan, who then uploads these spreadsheets into Google Sheets to share with you. Looking at the spreadsheets, we will initially focus on the following five datasets: `Sales`, `Sales lines`, `Employees`, `Products`, and `Promotions`. For now, refer to the `Sales` spreadsheet (shown in *Figure 8.1*):

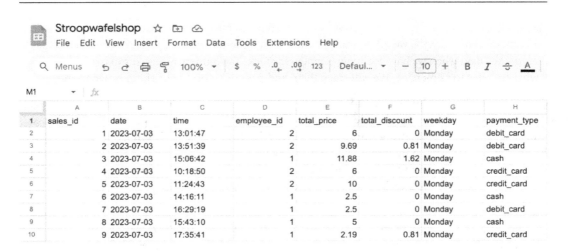

Figure 8.1 – Overview of the Sales spreadsheet

Each row here corresponds to a single in-store sale. Looking at the columns, we can identify `sales_id`, `date`, `time`, `weekday`, `employee_id`, `total_price`, `total_discount`, `weekday`, and `payment_type`. These attributes offer information about the date and time the sale occurred, as well as the payment method. Then, there are **meta attributes** or **keys**, such as `sales_id` and `employee_id`, that tell us something about the data itself.

> **Note**
> We use the terms field, column, and attribute interchangeably when referring to the properties of a record of data (for example, a row in a table).

It appears that each sale is tracked by a `sales_id` value. Looking at it, you can see that it is an incrementing number, most likely autogenerated for each sale-furthermore, `employee_id` hints at more employee information outside of the `Sales` dataset. Most likely, there is another table containing this information that can be connected using `employee_id`.

It would have been possible to add all the information on an employee (for example, full name, date of birth) in each sales record, but since each employee will have multiple sales a day, this would mean a lot of duplication. Separating data into individual tables, such as `Sales` and `Employees`, to prevent such duplication is called **normalization**.

We discussed this back in *Chapter 5, Data Modeling*. Database normalization is a common technique to minimize duplication of data in each table and is very common in **online transaction processing** (**OLTP**) systems such as PoS systems.

Since we have been provided with the `Employees` dataset, we can take a quick look at it to confirm our suspicions:

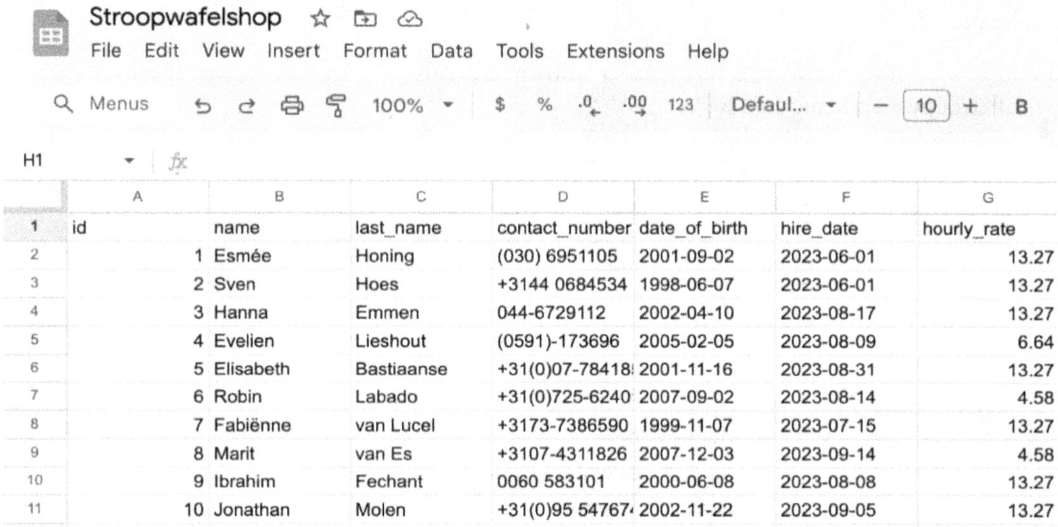

id	name	last_name	contact_number	date_of_birth	hire_date	hourly_rate
1	Esmée	Honing	(030) 6951105	2001-09-02	2023-06-01	13.27
2	Sven	Hoes	+3144 0684534	1998-06-07	2023-06-01	13.27
3	Hanna	Emmen	044-6729112	2002-04-10	2023-08-17	13.27
4	Evelien	Lieshout	(0591)-173696	2005-02-05	2023-08-09	6.64
5	Elisabeth	Bastiaanse	+31(0)07-78418	2001-11-16	2023-08-31	13.27
6	Robin	Labado	+31(0)725-6240	2007-09-02	2023-08-14	4.58
7	Fabiënne	van Lucel	+3173-7386590	1999-11-07	2023-07-15	13.27
8	Marit	van Es	+3107-4311826	2007-12-03	2023-09-14	4.58
9	Ibrahim	Fechant	0060 583101	2000-06-08	2023-08-08	13.27
10	Jonathan	Molen	+31(0)95 54767	2002-11-22	2023-09-05	13.27

Figure 8.2 – Overview of the Employees spreadsheet

The extract from the `Employees` dataset shows that this is the case. There are 10 IDs, one for each unique employee working in the store. This means that the `employee_id` value in the `Sales` dataset is the one handling the sale, and additional information about them must be extracted from the `Employees` dataset. This is important information to know when we extract the data in an automated manner from the spreadsheet as it gives us insight into the relationships between datasets and the design of the source database system. Later, we can join these two datasets using these fields and extend each sale record with more information on the employee:

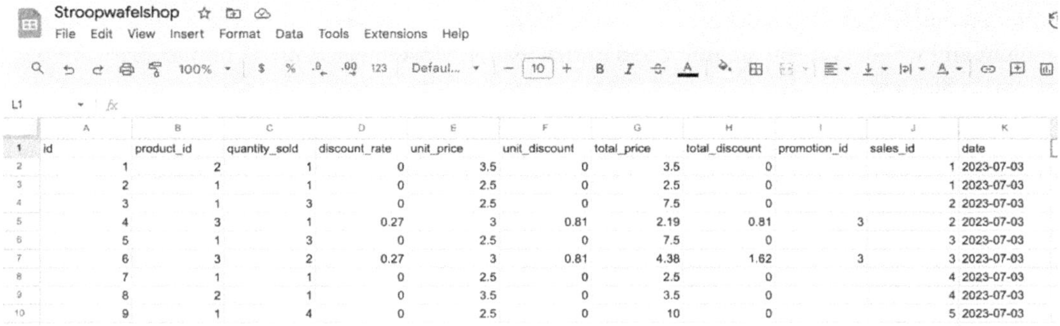

id	product_id	quantity_sold	discount_rate	unit_price	unit_discount	total_price	total_discount	promotion_id	sales_id	date
1	2	1	0	3.5	0	3.5	0		1	2023-07-03
2	1	1	0	2.5	0	2.5	0		1	2023-07-03
3	1	3	0	2.5	0	7.5	0		2	2023-07-03
4	3	1	0.27	3	0.81	2.19	0.81	3	2	2023-07-03
5	1	3	0	2.5	0	7.5	0		3	2023-07-03
6	3	2	0.27	3	0.81	4.38	1.62	3	3	2023-07-03
7	1	1	0	2.5	0	2.5	0		4	2023-07-03
8	2	1	0	3.5	0	3.5	0		4	2023-07-03
9	1	4	0	2.5	0	10	0		5	2023-07-03

Figure 8.3 – Overview of the Sales Lines spreadsheet

In the `Sales Lines` spreadsheet (*Figure 8.3*), we can see that each sale from the `Sales` dataset has been divided into multiple sale lines that define the quantity of each product sold in a single sale. This indicates that, in the source database system, the sales lines are stored in a different table than the sales records.

Now, looking at the `Products` spreadsheet (shown in *Figure 8.4*), we can see that there are three types of Stroopwafels being sold by Jan:

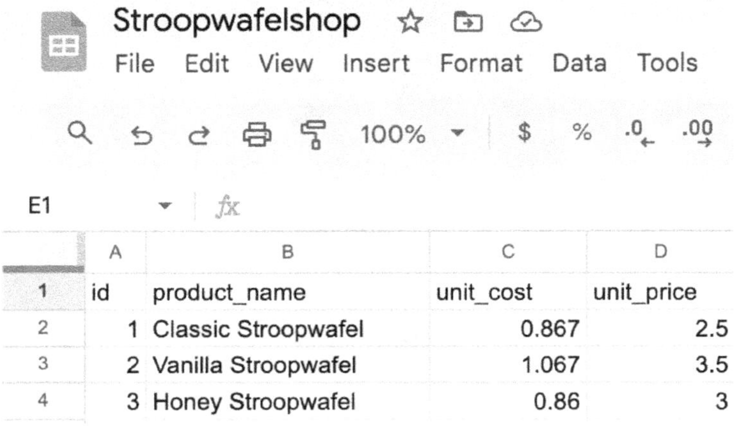

	A	B	C	D
1	id	product_name	unit_cost	unit_price
2	1	Classic Stroopwafel	0.867	2.5
3	2	Vanilla Stroopwafel	1.067	3.5
4	3	Honey Stroopwafel	0.86	3

Figure 8.4 – Overview of the Products spreadsheet

Again, each of these Stroopwafel products corresponds to a unique `id` value and can be linked to another table by this unique key. You will most likely encounter similar data designs when dealing with OLTP systems, and they are the basis for the **dimensional modeling** technique, which you will employ later in this chapter to model the data. For now, it is enough to understand that separating business events and entities, such as a sale or an employee, into separate tables and referencing them by unique keys is a staple in the database systems you will encounter in the workplace.

In the meanwhile, you notice you have received an email from Jan. He states that he should have mentioned that he has a spreadsheet containing the daily shifts for each employee, which he tracks manually, and wonders if you are interested in that as well. Absolutely! You ask him to share this as well, which he does:

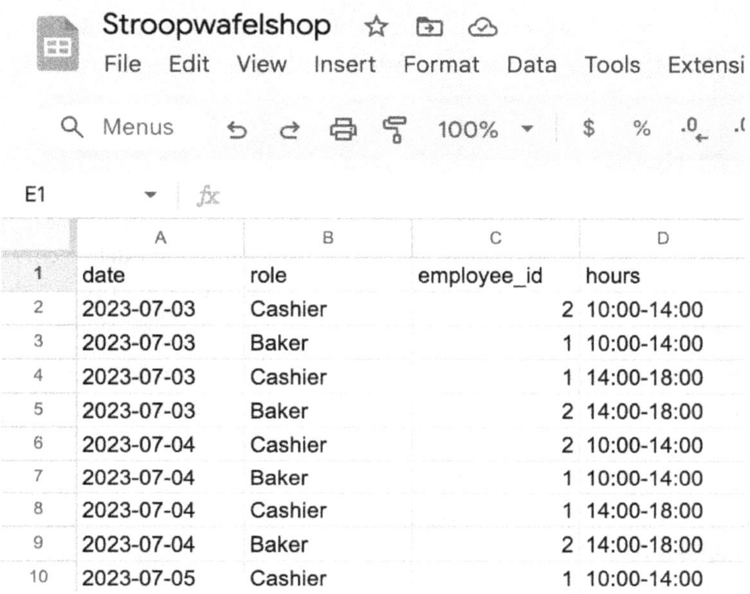

	A	B	C	D
1	date	role	employee_id	hours
2	2023-07-03	Cashier	2	10:00-14:00
3	2023-07-03	Baker	1	10:00-14:00
4	2023-07-03	Cashier	1	14:00-18:00
5	2023-07-03	Baker	2	14:00-18:00
6	2023-07-04	Cashier	2	10:00-14:00
7	2023-07-04	Baker	1	10:00-14:00
8	2023-07-04	Cashier	1	14:00-18:00
9	2023-07-04	Baker	2	14:00-18:00
10	2023-07-05	Cashier	1	10:00-14:00

Figure 8.5 – Overview of the Shifts spreadsheet

As we can see, a day can have two shifts: the morning shift from 10:00 to 14:00 and the afternoon one from 14:00 – 18:00. It seems that there are two employees per shift working together: a cashier and a baker. Furthermore, we can now assume that the `employee_id` value will match the `Employees` data to see what employee was working the shift. This will enable you to count the total shifts and hours worked by the employees, and the quantity of sales they made together. We just gained more insight into the daily operations of the store. For now, we will want to start moving the data into our data warehouse. Now, you might feel the need to ask why we do not just use Google Sheets or Microsoft Excel to do the modeling and analysis.

Excellent question. Let's discuss this.

The thing about spreadsheets

At its current size, the Stroopwafelshop could manage just fine using a spreadsheet such as Excel for basic analytics and reporting. Excel is user-friendly, and Jan is already familiar with it. However, the limitations of Excel become glaringly apparent as the business grows. It can't be scaled to larger datasets and more complex analytics needs.

Moreover, it lacks the robust security features and automation a data warehouse can provide (refer to *Chapter 4*, *Data Warehousing*, for more details). Furthermore, a data platform such as the one described in *Chapter 2*, *The Modern Data Stack*, can support real-time dashboards, better integrate with other specialized analytics tools, and even support advanced machine learning algorithms. So, while Excel may be the path of least resistance now, opting for a data warehouse from the start sets the business up for scalable, long-term success. And with the pay-as-you-go offerings that modern cloud vendors provide, you can do so affordably.

What about BI tools?

Another possibility is to load the data into a popular BI tool such as Tableau, Power BI, or Looker. These are powerful tools that are capable of loading, transforming, and modeling data directly from sources, allowing you to create beautiful visualizations and present them to stakeholders. It seems logical to use the BI tool for everything.

However, the problem is that these tools can quickly become a mess of indecipherable reports. Many BI tools provide a drag-and-drop interface with a custom language for writing transformations but offer limited version control and reviewing capabilities. The combination of these factors can lead to analysts creating complex reports very quickly.

While this might deliver business value in the short term, these lone-wolf reports will be hard to understand and maintain once transferred to others. Peer-reviewed code is a staple of successful software engineering and its absence often leads to "spaghetti code" that only makes sense to its original author. The same holds for analysts working alone in a BI tool.

The consequence is that in the worst case, the report, or parts of it, must be recreated by the next analyst, who might then fall into the same trap. Analytics engineering is all about creating reproducible, well-documented, and high-quality datasets. Consequently, using just a BI tool is not going to cut it. The mantra is to pick the tools that are good at what they do, but not to expect one tool to do it all.

The tooling

If we want to start this analytics adventure in a scalable way, we should match it with the right tooling. A common way to think about the tools is to see where they fall in the layers of a modern analytics stack (shown in *Figure 8.6*):

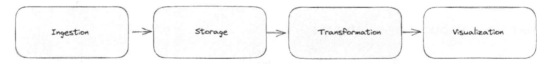

Figure 8.6 – Basic layers of a modern analytics stack

Modern analytics stacks consist at the very least of the following layers:

- There's an **ingestion layer** to load data from various sources into a storage layer, usually a data lake or a data warehouse

- There's also the **transformation layer**, which is where the data in the **storage layer** will usually need to be cleaned and transformed

- Lastly, there will most likely be a **visualization layer**, where visual representations of the data, such as dashboards are created to serve business users

There are many other auxiliary layers, such as support for event-streaming, but for basic reporting purposes, they are not strictly necessary.

For each of these layers, tooling exists, as we have discussed in the previous chapters. Now, we will use this tooling to create our data platform.

To work with the source data, transform it into a usable model, create metrics, and visualize them in a dashboard, we will use an ensemble of the best-in-class data tools. There are many different tools out there, some would even say too many to keep track of. All of these tools have their advantages and disadvantages and we will not make a comparison between them all. We have chosen the tools based on their popularity, ease of use, and because they are free either permanently or for a trial period and without requiring payment information.

Here's a quick rundown of the tooling we will use in this chapter:

- **Airbyte Cloud for ingestion**: This is a SaaS product that offers a no-code/low-code way of performing data ingestion. Airbyte provides hundreds of connectors to various source systems, with support for major, well-known systems. This means you are not required to write custom data ingestion code to extract data, given the already available source connector. Many of these connectors have been developed by community members, and it is possible to create them yourself. Airbyte offers a free trial, as well as the possibility to pay for credits. We will use the 14-day trial period to move the data into our data warehouse. See `https://airbyte.com/pricing` for more information on the pricing.

- **Google Cloud BigQuery for storage and processing**: We discussed Google's powerful data warehousing solution in *Chapter 4, Data Warehousing*. BigQuery is a fast, scalable, and cost-effective tool for analyzing massive datasets. Being serverless, it requires zero maintenance, letting us focus solely on data analysis, and not the engineering part.

- **dbt Cloud for transformation**: dbt is a data transformation tool created by dbt Labs that enables analytical engineers. It provides a robust way of writing SQL, combined with built-in documentation and testing. In the ELT architecture, as discussed in *Chapter 6, Transforming Data*, the raw data is loaded into the data warehousing/lakehouse solution, and then transformed using a tool such as dbt. dbt Cloud offers a free plan for a single user, perfect for our needs. See `https://www.getdbt.com/pricing/` for more details on other offers. We will discuss dbt and dbt Cloud in more detail once we have ingested the data into Google BigQuery and are ready to transform the data.

- **Tableau for visualization**: We will use Tableau for creating dashboards. Tableau holds a large market share in the data visualization scene, offering a desktop client to create interactive and shareable dashboards. Its intuitive drag-and-drop interface makes it accessible to users of all skill levels. Tableau offers a 14-day trial without any commitment. See `https://www.tableau.com/products/trial` for more details. We will dive deeper into Tableau when we create the dashboards.

- Lastly, remember that dedicated tools exist for orchestration, such as Apache Airflow or Dagster. These tools are popular due to their powerful and intricate functionality for executing jobs by creating a **directed acyclic graph** (**DAG**), in which dependencies between jobs are defined. This way, tasks are executed in a specific order, ensuring that one task finishes before another dependent task begins. They can even call tooling such as Airbyte by leveraging its API. Once a project grows larger and requires the execution of custom code in combination with calling different APIs, it may be wise to explore these tools. For small projects such as ours, they are unnecessary and only add more complexity. However, it is good to evaluate the scheduling aspect of your projects. If none of the tools you use offer adequate scheduling, or every tool has its own scheduler and this becomes overwhelming, it might be worth investigating a dedicated scheduling tool.

Next, we will prepare Google Cloud so that it can use BigQuery.

Preparing Google Cloud

Since we will use Google BigQuery as our data warehouse, we will need a Google account to prepare BigQuery for loading the Stroopwafelshop data. For this, you will need the following:

- A new Google Cloud Trial account with $300 in free credits. Alternatively, you can reuse your existing Google Cloud account (in that case, any costs that are incurred, although likely minimal, are at your own risk)!

- A Google Cloud project named stroopwafelshop.

- A BigQuery dataset named stroopwafelshopdata.

- Three service accounts, assigned with IAM roles:

  - A service account named `airbyte` that's been assigned the BigQuery Data Editor and BigQuery User roles.

  - A service account named `dbt-cloud` that's also been assigned the BigQuery Data Editor and BigQuery User roles.

  - A service account for Tableau, including the BigQuery Data Viewer role for read-only access

- For each service account, you will need to create and download a key in JSON format. These will be used to authenticate from the tools.

If you are already familiar with these concepts, feel free to create them and move on to the next section. If not, rest easy! We have a step-by-step guide that will help you create them and explain the concepts along the way: https://github.com/PacktPublishing/Fundamentals-of-Analytics-Engineering/blob/main/chapter_8/guides/setting_up_gcp_and_bigquery.md.

Next, we'll move on to Airbyte.

ELT using Airbyte Cloud

We will use Airbyte Cloud to directly connect to our data sources, extract the data, and then load it untouched into our destination, BigQuery. Unlike traditional tools that transform the data during the ingestion process, Airbyte will keep the data in its original, *raw* form. In *Figure 8.7*, we can see where Airbyte Cloud and Google BigQuery fit into the architecture:

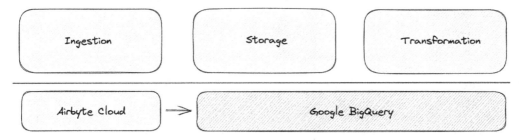

Figure 8.7 – Airbyte Cloud and Google BigQuery

Traditional tools often mix the data ingestion and transformation steps in their product, requiring developers to understand and adapt to their interfaces. These interfaces can range from specialized programming languages to drag-and-drop UIs. While it can be convenient to perform the **extract, transform, load** (**ETL**) steps in a single tool, they can also trap developers within their ecosystem, a scenario referred to as "vendor lock-in." This can lead to costly licensing fees and the need for specialized training, especially if the tool is not widely adopted.

Modern cloud data warehouses, such as BigQuery, can handle and transform vast amounts of data using just SQL. This capability has led many to switch from the traditional *ETL* to **extract, load, transform** (**ELT**), where data is first extracted, then loaded, and finally transformed within the warehouse itself. This change means the data warehouse, which is optimized for such tasks, executes the transformation workload instead of specialized ETL tools.

SQL is the de facto industry standard for working with tabular data, and often the first programming language that data professionals learn. Although there are many popular programming languages in the data engineering space, such as Python, Scala, and Java, SQL is the most widely used. Hence, it is no surprise that businesses are adopting a *SQL-first* approach, favoring it over proprietary tools and languages.

Recognizing this trend, tools such as Fivetran and Airbyte have emerged. They focus on connecting to various data sources to extract data without meddling with its structure. The transformation responsibility is handed over to the data warehouse. Further assisting in this process, tools such as dbt, Dataform, and SQLMesh offer frameworks to help organize and execute data transformations. However, the heavy lifting – the actual data processing – is done by the data warehouse itself. Now that you know the theory behind our data loading and transformation approach, let's start by setting up our data warehouse.

Loading the Stroopwafelshop data using Airbyte Cloud

Now, we will perform the following steps to load the Stroopwafelshop data into the cloud:

1. Create a free, 14-day trial account in Airbyte Cloud.
2. Set up a source connection to Google Sheets, connecting to the Stroopwafelshop spreadsheet provided earlier.
3. Set up Google BigQuery as the destination, using the security credentials you created earlier.
4. Load and store the data from Sheets into BigQuery, in its original form.

A step-by-step approach can be found at `https://github.com/PacktPublishing/Fundamentals-of-Analytics-Engineering/blob/main/chapter_8/guides/setting_up_airbyte_cloud.md`.

At this point, you have successfully synced the data into BigQuery and explored some of the key features of an ELT tool such as Airbyte. The next step is to start working with the data!

Modeling data using dbt Cloud

With the raw data in BigQuery, you might want to jump right in and start uncovering those key business insights. But before you start building those queries, take a moment to think about the tools and strategies available. Remember, there is often more than one way to tackle data analysis.

The shortcomings of conventional analytics

BigQuery and platforms of its kind are built to manage massive data volumes at impressive speeds. Still, this does not iron out every hurdle for analysts. They frequently receive ad hoc requests for data queries, such as dissecting sudden changes in sales patterns, forecasting next week's inventory requirements, or explaining yesterday's customer behavior. Analysts address these tasks diligently aiming to enhance business insights. Often, they might pull SQL from one of their past analyses and repurpose it for a new one. This new analysis could be stored away in a Word document on a shared network drive or, if available technology supports it, within the data warehouse's interface.

While this approach might seem efficient at first, it becomes less so as the team grows. New analysts might struggle to access or decipher the work of their predecessors. Many data professionals, including analysts, tend to write and document their code in a way that is clear to them but might be confusing for others. On top of that, understanding the data is not just about the numbers; it often demands knowledge of the business domain. In the absence of a consistent framework, there is typically a lack of thorough documentation. This can leave new team members piecing things together on their own, sometimes revisiting challenges that others have already successfully tackled.

Additionally, analysts crafting one-off reports might not be well-versed in managing data quality challenges. The longer a dashboard stays in use, the higher the likelihood of it encountering issues, such as changes in the original data source. This could result from fields being renamed, data types being altered, or unexpected data entries such as **NULL** values (the lack of a value) or duplicates (the same value more than once). Moreover, there could be errors in the initial analysis that only surface later. Addressing these data quality issues can be quite a task.

The role of dbt in analytics engineering

As previously discussed, dbt emerged as a solution to the challenges relating to data transformation faced in data analysis. Initially crafted as an open-source Python package, dbt aimed to bring software engineering best practices to the world of analytics.

Over time, dbt matured beyond just a package, becoming a versatile cloud service. While the open-source package remains available and actively supported, dbt now offers a cloud-based version, packed with features such as an **integrated development environment** (**IDE**), scheduling tools, data lineage trackers, and hosted documentation. This is especially valuable for analysts who might not have a deep software engineering background.

For more information on dbt's history, read `https://www.getdbt.com/blog/what-exactly-is-dbt`. We will use dbt Cloud, which offers a free tier for a single developer: that's you! You can learn more about its pricing here: `https://www.getdbt.com/pricing`.

dbt seamlessly integrates into the ELT architecture. It does not store or process data but serves as a bridge between analysts and the data warehouse. *Figure 8.8* shows dbt's position in a data stack as an intermediary in the transformation layer:

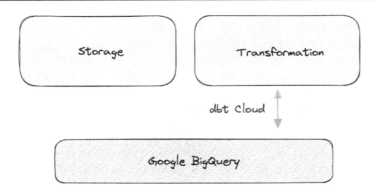

Figure 8.8 – dbt's position in the data stack

This is how it works: analysts draft SQL queries, enhanced with dbt's unique capabilities. dbt then translates this specialized SQL into the native SQL of the data warehouse and dispatches it for execution. All the transformed data and results remain within the data warehouse, making dbt a lightweight yet powerful tool in the analytics toolkit.

Because of dbt's pivotal position in analytics engineering, we will spend more time discussing its features and zooming in on best practices.

First, we will set up dbt for our use case.

Setting up dbt Cloud

The following steps are required for dbt:

1. Creating a dbt Cloud account.
2. Setting up a connection from dbt Cloud to BigQuery.
3. Testing the connection by querying the data using dbt Cloud.

Follow the step-by-step instructions here: `https://github.com/PacktPublishing/Fundamentals-of-Analytics-Engineering/blob/main/chapter_8/guides/setting_up_dbt_cloud.md`.

Now, let's focus on the various **data layers in dbt**.

Data layers in dbt

It is a widespread practice to separate the data we use for analytics into layers. This helps data practitioners communicate the distinct parts of the data transformation process. Broadly speaking, the process will fall into **three layers in dbt**, as shown in *Figure 8.9*:

Figure 8.9 – Data layers

Let's take a closer look:

- **Raw layer**: The source data is stored in the form it arrives in. Whenever you receive data, it should be stored as-is so that you have a backup in case something goes wrong during the transformations. When you copied the Excel sheets using Airbyte, they became part of the raw layer inside BigQuery.

- **Preparation layer**: In the second layer, the raw data is cleaned, deduplicated, and transformed to conform to naming conventions and other rules. For our data, this could mean renaming fields for readability and standardizing sales figures from cents to euros.

- **Business layer**: In the final layer, business rules are applied to the prepared data, and different data is joined and modeled into datasets that are ready for consumption by BI tools and stakeholders. In our case, we might add a business rule to disregard negative sales amounts when summing the total stroopwafels sold, as these are likely an error. The resulting data can then be served to the BI tool for dashboarding.

In dbt, these layers are present but with a slight difference, as shown in *Figure 8.10*:

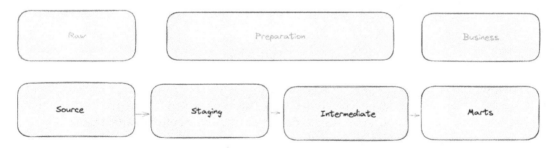

Figure 8.10 – Data layers in dbt

In dbt's terminology, the **source layer** contains the raw data in your data warehouse, nothing more. The next layer, where this source data is cleaned and prepared, is called **staging**. The name comes from a **staging area** in a warehouse, where goods are stored temporarily before moving toward their destination. In this layer, the data is cleaned but no complex business rules are applied. Next is an **intermediate layer**, which is where business logic is applied in a modular manner. Finally, the **marts layer** is where intermediate and staging data are combined, certain data are aggregated and all necessary business logic is applied. This data can be presented to the business.

It is vital to understand these layers since as a developer in dbt, you will be moving the data through these layers, working your way up from **source** to **mart**.

dbt project structure

Coming back to the dbt Cloud IDE, you can see the project files on the bottom-left corner of the screen, as shown in *Figure 8.11*. These files and folders are the scaffolding for each new dbt project, and you will need to update and add to them for your specific needs:

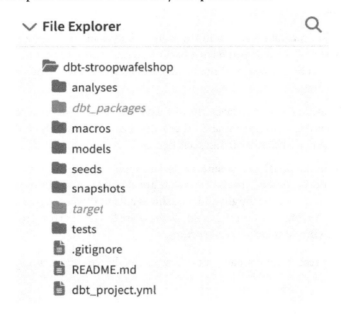

Figure 8.11 – dbt project files

For a comprehensive explanation of the structure of the dbt project, including an explanation of the different files and folders, take a look at `https://docs.getdbt.com/guides/best-practices/how-we-structure/1-guide-overview`. The most important thing for now is that we will create `staging models` in the `models` folder.

In there, we will place all the files that contain the SQL to model our data. Each file should be considered a separate dataset, or **model**, that can be referenced and built upon by other models. Looking at dbt's layered approach, the first layer we will build is **staging models**, which reads from the source layer. To do this, we will need to create some folders and files.

> **Models in dbt terminology**
>
> In dbt, *models* are a fundamental concept. A model, in this context, is a file composed of a SQL statement that processes data, applies transformations, and yields a resulting dataset. This interpretation is somewhat different from the general use of the term "data model" in the field, which usually implies a composite of various datasets that have been merged and formed into a unified model.

First, we will create subfolders in the `models` directory: `models/staging/stroopwafelshop`. dbt's convention is to create a subfolder for the `staging`, `intermediate`, and `marts` layers. Then, inside the `staging` folder, we will create a subfolder called `stroopwafelshop` to indicate the source of the data, which is the store.

Defining sources

Looking at dbt's guide on staging models (`https://docs.getdbt.com/guides/best-practices/how-we-structure/2-staging`), we will need to create a so-called source to reference sources. This source file, alongside other configuration files in dbt, uses a specific formatting language called **YAML**.

YAML is a popular configuration language that's used in software programs that is both human and machine-readable. We will not go over the specifics of the YAML language; it should be simple enough to pick up by following the examples. If you want to have a more extensive look into the language, take a look at the guide at `https://docs.ansible.com/ansible/latest/reference_appendices/YAMLSyntax.html`. In dbt, the file extension for YAML is `.yml`.

Moving on, we will create a source file in `models/staging/stroopwafelshop/_stroopwafelshop__sources.yml` (shown in *Figure 8.12*) that contains the code provided at `https://github.com/PacktPublishing/Fundamentals-of-Analytics-Engineering/blob/main/chapter_8/dbt_stroopwafelshop/models/staging/stroopwafelshop/_stroopwafelshop__sources.yml`:

_stroopwafelshop_sources... ⚙

models > staging > stroopwafelshop > _stroopwafelshop_sources.yml

```
 1    version: 2
 2
 3  ∨ sources:
 4  ∨   - name: stroopwafelshop
 5        schema: stroopwafelshopdata
 6  ∨     tables:
              Generate model
 7  ∨       - name: employees
 8            identifier: Employees
 9            description: "The employees table contains information about
10  ∨         columns:
11  ∨           - name: _airbyte_raw_id
12              data_type: string
13              description: "Unique identifier for the record"
14  ∨           - name: _airbyte_extracted_at
15              data_type: timestamp
16              description: "Timestamp of when the record was extracted"
17  ∨           - name: _airbyte_meta
18              data_type: json
19              description: "Metadata about the record"
20  ∨           - name: hourly_rate
21              data_type: string
22              description: "Hourly rate of the employee"
```

Figure 8.12 – Source YAML file

This defines a source named `stroopwafelshop` containing several tables, such as `Employees`. Sources help to distinguish all the source data in a central place. This helps other developers identify the sources used in your project and enables other dbt functionality such as documentation, testing, and data freshness checks. If you want to learn more about defining sources and their features, read up on dbt's documentation (`https://docs.getdbt.com/docs/build/sources`).

Creating staging models

The next step is to create a **staging** model for each source. Let's start with the `Employees` table by creating a file in `models/staging/stroopwafelshop/stg_employees.sql` and inserting the SQL found at `https://github.com/PacktPublishing/Fundamentals-of-Analytics-Engineering/blob/main/chapter_8/dbt_stroopwafelshop/models/staging/stroopwafelshop/stg_employees.sql`:

```
_stroopwafelshop__sources....        stg_employees.sql              ⊙

models > staging > stroopwafelshop > stg_employees.sql
 1    with
 2        raw_source as (select * from {{ source("stroopwafelshop", "employees") }}),
 3
 4        employees as (
 5
 6            select
 7                -- ids
 8                id as employee_id,
 9
10                -- strings
11                contact_number,
12                name as first_name,
13                last_name,
14                concat(name, ' ', last_name) as full_name,
15
16                -- numerics
17                cast(hourly_rate as numeric) as hourly_rate,
18
19                -- dates
20                date_of_birth as birth_date,
21                hire_date as hired_date
22
23                -- meta
24                _airbyte_extracted_at,
25                _airbyte_meta,
```

Figure 8.13 – The Employees staging model

Looking at the SQL, as shown in *Figure 8.13*, there are some things to note. First, the top SQL statement starts with the following code:

```
with  raw_source  as (
  select *  from {{ source('stroopwafelshop',       'employees')}}),
```

The with raw_source as statement defines a **common table expression** (CTE) named raw_source, and wraps a select statement using round brackets ((and)).

A CTE is essentially a named select statement that exists for the duration of your query. It is a way to organize complex SQL logic into a more manageable form, making your queries more readable and modular. CTEs allow you to break down your SQL queries into simpler parts, which can then be reused or referenced by other parts of your SQL code. CTEs can be referenced by other SQL statements, including other CTEs.

Notice how the next CTE, called `employees`, selects from the `raw_source` CTE. When writing dbt models, using CTEs is a best practice that makes your models more readable and can prevent duplication. You can read more about the use of CTEs at `https://docs.getdbt.com/terms/cte`.

Secondly, if you are familiar with ANSI SQL, the common standard of writing SQL, you might be puzzled by the use of curly brackets (`{{` and `}}`) and the `source` function. These are indeed native to dbt and not valid in regular SQL.

Jinja and dbt

The curly bracket syntax is used when we want to combine SQL with Jinja, a templating language that makes it possible to add more traditional programming features such as looping, setting variables, and calling custom functions, which are called **macros** in Jinja terminology. This is one of the most powerful features that dbt offers since it enhances SQL in a way that minimizes code duplication and verbosity.

Within these curly brackets, we can write Jinja code and call macros. The `source` macro called here is created by dbt and provides custom functionality that is not present in SQL. You can either make use of built-in macros provided by dbt, create your own custom macros, or even use third-party macros by using **packages**. You can read more on the use of Jinja and macros at `https://docs.getdbt.com/docs/build/jinja-macros`.

The `source` macro is used to reference the data sources that have been defined in the `sources` YAML file. Specifically, we are referencing the `Employees` table as part of the `stroopwafelshop` source. Looking at the `_stroopwafelshop__sources.yml` file, we can see that this matches the `Employees` table. It is a recommended practice to always use the `source` macro in your staging models so that it becomes clear what data is being used in your project and where a developer can find more information by looking at the `sources` YAML. Only staging models should use the `source` macro since the source data should only be read by staging models (that is their purpose). Further models, such as marts, build upon the staging models but should never read from sources directly.

Best practices for staging models

We should apply some of dbt's recommended best practices concerning staging models:

- We should define our sources at the top of our model as separate CTEs for clear separation and readability.

- The next CTE, called `employees` in our example, will read the source data, define the fields that we want to expose to the staging model, and apply any minimal transformations. These best practices are further described at `https://docs.getdbt.com/guides/best-practices/how-we-structure/2-staging` and are recommended reading.

- Next, look at the naming and order of the columns in the employees CTE. For consistency and readability, we'll follow dbt's style guide, which is provided at https://docs.getdbt.com/guides/best-practices/how-we-style/1-how-we-style-our-dbt-models.

You can choose whatever style options you like, so long as you stick to a consistent method. This will help when you're working together with others (and yourself) in the future. While you are at it, take a look at the SQL style guide for a more comprehensive view into writing SQL: https://docs.getdbt.com/guides/best-practices/how-we-style/2-how-we-style-our-sql.

Materializing models

To realize the transformations, we need to **materialize** them. This means we must run SQL and store the results in the data warehouse. We will discuss different materialization types later. Whenever you see the word, think of it as executing a dbt model and storing the result inside BigQuery so it can be queried.

In dbt Cloud, you can use the **Preview** functionality to execute the SQL statements and return the results in the browser. Running this will *not* materialize the model yet. In contrast, the **Build** functionality stores the model's results in the data warehouse, materializing them, as shown in *Figure 8.14*. Now, build the models yourself to achieve this:

Figure 8.14 – Building the model

You should be able to view the newly minted BigQuery dataset now. Notice how it has been created with your dbt schema name (for me, it is dbt_lbenninga), as shown in *Figure 8.15*:

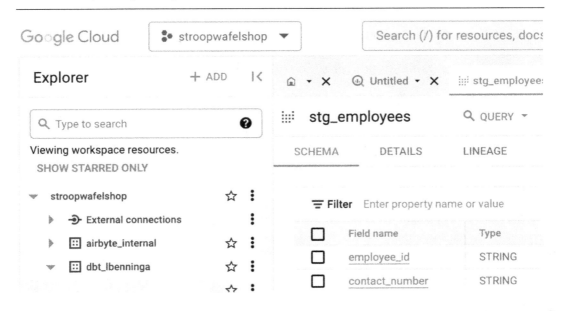

Figure 8.15 – Viewing the new BigQuery dataset

By default, dbt materializes the data as a **view**. Views do not contain data, only SQL. This means that when you query the view, you are executing its SQL, which can, in turn, reference a table or another view, repeating the process.

In dbt, a common guideline is to initially materialize staging models as views. This approach is favored because views offer a real-time snapshot of the underlying data, ensuring that the most current data is always presented. However, as the complexity and volume of data increase, the performance of these views can degrade, especially if the transformations they perform are resource-intensive. When this performance issue becomes noticeable, it's advisable to switch the materialization of these models from views to tables. This change can significantly improve performance when querying the materialized models since no transformations are required (as was the case with views).

There are nuances to these rules of thumb, and more advanced materializations exist, such as *incrementally* materializing a table. You can read up on the different types of materializations at https://docs. getdbt.com/docs/build/materializations.

Creating the other staging models

Next, create the staging models for the other source tables. You can practice creating the staging models yourself by looking at the different source tables in the stroopwafelshopdata dataset and writing the SQL (do not forget to use the source macro), or you can grab the code here: https://github. com/PacktPublishing/Fundamentals-of-Analytics-Engineering/tree/main/ chapter_8/dbt_stroopwafelshop/models/staging/stroopwafelshop. Notice that we follow the naming best practices that are defined by dbt when modeling the data.

Once you have added all the staging models, build the models to materialize them into BigQuery. The result (shown in *Figure 8.16*) means that six staging models have now materialized in your dbt dataset – one for each source table:

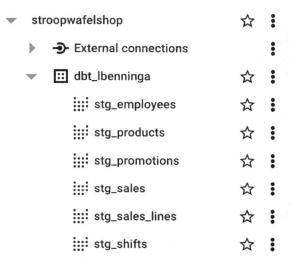

Figure 8.16 – Materialized dbt models in BigQuery

Next up, we will create models for the *business layer* that will be consumed by the BI tool.

Data marts

The staging models we have created serve as the foundation for our dbt project. The next step is to prepare the data for consumption by the BI tool. This consumption layer is called **marts** by dbt. It references the old term, where datasets would be placed in separate databases called **data marts**. In dbt, we store the data from the raw layer to the business layer in the same data warehouse but model the data according to the purpose of the different layers.

This means that we will need to create additional models and place them in a separate folder. But first, we need to decide on the modeling technique we will use to create the marts.

Dimensional model for analytics

As we discussed in *Chapter 5*, *Data Modeling*, there are different modeling techniques. For our analysis, we will choose dimensional modeling, a popular technique for analytics.

The **dimensional model**, popularized by Ralph Kimball, is a decades-old, time-tested technique that is still often used in the world of data warehousing due to its flexibility. Specifically, we will create a so-called **star schema**, consisting of **fact** and **dimension** models, by following the Kimball Group's four steps, as stated earlier in *Chapter 5*, *Data Modeling*.

Following these steps, we will know how to model our data marts:

1. **Choose the business process**: First, we need to pick the **business process** we are interested in. Looking at the datasets, the sales transactions seem like the most logical business process to start with. By choosing the **sales process**, we aim to gain insight into the store's performance.

2. **Define the grain**: The **grain** is another word for the level of detail of a dataset. In our sales process, we have multiple levels of detail. A sale consists of multiple sales lines, and since we have both datasets, we will have to make a choice. A rule of thumb is that the lowest grain is often more useful since you can always aggregate to a higher grain. Going from a higher grain back to a lower one is difficult, if not impossible. For instance, if I provide you with a day's worth of sales data you can tally them to give me the daily total spent. However, if I had only provided you with the daily total, you could not have deduced the number of sales. If we choose a sale as the grain, we will lose the information concerning the items sold unless we aggregate them. For simplicity, let's choose the individual sales line as the grain so that we can always aggregate to a sale later.

3. **Determine the dimensions**: **Dimensions** provide context to the business process. In our case, we can quickly identify them by looking at the data to see how they fit in the sales process. This data does not contain sales events (such as a transaction) but rather provides additional information for each sale. In our case, the dimensions are as follows:

   - **Employees**: Contains information on the employee who worked during the sale

   - **Products**: Information on the products that were sold

   - **Promotions**: The promotions that were held during the period

   - **Shifts**: Employees work in shifts, and a shift can be tied to a sale

4. **Identify the facts**: **Facts** are measurable business process events, such as a sales transaction or a page visit on a website. Identifying the facts for the sales process is quite straightforward. Since a sale is the central business process we are looking at, we need to look at the models that contain sales measures. **Measures** are numerical values that we can aggregate (when it makes sense to do so):

   - **Sales**: Central to the sales business process are the individual sales. Here, we can find measurements such as the total sales amount. We can aggregate all total sales amounts for a given day to find the daily total.

   - **Sales lines**: A sale consists of one or more sales lines. Within a sales line, we find information on the quantity of products sold and their prices. By aggregating the quantity and prices, we can get a daily overview of individual product sales.

This means that the sales and sales line models are both valid facts and we can even combine them to get a more detailed overview. Since we decided on the sales line as the grain detail, we will take the sales lines and combine them with their corresponding sales to create a single fact table relating to sales.

> **Dimensional modeling in dbt**
>
> You can read more about dimensional modeling in dbt here: `https://docs.getdbt.com/terms/dimensional-modeling`.

Naming convention

Similar to the naming convention of the staging models, we will shorten the names of the dimensional models in dbt. **Fact Sales** becomes `fct_sales`, and **Dimension Employees** becomes `dim_employees`. From now on, we will reference the models by their shortened names.

Star schema

The `fct_sales` model will be the main entry point for our analysis, meaning that we will query this model and join the dimensions for additional information. For example, if we want to count the number of sales per product, we would query the `fct_sales` model and join `dim_products` using the `product_id` field available in both models. Then, we can sum the number of sales to a daily aggregate, per `product_name`.

The process of joining dimensions to the central fact is also called a **star schema** due to its star-like shape. In our case, it will end up looking like what's shown in *Figure 8.17*:

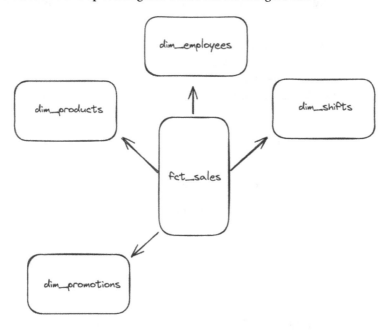

Figure 8.17 – The Stroopwafelshop "star schema"

Although this does not exactly resemble a star due to the missing fifth dimension, the idea remains the same. With the rough outline of the star schema in place, we can start to create the marts.

Creating the marts

First, we will create the models/marts folder. Here, we will place our mart models. Like the staging models, we will create a model for each mart.

We will then create the following models:

- The fact model, fct_sales, which will combine the stg_sales and stg_sales_lines models, and expose relevant fields.
- A dimension for each staging model: dim_employees, dim_products, dim_promotions, and dim_shifts. These are mainly continuations of the staging models, but we will expose the relevant fields and add necessary new ones.

When creating dimensional models, we need to make note of their **join keys**, also known as foreign keys, which make it possible to identify a record in another model and join it to the current models' records. For instance, employee_id in the stg_employees and stg_sales models is an example of a join key that connects an individual sale to the employee who performed it. Usually, these join keys are created by the source system you are loading from. In our case, we need both the fact and dimensions to have a join key so that we can combine them.

You can find the code for the marts here: https://github.com/PacktPublishing/ Fundamentals-of-Analytics-Engineering/tree/main/chapter_8/dbt_ stroopwafelshop/models/marts. You can copy the code for the marts and create them as SQL files, as shown *Figure 8.18*. Then, you can build the models in dbt Cloud, just like you did for the staging models:

Figure 8.18 – The mart models in dbt Cloud

Notice the following changes from the staging models:

- We do not take any of the Airbyte metadata fields, such as `_airbyte_raw_id`, since end users are generally not interested in this type of information.

- The `fct_sales` model combines the sales and sales lines, taking the individual sales line granularity but adding the `employee id`, `payment type`, and `date` properties of `sale`, which are not available on the sales line. Additionally, since a sale does not always have a promotion, this value can be NULL. We can check for that by creating a Boolean `has_promotion` column.

- We configure our marts to be materialized as tables by setting a folder-level materialization in `dbt_project.yml`. This improves query times for the BI tool for all our marts. You can read more about configuring materializations at `https://docs.getdbt.com/docs/build/materializations#configuring-materializations`.

> **Structuring the marts**
>
> You can read more about marts in general at `https://docs.getdbt.com/best-practices/how-we-structure/4-marts`.

Additional dbt features

Now that we have created the marts, we are ready to move from dbt to our BI tool so that we can start consuming them. Before we do, it is good to be aware of some other dbt features that are helpful but are not essential for our current use case:

- **Testing**: You can define data tests in dbt to assert that certain fields in your models contain expected values. For example, you could test that `sales_id` is never **NULL** and always unique, or that the sales total should be positive. By declaring them in the `sources` and `models` **YAML** files, when you run the `dbt build` command, dbt will first materialize (build) the models, and then run the tests. When a test fails, it can prevent loading erroneous data into downstream models. You can read more on testing here: `https://docs.getdbt.com/reference/resource-properties/data-tests`.

- **Documentation**: We have added descriptions to the staging models' fields, which is a good practice to help with understanding the data. Additionally, dbt Cloud provides a feature to view the documentation on a web page called **dbt Explorer**. It can show all the project's models, fields, and descriptions in a single interface. You can find out more about the dbt Explorer feature here: `https://www.getdbt.com/product/dbt-explorer`.

- **Incremental materialization**: While the Stroopwafelshop's volume of data is still small, in the thousands of records, performance optimizations are hardly necessary. However, when you encounter dbt projects that load sources with millions of records on a daily schedule, you might start to notice that your dbt build times slow down drastically. This is due to the way dbt reprocesses all records for a table on each build. The **incremental** materialization type counters this by only processing new records based on a unique identifier. You can read more about this topic at `https://docs.getdbt.com/docs/build/incremental-models`.

- **BI Tooling**: Now that we have cleaned and modeled the data, we can move forward to creating insights from them using a BI tool. Ideally, analysts should be able to pick up the marts and turn them into charts without spending time cleaning, renaming, and transforming the data. Mostly, they should aggregate and filter the data across dimensions, and turn these aggregations into charts.

Next, we will visualize the data.

Visualizing data with Tableau

Once the data has been cleaned and transformed and is available in your data warehouse, it is time to use this data to generate insights. In this section, we will walk you through the basics of using Tableau and how you can create dashboards. Additionally, we will expand on how the Stroopwafelshop can use dashboards effectively to answer different business questions.

Why Tableau?

Tableau stands out in the business and analytics world for its straightforward but powerful data visualization features. Its ease of use appeals to a wide range of users, not just tech experts, enabling them to create engaging and interactive charts and graphs. It is versatile, working seamlessly with various data sources and offering advanced functions like trend analysis and forecasting. Tableau's active online community is a big plus, offering learning and networking opportunities. Furthermore, constant updates keep Tableau at the forefront of data visualization trends, making it a reliable and dynamic tool for anyone looking to present data.

Want to learn more about Tableau?

Please note that this is not an in-depth tutorial of Tableau's features. If you want to learn more about Tableau, you can go to Tableau's official resources (`https://www.tableau.com/resources`). In there, you can find anything from webinars and self-paced tutorials to official in-class training.

We will need to perform the following steps before we can create a dashboard for Jan in Tableau:

1. Download and install Tableau Desktop.
2. Connecting Tableau to BigQuery.
3. Create the relationships between the dbt models.

A step-by-step guide is available at `https://github.com/PacktPublishing/Fundamentals-of-Analytics-Engineering/blob/main/chapter_8/guides/setting_up_tableau.md`. After performing these steps, we should get back to Jan and start gathering requirements for our visualizations.

Selecting the KPIs

You proudly tell Jan that all the tooling is now in place to create a dashboard! The most important thing now is to get his input on what to start measuring. As stated earlier in this chapter, Jan values healthy financial growth and customer satisfaction. He can also see the importance of monitoring these objectives as they evolve. After careful consideration, Jan has decided which KPIs are the most important for his business and how he is going to monitor them in a dashboard.

Here's an overview of the KPIs that have been selected:

- **Sales revenue**: The total revenue generated during a given period. This is a fundamental KPI for any retail business, providing a basic measure of its financial performance.

- **Sales volume**: The total number of waffles sold during a given period. It should be tracked in total and broken down by different waffle types.

- **Gross profit**: This is calculated as sales revenue minus the product's unit price (cost of goods sold). It's important for understanding the profitability of the products.

- **Number of transactions per day**: Tracking the number of sales transactions can provide insights into customer foot traffic and purchase frequency.

- **Average transaction value**: The average amount spent by customers per transaction. This helps in understanding the spending behavior of customers.

With these KPIs, which are common points of interest for retailers, Jan will be off to a flying start with his first dashboard.

First visualization

We'll start by creating a new **worksheet**, which is a blank canvas for visualizations. On the left-hand side of the screen, we can find the models and fields from the data model. Search for the **Quantity Sold** field and drag it into the **Columns** section at the top of the screen. Then, find **Sold Date** and drag it into the **Rows** section. That should autogenerate a line chart plotting the number of stroopwafels sold over time, as shown in *Figure 8.19*. Notice that Tableau automatically decides on the **SUM** aggregation type for **Quantity Sold** to help the developer. You can always change the aggregation type if you wish:

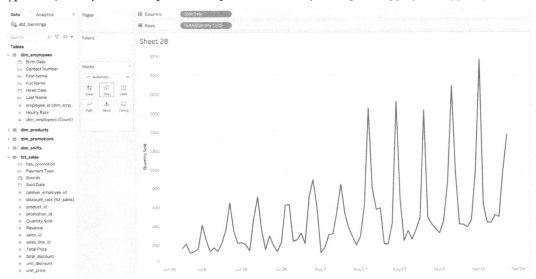

Figure 8.19 – Autogenerated visualization

You can change the visualization type by clicking the **Show Me** button at the top-right corner and selecting another type, such as **Stacked Bars**. You can play around with the different types to get a feel for the possibilities (shown in *Figure 8.20*):

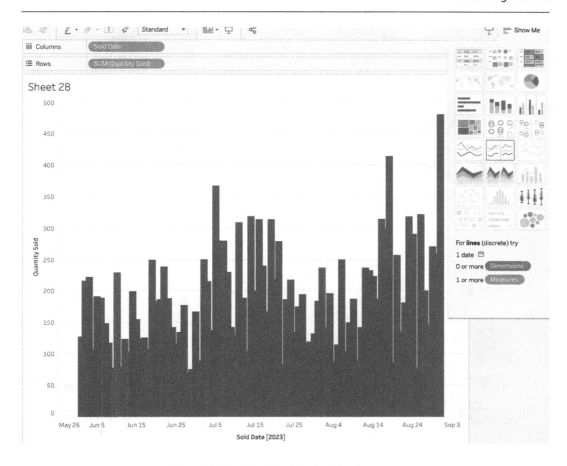

Figure 8.20 – Changing the visualization type

Creating measures

So far, we have added some fields and made some transformations to the source datasets using dbt, but we haven't created any aggregations using SQL. A popular practice is to keep the dimensional models at a high level of detail and not to perform aggregations in dbt, and instead let the BI tool take care of this. BI tools are often very capable of aggregating data on the fly and letting the user drill down from a summarized overview to a more granular level of detail. For example, a visualization might display the yearly aggregated sales values with the option to drill down to individual sales transactions.

These aggregations can often be defined in the BI tool and are commonly known as **measures**. A measure is similar to a formula that states the fields that are to be aggregated, and the type of aggregation. For instance, SUM(Quantity Sold) is a measure that Tableau created automatically when you dragged the Quantity Sold field into the visualization. Measures are dynamically calculated for the current visualization type.

If you change the measure's granularity from **year** to **day** in the visualization, the underlying data will be re-queried and returned for the appropriate aggregation level. This makes it very powerful since users can interact with visualizations and change filters and aggregation levels without the BI developer needing to define all supported aggregation levels. Replicating the same in the SQL model would mean having to precompute these levels – for example, daily, monthly, and yearly – and consumes far more compute and storage resources.

We can create measures by right-clicking on the data panel and selecting **Create Calculated Field**. Then, we can add the **[Quantity Sold]** * **[Unit Cost]** formula and name it Cost Per Sale, as shown in *Figure 8.21*:

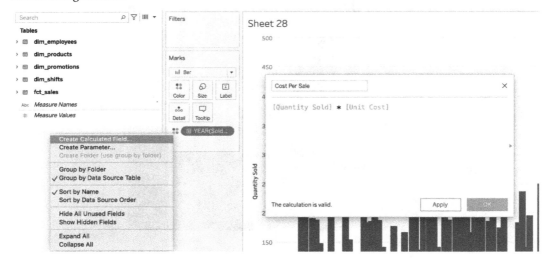

Figure 8.21 – Creating a measure

The resulting measure will appear in the data panel and can then be used inside visualizations similar to the other fields. Drag the field into the visualization to test it out. Changing the Sold Date's level from year to month will recalculate the measure. Try it out!

Now that you know how to create one, let's create measures for the KPIs defined by Jan and match them with the following formulas:

- **Sales revenue**: [Total Price]
- **Sales volume**: [Quantity Sold]
- **Gross profit**: [Total Price] - [Cost Per Sale]
- **Number of sales**: COUNTD([sales_id])
- **Average transaction value**: AVG([Total Price])

With these measures, we can create the visualizations we want in a dashboard.

Creating the store growth dashboard

In Tableau, a dashboard is an interactive tool that allows you to visually display and analyze data from multiple sources. It is essentially a canvas where you can combine various Tableau views (such as worksheets) along with other components such as images, texts, and web content to create an interactive data visualization.

Dashboards in Tableau are powerful because they enable users to present a cohesive story by bringing together different data visualizations that are connected. This means that when you interact with one component of the dashboard, such as selecting a specific item in a chart, other components can update based on that selection. This interactivity allows for deep exploration and insightful analysis of data, making it easier to uncover trends, patterns, and outliers.

Now that you know how to create worksheets and measures, take a look at the online Stroopwafelshop dashboard, which combines these different aspects into a single view (`https://public.tableau.com/app/profile/jmperafan/viz/StroopwaffelShopStoreGrowthDashboard/StoreGrowthDashboard`):

Figure 8.22 – Store growth dashboard

Here, as shown in *Figure 8.22*, we show the most important KPIs, with weekly and daily trends. You can try to replicate the dashboard based on the knowledge you have gathered so far by creating worksheets with visualizations for each of the different views. If you get stuck, download the worksheet from the URL and open it in Tableau Desktop to look at the dashboard's components. Give it a try!

With this dashboard, Jan has a pretty good idea of the daily and monthly performance of his store. It seems that there has been a downward trend in revenue in the last period, which Jan needs to investigate. Hopefully, he is not too concerned. Perhaps we can even help him with some analysis if he wants. For now, let's hand over the dashboard to him and see what he thinks.

A challenge for you

You might have noticed that we hardly discussed the `promotions` dataset during this chapter. If you want to practice with Tableau, look at the data and see where you can incorporate it into a visualization. Perhaps you could look at which employees benefited most from working during a promotion.

What's next?

The ever-evolving world leads to more need for insights. Perhaps a competitor opens a store nearby, prompting Jan to compare sales on the days that both stores are open. Maybe the Stroopwafelshop launches a new type of product and wants to measure its success. There are many opportunities for additional insights, requiring the analytics engineer's skillset.

With the robust tooling for data ingestion, transformation, and visualization that we set up, we have kickstarted the Stroopwafelshop's analytical capabilities and hope to make future analysis much easier.

Summary

In this chapter, we transitioned from theory to practice by focusing on analytics engineering in a real-world context. The Stroopwafelshop case study guided you in assisting the store's owner, Jan, with understanding and analyzing his business data. This case study served as a practical example, demonstrating how to apply analytics engineering techniques and tools in a business context.

Powerful tools such as Airbyte Cloud, Google BigQuery, dbt Cloud, and Tableau were introduced and used. This hands-on approach has not only equipped you with the necessary skills to tackle real-life analytics engineering challenges but also culminated in the creation of an insightful dashboard for the Stroopwafelshop. This combination of theory and practice has offered a glimpse into the daily activities of an analytics engineer, underscoring the importance of comprehending metrics and KPIs to add value to the business.

In the next chapter, you will delve into the importance of monitoring and understanding your data by focusing on its quality and observability.

Part 4: DataOps

In this section, the spotlight shifts to refining the skills of analytics engineering, focusing on quality assurance, collaborative coding, and streamlined workflows. The emphasis extends beyond merely constructing functional data pipelines; it prioritizes implementing safety measures, ensuring reliability, fostering collaboration, and optimizing processes for a more secure and efficient analytics workflow. Consider this knowledge as the differentiating factor between experienced analytics engineers and aspiring ones.

This section has the following chapters:

- *Chapter 9, Data Quality and Observability*
- *Chapter 10, Writing Code in a Team*
- *Chapter 11, Automating Workflows*

9

Data Quality and Observability

Have you ever wasted time or money because you made a decision based on incorrect data? Or because someone had a different definition of a **key performance indicator (KPI)**? If you have, you are familiar with the importance of data quality. In this chapter, we will cover not only the problem of data quality but also some solutions in the form of tools and techniques that can help you overcome this problem.

You will learn about three main areas of data quality: the potential data quality issues in source systems, the issues in infrastructure and pipelines when moving data between systems, and the issues related to data governance. You will also learn why data lineage and understanding the journey of your data as it moves through systems is a crucial part of guaranteeing data quality.

After learning about the problem of data quality, we will investigate data observability as a solution to addressing data quality issues. We will then discuss how data catalogs and semantic layers are separate techniques to help you tackle the issues of shared definitions and the discoverability of data that are crucial for guaranteeing good quality data.

In the end, you will have a good grasp of the problems around data quality as well as potential solutions to those problems. In summary, this chapter will cover the following:

- Understanding the problem of data quality at the source, in transformations, and in data governance
- Finding solutions to data quality and data lineage issues – observability, data catalogs, and semantic layers

Understanding the problem of data quality at the source, in transformations, and in data governance

It is hard to understate the problem of data quality and its impact on you, your organization, and even society. Let us consider a few examples to understand the breadth and impact of data with problematic quality:

- Has your dentist or doctor's appointment ever been moved because of a double booking or scheduling issue? This is due to a simple data quality issue with inconsistency between the two systems.

- Over the last two decades, the academic fields of medicine and psychology have been shaken. Many previously accepted findings suddenly became questionable when other researchers could not reproduce the same results. This so-called replication crisis had, at its foundation, a misunderstanding and too much trust in the statistical concept of significance. It serves as a lesson for all of us: truly valid methodologies for any statistical measure are hard to come by.

- In the 2000 US election, the voting ballot with a so-called butterfly design became a contentious issue, leading to widespread concern among voters. The design was supposed to have led voters to attribute their votes to the wrong candidates. It serves as a reminder that you can never assume the collected data you are working with are 100% correct.

- The 2008 financial crisis started with a fundamental misunderstanding of the value of mortgages traded in mortgage-backed securities. These batches of mortgages were rated AAA for quality, but as we now know, this could not have been further from the truth. Whether intentional or unintentional, the bad data quality of these ratings had a tremendous monetary and societal impact.

It is unlikely that you are the analyst whose reports will bring down financial markets in the next crisis due to data quality issues. However, a lesson from the 2008 financial crisis is that nobody's job depends on data quality until everybody's job does. The impact of the data you work with may not be on the scale of some of these examples, but everybody has seen firsthand how a data quality issue has led to wasting time or money.

In every business decision, we use data combined with experience to determine the course of action. With time, the data part overtakes the experience part of that equation. Combine that with the increasing number of decisions based on automation and machine learning, and data quality becomes more critical than ever. At the same time, a lack of data quality will erode the general trust in data. Let us see which data quality issues you may encounter.

We define three main areas where data quality issues can arise when you use data for analysis, decision-making, or machine learning:

- **In the source system**: Here, data quality issues can arise because, by definition, this system is separated from your central data warehouse. That means that any decision and assumption made by the developers of the source system when collecting or designing the data model of the system might not be communicated properly to any consumers of this data.

- **When you move data from a source system to a target system**: An example of this might be moving data from your sales system to your central data warehouse. In that process, you can create issues around the integrity or completeness of the data or make errors in the transformations applied to the data.

- **In the governance of data quality**: Here, additional issues can arise, for example, a misunderstanding of documentation, a lack of metadata, such as the time of extraction, or unclear ownership are all data governance-related issues that can impact data quality down the line.

We will now discuss each of these sources in detail.

Data quality issues in source systems

In all source systems, decisions have to be made by developers, product owners, and stakeholders on how to collect data and how to implement the collection and storage of that data. If you are unaware of those decisions, inaccuracies and data quality issues can creep into your data platform. To understand the discrepancies between a source system and a data platform more concretely, let us look at an everyday use case: a **customer relationship management (CRM)** system.

Every business has customers or partners, so every business has a way of managing customer relations. It can be as simple as one person with an email inbox or as complicated as a custom application for a multi-national enterprise with millions of customers. For both systems, however, a common question is, when was customer X last contacted? Some companies' systems are so poorly equipped to handle these types of questions that the only way to get an answer to them is to contact company X and ask them. For now, let us assume that they can answer this question. Even then, there are still a wild number of places where getting a correct answer could go wrong. As a little thought experiment, take the concepts in this question that we take for granted:

- **Customer**: Many companies do not actually know their customers, especially in the business-to-business space. For example, is a customer still a customer if the company gets acquired by another company? What happens if the company moves to a different location or opens a new branch? What happens if the contact person changes companies? What happens if a company splits? What happens if the legal entity is different from the operating name? Those are just external factors, but internally, there are just as many questions: Is someone a customer when they have not paid yet? Is someone a customer when they are just on your mailing list? Can company X have multiple customers at once?

- **Contact**: Just like the customer example, the concept of contact can also be interpreted in various ways. Is automated contact good enough? Or does it have to be in person? If it is by phone or email, does a contact need to pick up or read it? Is contact conducted by department A or department B? The customer might perceive your company as one, but internally, you could have departments that do not communicate well.

- **Time**: This is another concept that seems simple at first but always complicates things. Your system might not take time zones into account, or maybe you use different definitions of what a week is. Particularly, the last week of the year will have a different number depending on your chosen standard.

It is easy to be philosophical about these topics and think about all the different possibilities, but in practice, these concepts are implemented even if you are not aware of the specifics. What you should take away from this is that in every system you use as a source for your data platform, someone has made a decision about the concepts and entities that are relevant to your data platform and directly impact data quality.

If you want to stay ahead of data quality issues stemming from source systems, you have to know what aspects to check and discuss with their owners. We define five relevant aspects for this matter: **completeness, consistency, reliability, integrity,** and **relevance.**

Completeness

The simple question, "when was company X last contacted?" implies that we at least have some record of contact. It is not uncommon, though, for organizations to have very fragmented records or even no records at all of customer contact. Sometimes, this is due to different channels that are just not connected (chat, email, or phone), and sometimes, it is due to the absence of a process or the complexity of creating a record. For example, imagine a call center employee who has to create a summary of a phone call in a system where it takes eight clicks and five seconds per screen to do so; they will probably drop that task when the next customer is already on the line.

The same issues arise in many other fields. For example, a **smart** humidity measurement device stuck in a nuclear bunker-like parking garage will have a hard time communicating its measurements over 5G. This will lead to missing records, making it hard to analyze the data.

In both examples, you might still have some data coming in, but the missing data may introduce some bias. Often, you do not know what you do not know, and if there is no visible change in your data, you might have incomplete data for years. Countering incompleteness will sometimes mean accepting you cannot have perfect data quality and documenting uncertainty, especially when you have limited control over the data collection. In other cases, you may still be able to test your source data or algorithmically detect anomalies.

Consistency

The examples in completeness can also impact another aspect: consistency. A smart device that sends data intermittently will probably be inconsistent over time. Both factors will lead to similar results: bias, uncertainty, and, eventually, less accuracy in decision-making. The consistency of data, however, can be checked in different ways. First, a data source can be checked against itself over different dimensions. Is it consistent over time or when comparing different groups, such as countries or states? Second, some data is available from different sources. For example, data on online ads might be available from your advertising platform, the entry campaigns in your web analytics tool, and third-party reports on web traffic or search keyword volume. Each of these will have a slightly different aspect, but you can expect consistency over time.

If you want to check your data for consistency, a tool such as **Datafold** (https://www.datafold.com/) can help you understand the differences between datasets. For example, you could easily check the changes between data in your development and production environments to understand the effects of a new feature in your code. Many observability and data quality tools, such as **Soda** (https://www.soda.io/), **Monte Carlo** (https://www.montecarlodata.com/), or **Masthead** (https://mastheadata.com/), have built-in anomaly detection that can quickly identify consistency issues when ingesting and transforming data. Even simple tests or data freshness checks written in Python, dbt, or SQL can help you do quick sanity checks for consistency.

On the other hand, if you wish to understand the consistency of a specific source data, you must find tools and data providers specific to your source. For example, when you want to understand your web traffic or online advertising data, you could use tools such as **Ahrefs** (https://ahrefs.com/), **Moz** (https://moz.com/), **Semrush** (https://www.semrush.com/) or **SimilarWeb** (https://www.similarweb.com/) to, for example, better understand and compare the metrics of your website and advertising campaigns against other sites. Some sources will have similar tools and providers available, usually at a price, but, especially for proprietary data, this might not be the case, and you will have to rely on internal tests and anomaly detection.

Reliability

Sometimes, you have little or no access to the data collection process, or it might be so complicated it requires a PhD to understand it. In that scenario, you will have to ensure the source is reliable. As we have seen in the examples at the start of this chapter, the data quality in the source system can be impacted in many ways.

As we saw in the case of the mortgage-backed securities that were the catalyst for the 2008 financial crisis, there was an assumption of quality and reliability in the rating agencies that rated these securities as AAA. You cannot always take the time and effort to go into the underlying raw data of every source system. You must accept that every system can have errors and mitigate their impact as much as possible.

There are various ways to determine reliability that we cannot cover, but here are some simple heuristics you can use. For starters, you can test your assumptions about the source system. Simple tests on uniqueness, NULL values, or data freshness may suffice. Secondly, as the famous saying goes, "Follow the money." If there is an incentive for your source to over or under-report (for example, Facebook did this multiple times with ad impressions over the years), this will likely happen. So, if you do not have that PhD to understand the data collection system, it could help to hire an independent consultant who assesses the system.

Integrity

The fourth aspect when looking at data sources is integrity. Even when your data collection process is bulletproof, and your source is reliable and consistent, you may still run into trouble. For one thing, if you just did an analysis on that perfect dataset but the users from whom that data was collected did not consent to its use for analytics purposes, you might have to throw out your data altogether. Legislation and compliance are important factors regarding data integrity, and they can definitely affect your process if you do not consider them.

Integrity also refers to whether or not your data may be compromised. In the worst case, malicious actors might mess with your data; in other cases, bots, automation, or spam might ruin your data. Some organizations unknowingly open the gates to data hell by asking the public for input. When the data collection system is poorly designed, some people will not use it as intended. One such case was the naming of a new British research ship for which the public was asked for input and a vote. The result of that vote was the name Boaty McBoatFace, which was not exactly the intended outcome.

Relevance

When you ask a stakeholder in your organization what they would like to measure, the most annoying answer you can get is "everything." It is often appealing to capture as much data as possible, but that is a recipe for disaster. Adding more and more data to your data lake will end up creating a data swamp. Data without context and meaning is just noise. Not only that, it will be detrimental because every additional dataset, source, or metric adds more complexity. Imagine explaining to a new team member the ingestion process, data model, and other intricacies of a specific source when only 5% of the data is used in any business reporting. On the other hand, when you start with the end goal of how you want to run a business or project, you can create a set of relevant indicators to understand how close you are to that goal. From there on, you can determine the data and measures you will require to report on those indicators. Sometimes, noise is unavoidable, as you might not have the perfect data for reporting. That means you will likely rely on a proxy for your metrics instead. Regardless, starting with the project or business goals, instead of going with whatever data is readily available, can make all the difference in bringing better quality data to your consumers and stakeholders within the organization.

The availability or absence of clear business goals will also make or break your data definitions. It is common to see definitions and metrics based on the source data instead of the target metric or indicator. That leads to a wild growth in definitions for the same metric or indicator. As a consequence, these definitions will have to be aligned later in the process, leading to additional business logic and complexity.

These source-based metrics are common in places where a specific tool or source system is prevalent across teams. For example, a call center might use a single system for call distribution, interactive menus, and CRM. They will often determine their metrics based on this system because it is easy to measure things such as call time. In practice, the business needs an overall view of success across multiple channels. Of course, this is a lot harder to measure than call time. Similarly, when working with marketing teams, it is easy for each team to report conversions or **return on investment** (**ROI**) for the specific marketing channel they are responsible for. However, getting a clear measurement of how to attribute value across digital and even offline marketing channels is something very few organizations do successfully, even though that would be the true measure of success for their marketing department.

Data quality issues in data infrastructure and data pipelines

So far, we have looked at how issues at the source influence data quality, but many other things can go wrong when moving your data from a source system to your data lake or data platform. These infrastructure-based data quality issues usually come from errors in the extraction and loading or in-process transformations applied to the data. We will now look at five important types of **data quality issues** in the data infrastructure.

Timeliness

Nearly every dataset has a time component or at least a time-relevancy component. In other words, we care either about observations over time or before a specific moment in time. That means that when data do not arrive **on time**, it poses a problem for decision-making.

Imagine you run a bike factory. Each bike consists of many different components, most of which are imported. Since importing the components takes time, having good forecasts of your bike sales is essential. If the sales data take a lot of time to arrive, for example, because they have to be manually collected from bike shops, your estimates might be off by an order of magnitude. This problem gets hairier when multiple employees order components, and the status of those orders is not updated in time for adjustments to be made. Not only might you miss valuable sales, but in the worst-case scenario, your factory could have downtime because bikes cannot be finished due to a lack of components.

Whether it is order data, operational data, or stock data, your data must represent the current state of affairs. The **timeliness** of the data becomes an issue if the data is stale or outdated because your decision-making will also be limited and potentially inaccurate.

Integrity

When speaking about data quality issues at the source, we addressed the issue of integrity. This is equally important when looking at data infrastructure. **Infrastructural integrity** requires the assurance that data is not corrupted over its entire lifecycle. In the pipeline, data integrity can be compromised in many different ways. Just think about how to manage extracting a batch of order data when the internet connection drops and a retry has to take place. This could lead to duplicates or missing rows if the exception is not handled correctly. Most of the time, this is not a problem, but the goal of a data team is not to be correct most of the time; it is to be correct all the time.

Dropped connections are not the only problem. Many issues arise from mismatches between environments, for example, when certain settings, such as filters or access keys, accidentally leak between a local, development, or production environment. Similarly, authentication is a big problem for infrastructural integrity. It could be an expired access key or the use of the personal credentials of an employee who is no longer with the company. But even smaller issues than authentication, such as inconsistent settings, timeouts, or the libraries used, can lead to environments drifting apart. If that is the case, your development or acceptance environment might not accurately reflect your production environment and cause data quality issues that can go undetected for a long time.

Completeness

As a direct consequence of infrastructure integrity problems, issues with completeness can occur. We saw that completeness can be an issue in source systems, but it can also happen at this stage. You might miss some data in your pipelines because a filter is too strict or your code incorrectly assumes an array is one-based instead of zero-based. In other cases, completeness is not just about missing rows but about missing datasets altogether. It could be that your team and your stakeholders are unaware of the existence and availability of certain data that could be useful.

Completeness is especially an issue because it is often a so-called "**unknown unknown**." That would be the case for missing rows or even entire datasets. Finding out about these issues usually involves a combination of anomaly detection tools and human scrutiny.

For other issues, you can write tests and checks, even though you are uncertain about their future state; for example, whether a column has NULL values, unique values only, or if it is of type float or Boolean. These are what we call "**known unknowns**." For issues such as missing rows or even entirely missing datasets, this might be harder because, oftentimes, we do not know what we do not know. These are the unknown unknowns, and detecting them will often be a combination of anomaly detection tools and human scrutiny.

Precision

Sometimes, transformations happen while moving data from one place to another. Ideally, a transformation is idempotent, that is, independent of when and how often you run the transformations. For example, if you have a raw dataset of orders that you aggregate daily, creating a new dataset for the aggregate instead of changing it in place makes sure that the process is idempotent and, thus, repeatable when it fails or when a change, such as the removal of a few orders, has to be made to historical data.

Idempotency does not have anything to do with **precision**, but it reminds us that not all data consists of pure, unaggregated, single observations. Some data is transformed in the process because it would otherwise not be manageable or because the data provider has concerns about, for example, the privacy of users or intellectual property, such as custom analysis or unique insights. Consider the measurement of CPU temperature or a smart device capturing humidity levels. We take the sensor readings and aggregate them by seconds or minutes because there is no sense in storing the immense amount of raw data from sensor readings with very little added value. However, this brings us to a potential issue: if the granularity of our data is too low, we may not be able to perform the downstream analysis and aggregations that we would like to.

This issue of precision is like getting an image in a resolution that is too low. A common situation where this happens is for marketing campaign data. Third-party platforms such as Google, Meta, or TikTok, through which marketing campaigns run, do not usually share data on an individual level. Instead, they will provide campaign performance aggregates such as clicks, impressions, or cost per hour or day.

Finally, precision issues do not necessarily have to be time-related but can also occur in other dimensions. For example, you might only have data at the country level when you need it at the city level.

Cleaning

Another issue when dealing with data quality in data infrastructures comes from data cleaning. Since the move from ETL to ELT (discussed in *Chapter 1, What Is Analytics Engineering?*), it has become somewhat contentious to do any transformation on your raw data, including simple cleaning steps. The underlying recommendation is that you keep your raw data as is and do nothing more than load it into your data lake or warehouse. However, as we saw in *Chapter 3, Data Ingestion*, on data ingestion pipelines, there are some good reasons for applying transformations in your pipeline, for example, when these transformations are stateless (there are basically no dependencies on other data). For example, adding a column `year` based on an existing column with the date would be a stateless transformation. Similarly, splitting a comma-separated string into a list could be a valid use case when your source database does not have the list type, but your target database does.

That is not all. You can apply many data-cleaning processes during your transformation step: removing duplicates, removing outliers, renaming columns, standardization (e.g., Fahrenheit to Celsius), string (de-)escaping, flattening or normalizing nested data structures (e.g., JSON objects), and date and time formatting. However, with every adjustment or addition you make, you also introduce the potential for errors. For example, you could split a comma-separated string into a list but might miss the rows with `NULL` values if you do not account for those. Or you may be accidentally formatting timestamps based on the server's time zone instead of the co-ordinated **universal time (UTC)**.

Cleaning data implies making some assumptions about the data coming in. In general, this means balancing the time and effort it takes to clean the data in the pipeline itself versus cleaning it at a later stage. Often, it can be hard, confusing, or computationally expensive when this **dirty** data has to be cleaned at a later stage. However, the downside of cleaning it earlier is that it obscures part of the transformation process and can be hard to debug later when errors are introduced in this stage of the pipeline.

We will now discuss the role of data governance and its impact on data quality.

How data governance impacts data quality

The previous issues around data quality mainly focused on the impact on the data's accuracy, reliability, and consistency. However, even when those three areas are covered, it does not mean data is treated or leveraged as a valuable asset within an organization. To achieve that, we need an overarching strategy and collective practices to dictate data collection, storage, maintenance, and sharing within an organization; in other words, we need **data governance**. The absence of that strategy and practice can have a severe impact on compliance and accountability regarding collected data and on data quality itself. We will look at common problem areas where data governance (or the lack thereof) impacts data quality.

Documentation

One of the most obvious yet underappreciated areas where data governance impacts data quality is **documentation**. It is common to hear horror stories from new employees starting in a data swamp of hours-long ETL jobs and 1,000-line SQL queries after all previous staff have gone without leaving any documentation behind. This often reflects the inability of an organization to balance the short-term time investment in documentation with the long-term cost of debugging data pipelines. However, borrowing time from the future in this way is usually a terrible investment. Consider a simple example where the calculation of **active users** for an online dating platform is assumed to be users who have significantly engaged with the platform on a specific day. The actual metric, however, might not be about users but about active logins. In this case, if a user's session stays active for 90 days even without any activity, there would be a wild overreporting of active users relevant to the business. This would heavily impact any development of new product features, as well as the relationships with advertisers and investors.

Or take a healthcare business that heavily relies on freelancers and temporary workers but also has its own employees. Two departments must calculate their **productivity** metrics. One department might calculate it based on just the hours of the organization's employees, while the other department also includes freelance and temporary workers. If this remains undocumented and undiscovered, there will be a massive bias in decision-making toward one or the other, even though both metrics can be justified in certain ways.

In short, a lack of documentation can lead to data quality issues that directly impact decision-making and limit the future productivity of engineers.

Consensus

Have you ever encountered a situation where you present a report with some numbers, and someone from a different team says, "But my Excel sheet here shows a different number"? Getting a single source of truth, or consensus, in your organization is very hard to achieve, as different teams rely on different operational tools with different types of data collection and definitions. Sometimes, even getting a consensus for one data source is hard. Here are some common occurrences of a lack of consensus or discrepancy between source systems:

- If you have ever worked with web analytics data, you know that different platforms report different numbers. Whether it is simply because advertisers have an incentive to overreport their numbers or because of conversion attribution, having multiple platforms measure the same thing has been a source of disagreement for many marketers.

- For sales and customer support, the reason for discrepancies is usually slightly different. Their CRM system might be hard to use; so, instead, they record everything in an Excel sheet. This leads to the data team reporting one thing and the sales or customer support team then magically revealing the "real" numbers in a quarterly meeting.

- Even when the measurements are accurate, there might still be disagreements. If you have been to Northern Europe or the United Kingdom, you know that weather services will frequently disagree on whether or not it will rain tomorrow or even in the next hour.

Nonetheless, **consensus**—or lack thereof—is usually not as trivial as disagreeing about weather reports. It can lead to painful losses when the business realizes they have spent millions on marketing campaigns or assembly line change, only to discover that the **positive** result might not be so positive after all. It is usually only when two systems disagree that the underlying assumptions of both systems are questioned.

Accountability

A crucial part of data governance is the **ownership** and **accountability** of data. We have already seen in this chapter how dependencies on source data or other teams can create data quality issues and confusion, and those dependencies become even harder to manage when there is no clear owner of the underlying data. When you clearly see issues with the data that you need to work with but no one is willing to address them, or it is unclear who should take accountability for addressing the issues, data quality will suffer.

Of course, the mere understanding of ownership is just the start. Once it is established, you also want the person responsible to address any issues regarding the data, preferably before you notice them. Ideally, together, you write down how the owner of a dataset takes responsibility for any issues with the data and within what timeframe they should be fixed. These days, this is often called a **data contract**, but you might also hear the term **service-level agreement (SLA),** which is a more commonly used term within software development.

Establishing a clear chain of accountability helps foster a culture of proactive data management within an organization. When individuals or teams know that they are directly responsible for the quality and accuracy of a dataset, they are more likely to implement rigorous checks, validations, and safeguards to maintain its integrity. This proactive approach can significantly reduce the occurrence of data anomalies, inconsistencies, and inaccuracies.

Merely designating ownership is not enough. For instance, as can be seen in *Figure 9.1*, in a nascent data organization, both the data team and the rest of the organization cannot yet benefit from well-established processes. This means that communication lines are not as clear yet and end users will often bypass the data owner and talk to the engineering team directly, prioritizing issues from the most vocal users instead of addressing the most important issues.

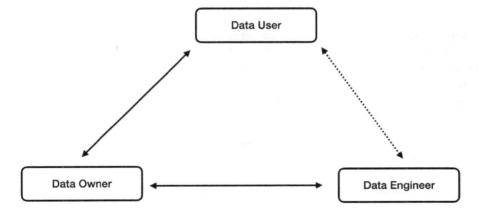

Figure 9.1 – Accountability in a nascent data organization

There needs to be continuous communication and collaboration between data owners, data users, and other stakeholders. Regular feedback loops ensure that data owners are aware of the challenges faced by data users and can make necessary adjustments in real time. Structuring this collaborative approach correctly not only ensures high data quality but also builds trust among different departments in the organization. Mature data organizations, as seen in *Figure 9.2*, will often appoint a data product owner to oversee the processes and communication required. Especially when the complexity of the data product grows and touches more data sources and, thus, more data owners, it is vital for an organization to structure product development and feedback loops efficiently.

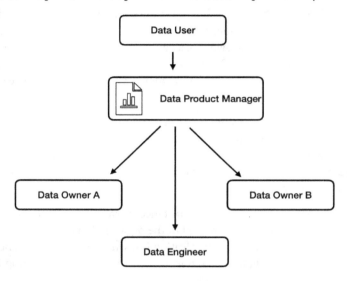

Figure 9.2– Accountability in a mature data organization

Additionally, with the evolving nature of data and its sources, the concept of ownership should not be static. As business goals, technological landscapes, and organizational structures change, there might be a need to re-evaluate and possibly reassign data ownership to better align with these changes. Periodic reviews of data ownership roles, combined with training and awareness programs, ensure that the organization remains agile in its data governance efforts.

In the grand scheme of things, accountability and ownership are not just about fixing data issues. They are about instilling a sense of responsibility and creating a culture where everyone understands the value of high-quality data and works collectively toward achieving it.

Metadata management

Metadata, which is nothing more than data about data, gives context to your datasets. Metadata can detail when, how, and by whom data was collected, transformed, or accessed. Without robust metadata management, teams can struggle to understand data relevance and quality, leading to potential misuse or misinterpretations during analysis.

Metadata might seem like it is not as valuable as the actual data, but consider the privacy discussion around how long metadata from your messaging apps can be stored. How much does such an app know if it does not have the actual message but does have the following?

- The exact time at which the message was sent and received

- The identifier of the sender and receiver

- The exact geolocation of the sender and receiver

- Details about the device from which the message was sent

This is **just** metadata, but it can give a very good idea of where you live, what places you have visited and with whom, who your friends and family are, and how much you are willing to spend on a phone.

For example, in the case of a ride-sharing app, those data could be leveraged to increase prices when you are abroad, when your device is unplugged, and when your battery is low (*Figure 9.3*). Hopefully, the data you collect about your data is not up for a similar debate on privacy, but it can still be very valuable to your organization:

Key	Value
deviceModel	Apple iPhone 15 Pro
networkType	mobile
batteryLevel	0.08
batteryState	unplugged
resolution	1200x900
physicalMemory	8000
language	FR
carrier	AT&T

Figure 9.3 – Example of mobile device metadata from a ride-sharing app

The value of metadata in an organization can be leveraged in many different ways, many of which relate to what we have already discussed in this chapter so far:

- It might give you an understanding of which datasets or transformations depend on one another; in other words, the lineage of data

- You can monitor if there is a discrepancy in the normal start time or duration of a data ingestion process or whether the number of rows ingested is wildly different from previous times

- Understanding and keeping track of access to data might be needed to protect valuable pieces of information or personally identifiable information

- Opening up metadata from datasets, such as the owner, descriptions, the columns, and the data quality status, might help end users to discover new datasets for their own needs and understand how the data might integrate with the data they have in their own systems

- You can tune and improve the performance of data pipelines both from an efficiency and a cost perspective by understanding how changes to your pipelines affect that performance and cost

Figure 9.4 shows an example of how metadata can be leveraged to monitor the transformations and lineage of a data pipeline:

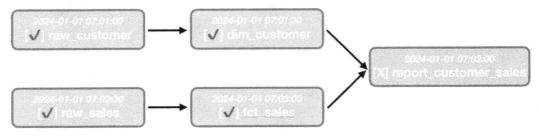

Figure 9.4 – A direct acyclic graph (DAG) showing the lineage,
status, and timestamps of models in a data pipeline

If, for example, a sales per customer dashboard is not showing any data, it is easy to see that the customer and sales data models have all run successfully, but the model combining them has an error (indicated here with an [X]), providing a clear place to start debugging.

Cost management

A special type of data governance is cost management. These days, there are specialized firms and tools to help you mitigate your cloud computing costs, as they run into the millions of dollars. As you ingest and process more and more data, your pipelines might account for a substantial chunk of those millions. For some, that makes data or cloud cost management a goal in and of itself, but in essence, it is just another business expense. It is up to you to decide when it makes sense to spend time and money on reducing your cloud costs.

The first step, however, is one you should not skip: understanding how much you are spending. This is sometimes harder to understand than it looks when resources in the cloud or even on-premises are a mixed bunch owned by different departments or hidden behind confusing line items on an invoice from a cloud provider, and that is not even including the complexity of the people and their salaries in your data team or calculating the business value of a data team and data warehouse.

You could write an entire book on cost management for data, but often the biggest overspending comes from simple issues:

- **Ingesting and storing data you do not need or use**: For example, when you miss visibility or knowledge on legacy data ingestion processes that are still running.

- **Ingesting and storing more often than you need the data**: If your analysts are not in the office on the weekend, you might not need to run that expensive pipeline on the weekend. If they look at the data once a day, you might not have to run it every 15 minutes.

- **Over-engineering your data pipelines**: Just because Netflix, AirBnB, or Google wrote a blog about it, it does not mean you need to implement their solution for a problem you do not have. Keeping things as simple as possible will take you a long way in saving costs.

- **Under-engineering your data pipelines**: The biggest benefit of having data or software engineers on your team is that they can turn business rules and logic into code. Instead of clicking your way through the tool that's in vogue today, you can spend a bit more time and money engineering a solution that leverages programming and data languages that have been around for over 30 years, and that will likely be around for the next 30 years.

Data lineage

Considering the many places where issues can arise in moving data from one place to another, data lineage is a crucial aspect of data quality. In essence, it describes the journey of your data. However, the lack of proper implementation or even the absence of data lineage can cause severe issues or, at the very least, time-consuming debugging sessions. That makes data lineage both a problem area and a potential solution for data quality. Understanding data lineage can vastly increase the speed at which you can identify and solve data quality issues.

These are some common issues you might face when creating a coherent view of the journey and the lineage of your data:

- **Lack of visibility**: data lineage is inherently visual, as it is a mapping of the underlying dependencies of a dataset.

- **Time component of lineage**: Not every dependency of your dataset will have a well-documented, logged, and audited trail of the transformations and interpretations that took place along the way. A data lineage is not a static diagram; as the underlying data moves and changes, the lineage diagram will also change, especially for parts that may be outside of your control. Capturing this changing lineage is extremely hard.

- **Audit and compliance**: For some types of data, quality is not even the biggest problem. If your user has the right to request the deletion of or access to their data (for example, under GDPR or CCPA) or if the government requires you to turn over certain documents up to, let's say, 7 years, this can pose enormous challenges in tracing back the origin of data over a long period of time.

- **Undermining data governance**: A lack of (visibility into) lineage can also undermine data governance initiatives, as ownership or responsibility can be disputed or even unknown within an organization, especially when the data crosses multiple departments on their journey.

Now that we understand where in our data journey problems can arise, we must next consider how to use tools and processes to adequately solve them depending on the needs of our organization.

Finding solutions to data quality issues – observability, data catalogs, and semantic layers

In the first part of this chapter, we saw how data quality can be impacted in many different ways. Whether it is an issue in the source system, a problem with your data pipeline infrastructure, or a data governance challenge, making sure the quality of your data is on par is crucial for making better business decisions and creating trust in your data. Luckily, we have a set of tools and techniques at our disposal to overcome issues around data quality. By considering the problems we have identified in the first part, we will look at a few solutions to overcome them.

The first solution or technique is observability. **Observability** is a concept from the software engineering and DevOps fields, where consistently **observing** issues is helpful to minimize or prevent the downtime of application systems. When translated to the data world, this means a tool that will give you alerts and visual insights into the data dependencies of a given table or dashboard as well as any errors, anomalies, or data quality issues. A good observability tool will also allow you to monitor where and when they appear.

Second, a **data catalog** can help you overcome issues relating to the definitions, understanding, and discoverability of data. Where observability tools focus on errors and anomalies in your data, catalogs are a way to prevent issues coming from a mismatch in the definitions of metrics, dimensions, and datasets. A catalog can help define and document those metrics and dimensions as well as make it easier to discover meaningful and relevant data for analysis within a business.

Finally, a **metric store** or **semantic layer**, such as a data catalog, combats the issue of having mismatching definitions for crucial business data. This is especially true for the metrics and key performance indicators that are used throughout the business, where a metric store or semantic layer can help to harmonize data and make sure different departments are using the same metrics in their reports, analyses, and models.

Let us now look at *Figure 9.5*:

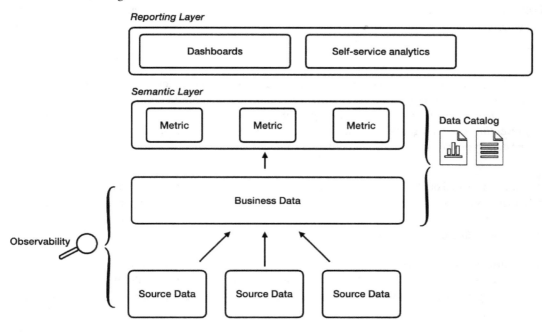

Figure 9.5 – The data analytics landscape showing the journey of data in a mature data organization

We can see that the observability tools capture the journey of data, a semantic layer creates a shared definition of business metrics, and a data catalog enhances a shared understanding and the discovery of data for all users. This, in turn, leads to consistent and reliable data in your reporting layer or any other data application you want to use in your organization.

Crucially, however, the biggest part of any data quality initiative is something that no tool will solve for you. If you want to guarantee the quality of data within an organization, you have to consider the processes and data maturity of that organization. To change perceptions about data ownership and responsible data production and collection, you have to manage the change in that organization. It is not something that happens overnight, but as you change the perception, usage, and responsibility of data quality, you will see that people, teams, and entire departments will trust the data more and more to make their decisions.

Using observability to improve your data quality

Data observability is a growing trend that borrows principles from software engineering and operational monitoring, adapting them to the nuanced needs of data management. Observability is a concept from the software engineering and DevOps fields, where being able to quickly and consistently observe issues is helpful to minimize or even prevent the downtime of application systems. When translated into the data world, this means having visual insights into the data dependencies of a given table or dashboard, as well as any errors, anomalies, or data quality issues, and being able to monitor where and when they appear.

> **Note**
>
> Yuliia Tkachova from the data observability company Masthead defines data observability as "*the ability of an organization to track and control its data landscape and multilayer data dependencies (pipelines, infrastructure, applications) at all times [...] with the goal of detecting, preventing, controlling, and remediating data outages or any other issues disrupting the work of the data system or spoiling data quality and reliability.*"

Of course, every tool out there for data observability will tell you its own version of what data observability is, but since we clearly defined the problems that we need to solve in the first part of the chapter, we can also start to see where an observability tool should be able to help us. Our data problems were roughly separated into three categories, where an observability solution can help in various ways:

- **Source system issues**: Detecting issues at the source is hard for any tool since part of the problem of a source system is that there is limited access and, thus, limited visibility in the first place. At the very least, identifying a source system as part of your data lineage should be something that every tool needs to do.

- **Data pipeline and infrastructure issues**: Detecting issues as you process, transform, and consume your data is the key strength of any data observability tool. This is done mostly through monitoring, testing, alerting, profiling, and anomaly detection. However, of course, every tool implements these elements in different ways.

- **Data governance issues**: Most data observability tools limit themselves to what is easily quantifiable; hence, getting insights into data governance issues is often harder to obtain from these tools. Costs might be the only exception to this, although this varies per solution.

Looking at observability solutions through the lens of data quality problems, we can see the contours of what a good data quality tool should look like and what features it should have. It is beyond the scope of this book to dive into the details of observability, but roughly speaking, your data observability solution, whether it is one or multiple tools, will need the following features:

- **Lineage**: Having a (preferably visual) understanding of how datasets, tables, and transformations depend on each other is the first step to identifying data quality issues. The most common way to do this is with a **directed acyclic graph** (**DAG**), as seen in *Figure 9.4*, which is a type of visualization that shows the linear flow of data from source to destination and, sometimes, even from column to column in a dataset. If the linear character does not work for your use case, you might be better off using something as simple as a heatmap or an entity-relationship diagram where relationship types, such as one-to-one or one-to-many between entities (the objects your business works with), are mapped out.

- **Testing**: Though never enough on its own, testing data against assumptions, such as uniqueness or non-null values, is great for quickly identifying issues as they appear. Many tools provide extensive testing solutions, sometimes even with machine learning and anomaly detection on top of them. While testing is great for providing guarantees about your data, it will not help you discover unknown problems with your data. Some examples of this are an orphaned pipeline where some data are still moved around in a valid way, but it is never used by a downstream dependency; a rogue dashboard that is created by another team in an environment that is not observed by the data team; or a legacy database query outside of the current system, created by an employee that no longer works at the company and that takes a long time to run.

- **Monitoring**: With your tests running and your pipelines turning, you need a way to see problems at a glance. Since this is a shared and common problem for many organizations, you can easily use the metrics and visualizations that tools provide. It could be as simple as the duration of a data ingestion pipeline, the number of rows that do not match a specified schema, or even whether a data loading job failed or succeeded.

- **Alerting**: While your monitoring solution might be running perfectly and detecting all your data pipeline problems, if no notification ever reaches you, it might all be in vain. An alerting solution, whether it is an email or a message on Slack, can alert you to act on data quality issues. The crucial part of any alerting solution is not just that it reaches you but that it also strikes the right balance between when to alert and when not to alert to prevent alerting fatigue.

- **Tracing**: Where monitoring and lineage give you a high-level overview of what went wrong and where the dependencies are, tracing can be a way to identify the errors or issues in specific transformations and functions that are applied to your data. It could be an issue with performance or timing, understanding when and where the error or culprit was introduced, or pinpointing the exact data transformation or function that is not operating as intended.

- **Profiling**: When working with data, not all errors are as easy to spot as failures in your program or function. Sometimes, a data transformation works well, but the outcome is not what is intended. There could be duplicates or missing values where none are expected. Profiling is a way to easily understand the makeup of your dataset by visualizing, often on a per-column basis, the number of NULL values, averages, maximum and minimum values, distributions, formatting, and similar insights to understand if your data makes sense in a single glance.

- **History capture**: A big problem with data transformations is that, over time, the data or the transformation might change with the business or the pipeline. Often, it is important to keep track of changes to the data for audit and compliance purposes, but similarly, you might want to keep track of data quality for debugging purposes.

- **Anomaly detection**: We have already considered how testing can help you with guaranteeing certain assumptions you have about the data. You can also try to detect anomalies in the unknown parts of known data. For example, when you ingest way more or fewer rows than you usually do or when certain values are out of normal bounds, this could be an indication of a data quality issue.

Apart from this, **data catalogs** also help in data discovery and maintaining data quality. Let's talk about data catalogs in detail.

The benefits of data catalogs for data quality

For a long time, the hardest part of analytics was the discovery and availability of data. We are at a turning point where the discovery and gathering of data is getting easier, but with increasing data volumes, understanding the quality of that data is getting harder. Data catalogs are intended to solve a big part of the problem around discovering data, including the quality and lineage of that data.

Let us take a common example. Imagine a shop selling Dutch stroopwafel delicacies worldwide, both online and offline. Now, a young analyst is looking to identify loyal customers for a special deal. Without a data catalog, finding the right data could be very hard. The data would be siloed, so while the analyst might be able to find, for example, returning visitors to their online shop, they might not be able to take into account the offline purchase data. This could create a huge bias in their dataset. If there was, for example, a big Dutch multi-national that bought all their employees in different countries a pack of stroopwafels every year for Christmas, this would likely not be reflected in just the online data. Having a data catalog would allow the analyst to discover datasets for every country, as well as customer support, invoicing, and online shopping. The catalog could also provide information on the definitions used in the datasets. For example, in some datasets, the local (country) branch of a company might be considered the customer, whereas, in other datasets, it would be the holding.

With these datasets and their varying definitions in hand, our young analyst is now able to create a much richer and powerful analysis for his organization. Even though the data itself might not be perfectly harmonized and cleaned, just being able to find and understand the underlying data saves hours and hours of valuable time. A well-implemented data catalog can provide a coherent view of data across the organization, enabling analysts and other data consumers to collaborate and combine datasets from different departments and teams with an understanding of the quality, value, and definitions of those datasets.

A **catalog** is not just valuable for data consumers. As we mentioned, with the increasing availability of data, managing data quality is more important for data producers as well. Having a catalog can provide a clear overview of all the data assets that a data producer is responsible for. That can significantly assist in compliance and governance, as a data producer is able to more easily manage permissions and access and understand the lineage, dependencies, quality, and potentially, the costs of their data.

That all sounds good, but implementing a data catalog that is actually useful and relevant for an organization is more than just clicking a button and filling out your credit card details. As we have seen in this chapter, a lot of issues around data quality depend on the data maturity of the organization. If the processes around data ownership, responsibility, and quality are not in order, no tool will be able to come to your salvation. Implementing something such as a data catalog is both a technical and a business problem and requires both a team capable of handling that as well as enough support from higher management.

Nonetheless, big parts of the implementation are becoming easier and easier. With the rise in machine learning and large language models, writing documentation, creating descriptions, and generating metadata have become more manageable tasks. While computer-generated descriptions might not be perfect, they are a great first step and can save a human a lot of time when improving those descriptions. Tools such as **Select Star** (`https://www.selectstar.com/`), **Atlan** (`https://www.atlan.com/`), and **Collibra** (`https://www.collibra.com/`) can automate a lot of the work that goes into creating a data catalog.

Thus, a data catalog can be a great solution for improving data quality by increasing the discoverability of data, creating an organization-wide understanding of data lineage, and documenting a shared understanding of data definitions. However, no tool will create those benefits unless you also have a process in place to embed the data catalog and the usage of the catalog within the organization's teams and departments.

Improving data quality with a semantic layer

In this chapter, we have seen how data quality is not just a technical problem but also a business problem. While a data catalog and good documentation help to overcome many challenges around creating shared definitions of data, this often lacks the practical implementation of going from a data model to a dashboard. A **semantic layer**—sometimes called metrics layer or metric store—is a translation layer that turns the complexity of data models into answers to business questions. As we have previously observed in *Figure 9.5*, the semantic layer functions as a gateway between modeled business data and data applications, such as a dashboard or report. If that is still too vague, consider the following example. Let's say our stroopwafel factory sells different stroopwafel flavors to different countries. The data are all there in the millions of rows in our orders table, but a business user from the sales team might find that too complex to query. A semantic layer would allow this user to easily create a "flavors per country per month" query without worrying about performance or the underlying data model.

A semantic layer, in essence, handles access controls, data modeling, metrics, aggregations, and caching so that drag-and-drop queries from business users can be translated to database queries regarding the raw data. It is not a replacement for your visualization tool, nor does it replace your transformation layer. Instead, it serves as an abstraction layer to centralize metrics within your organization. Whether it is for a local sales meeting or a meeting with the board of directors, knowing that your metrics and KPIs are the same across the organization can save many hours.

Traditionally, many metric calculations and aggregations are done inside BI and visualization tools. This can lead to a messy growth in metric calculations, as it is hard to re-use existing metrics across dashboard reports. This is somewhat manageable when your organization is small, and the number of metrics and dashboards is limited. However, with the increasing need for data across organizations and increasing data literacy required by the end users of your reports and dashboards, there is an increased need to self-serve this data. In the past, this need was likely fulfilled by emailing Excel sheets around, but, of course, ending a filename with `version5_final_final.xlsx` was never a viable alternative to the true re-usability of metrics across tools, dashboards, and reports.

The semantic layer, in that sense, is a key component of data democratization in your organization, and data democratization, of course, is intended to remove many of the traditional barriers to making informed decisions based on data. As you can imagine, just as for a data catalog, implementing a semantic layer in your organization has to go hand in hand with improving and growing data literacy in an organization and growing and improving data literacy requires having a support system from your data teams to answer the questions that will come from end users having increased access to data.

Summary

In this chapter, we have looked at both the problems of data quality and the potential solutions to improve it.

We saw that data quality issues come from three key areas. First, from the source system, where data might be incomplete, unreliable, or inconsistent. Second, from the infrastructure and pipelines that process and transform data as it is ingested. In that case, you might have issues with data quality because the data is too late, corrupted, or missing. It might also be that a mistake is made in the transformations, where, for example, we get the granularity or precision of the data wrong. Finally, data quality issues can arise from problems with data governance, most notably from inconsistencies in the definitions and documentation or a lack of access management, cost management, or metadata management. This all leads to a misunderstanding of the data and the data's lineage and dependencies, which, in turn, leads to suboptimal decision-making and increased costs for the organization.

Luckily, there are also solutions for improving data quality. Firstly, using data observability, we can improve the monitoring and detection of data quality issues throughout the data ingestion and transformation process. Secondly, using data catalogs allows us to create a shared understanding of the definitions within the data, as well as increase the discoverability of the data. Finally, a semantic layer can improve data democratization and better decision-making by improving the quality of metrics used throughout the organization and creating easy access for all end users to common metrics and KPIs.

In the next chapter, we will take our knowledge of data quality and data transformations and look at how to apply it in practice when writing code in a team setting.

10

Writing Code in a Team

Writing code individually and writing code in a team can be very different experiences. As your team grows, new challenges will arise from working together on the same code base. The most apparent challenges are about code quality, ownership, and accountability. Who works on what? How can you keep consistent coding styles and quality? How can you review code? How can you easily onboard new colleagues?

The clear separation of duties, version control, tracking issues and tasks, agreeing on and enforcing a coding standard, CI/CD, code reviews, and documentation are all ways to streamline maintaining a code base within a team.

Version control and CI/CD are tools and techniques that can help data professionals work more efficiently, collaborate more effectively, and maintain the integrity and reliability of their code and data assets over time. As analytics engineers, we should adopt these principles to make collaboration on the same code base more efficient.

In this chapter, we are going to cover the following main topics:

- Identifying the responsibilities of team members
- Tracking tasks and issues
- Managing versions with version control
- Working with coding standards
- Reviewing code
- Documenting code
- Continuous integration/continuous deployment
- Working with containers
- Refactoring and technical debt

Identifying the responsibilities of team members

Working in a data team requires having a clear separation of duties to streamline development work. This is like a musical orchestra, where each member—even within a wind, string, bass, or percussion section—can have a slightly different role to play. Similarly, in a data team, there will be members with different sets of skills and overlapping skills.

As analytics engineers, we might have to collaborate with both data engineers and data analysts or the consumers of data, either within the same team or across departments. It is crucial to define team responsibilities to prevent conflicts over tasks and ensure clear accountability.

The responsibility boundaries help create focus on a specific domain of work, which allows for the following:

- Mitigating the risks of overlapping work and redundant efforts, optimizing the team's productivity
- Fostering a sense of accountability and ownership among team members
- Helps promote a deeper understanding and mastery of one's designated area, leading to the construction of robust and efficient code
- It is essential for maintaining security and compliance

Let's say you work in a multidisciplinary team of data analysts and analytics engineers tasked with producing insights from some newly ingested data. These data are ingested already and need to be properly modeled in the data warehouse. Subsequently, the data analysts will build interactive dashboards using this data.

Let us first determine what sort of responsibilities there could be within such a team:

- Gathering and understanding the business requirements of the stakeholders
- Modeling the data
- Gathering insights from the data
- Responsibly overseeing the project, making sure the project is on track, and managing resources

When assigning these responsibilities to your team members, keep in mind the following:

- Divide responsibilities based on people's expertise
- Link up engineers with domain experts to avoid the misinterpretation of data and better task alignment
- Allow for direct communication channels

- Try to divide responsibility evenly among colleagues, as this establishes feelings of fairness and equality

- Limit access to certain sensitive data to only a few people on a need-to-know basis, as this reduces security risks

Having a clear separation of duties prevents ambiguity. Once you have clearly defined the roles and aligned the responsibilities, it is time to assign tasks to the team.

The following section will introduce issue and task tracking and explain some best practices around assigning tasks and structuring them.

Tracking tasks and issues

If the roles have been defined and assigned within a team, using issue and task-tracking tools with an Agile methodology, such as Scrum, can be an effective way to increase productivity within a team. We are not going to talk about Agile methodologies, but we encourage reading up on this topic, as doing task tracking and working in an agile way are quite related.

With the help of task and issue tracking tools, developers and project managers can collaborate more effectively, identify and address issues early on, and ultimately deliver high-quality data products that meet the needs of their users.

This sounds evident; however, in our experience as consultants, we have noticed that teams across different industries have implemented this practice to varying degrees. We have seen it all, from teams who do not do any issue and task tracking to teams who use the latest tools but have no coherent strategy for using these tools, and, thus, the tool quickly becomes obsolete. Therefore, a situation where teams do use a tool but without any internally established best practices can happen, which can add confusion and create friction within a team when it comes to how the tool is used. This section does not necessarily promote a particular tool, but rather, it underlines the importance of issue and task tracking to team performance.

Let us discuss the elements that constitute a mature business practice of issue and task tracking.

Tools for issue and task tracking

There are several tools that organizations use for issue and task tracking purposes. Tools such as **Jira** and **Azure DevOps** are frequently encountered in bigger corporates that already use the **Atlassian** or **Microsoft** stacks. Others, such as **Trello** and **GitHub Issues**, are more often used by smaller companies as they are easier to integrate into an existing stack and are relatively cheaper. The most prominent issue and task-tracking tools are the following:

- **Jira**: This is developed by Atlassian and is one of the most popular tools, known for its flexibility and powerful features. It supports Scrum, Kanban, and mixed methodology projects, allowing teams to create, assign, and track the progress of tasks and issues (https://www.atlassian.com/software/jira).

- **Azure DevOps**: Provided by Microsoft, Azure DevOps offers a suite of development tools, including task tracking and bug tracking, making it a comprehensive solution for anything from software development to data and analytics, particularly in a Microsoft-centric environment (`https://azure.microsoft.com/en-us/products/devops`).

- **Asana**: Asana offers a user-friendly interface to create and assign tasks, set deadlines, and track progress. It is well-suited for both small and large teams and supports project timelines, workspaces, and detailed reporting (`https://asana.com/`).

- **Trello**: This is also offered by Atlassian; Trello employs a card or a board interface, which is intuitive and easy to use, making it ideal for smaller teams or simpler projects. It's especially good for visual organization and quick task assignments (`https://trello.com/`).

- **GitHub Issues**: This is integrated directly within GitHub and is ideal for projects hosted on the platform. GitHub Issues allows for the easy tracking of bugs and tasks and is often utilized for open source projects (`https://github.com/features/issues`).

- **GitLab Issues**: Like GitHub, GitLab provides an integrated issue tracking system, with features such as issue boards, making it a viable option for data projects, especially those hosted on GitLab (`https://docs.gitlab.com/ee/user/project/issues/`).

Clear task definition

Now that you have become acquainted with some popular tools, let's look at **creating tasks**. Creating tasks seems like a straightforward activity, but getting the scope of tasks right is the tricky bit. How often do you find yourself struggling to find the right scope for a task while keeping in mind available resources and time constraints?

Therefore, always consider the following when creating tasks:

- Tasks need to be properly assigned to a person, not to multiple people

- Tasks need to have a clear description

- Tasks need to have a clearly defined scope

- Tasks need to have a clear **definition of done** (**DoD**)

- Tasks need to have a clearly defined deadline

Table 10.1 lists the considerations for task creation:

Consideration	Explanation
Assign a task to single person	This ensures accountability and ownership
Clear description	Avoids confusion about what the task is about
Clear scope	Avoid confusion about how much needs to be delivered

Consideration	Explanation
Clear DoD	This ensures a better understanding of what criteria this task requires to be finished
Clear deadline	This ensures accountability and that the project is on track

Table 10.1 – Considerations for task creation

Assigning tasks to a single person ensures accountability and ownership and a direct point of contact. Working with other colleagues on a task can be inevitable at times; in this situation, it is advisable to create better-scoped smaller tasks from out of the bigger task, with smaller increments of work that can be picked up by other colleagues. Following this advice will help you avoid the common who-does-what arguments and reduce the overhead of developers having to decide who takes up what task. Tasks need to have a clear description and scope; this avoids confusion on what needs to be done, and this goes together with the **definition of done** (**DoD**), which defines when a task is considered complete.

Categorization and tagging

Once created, tasks should be categorized and tagged to help organize, prioritize, and quickly find them. **Tagging** can be implemented by thinking about general themes corresponding to the product you're working on and then mapping the task to them.

For categorization, we suggest familiarizing yourself with task hierarchies and then labeling your tasks accordingly. Consistency will ease working with people coming from different companies or switching teams.

Many tools allow you to define a task hierarchy, quickly conveying how big or complex an item is.

For example, in Azure DevOps, you can create a certain **task hierarchy** that is frequently encountered in the Agile methodology; you may have heard this before.

Although different tools use different terms, the following list will guide you through the terminology you might encounter. The terms in an **Agile task hierarchy** are listed in order of a more specific task scope, from a general description to a specific description:

- **Epic**: An **Epic** represents a large, high-level **User Story** or feature that encompasses multiple related tasks. Epics are often used to group together work that contributes to a larger goal or objective.

- **User Story**: A **User Story** is a concise description of a software feature from an end-user's perspective. It represents a single piece of functionality that delivers value to the user. User Stories are often written in the following format: "*As a [user type], I want [an action] so that [benefit/value].*" For example, "*As a buyer, I want a portal so that I can see my past purchases.*" User Stories are more common in software development than in data teams. However, the format can be helpful.

- **Feature**: A **Feature** is a functional unit of work that delivers specific business value. It is a smaller, more focused User Story that is part of an Epic. Features are typically scoped to be completed within a single sprint or iteration.

- **Product Backlog Item (PBI)**: **Product Backlog Item** is a general term used to describe any item in the backlog, which can include Epics, Features, and User Stories. It represents a unit of work that needs to be prioritized and addressed by the development team. You will probably encounter PBIs more often than complete User Stories and Features as an analytics engineer, but it is good to understand the overarching terms as well.

- **Task or Work Item**: **Task or Work Items** are granular units of work that are derived from User Stories or Features. They represent the specific activities or steps required to complete a PBI or User Story or deliver a Feature.

- **Subtasks**: **Subtasks** are even more granular breakdowns of work within a Task. They represent the smallest units of work within a User Story.

Table 10.2 summarizes these categories and their relevance for analytics engineers:

Concept	Description	Scope/ Size	Typical Use in Development Process	Note for Analytics Engineers
Epic	A large, high-level User Story or feature that encompasses multiple related tasks.	Largest	Grouping related features or User Stories.	Epics are seldom encountered by analytics engineers, but they provide valuable context.
User Story	A concise description of a (software) feature from an end-user perspective, typically written in a specific format.	Medium	Defining single pieces of functionality.	Although more common in software development teams, they are useful for understanding the end-user perspective.
Feature	A functional unit of work that delivers specific business value. A smaller, more focused User Story that is part of an Epic.	Small to medium	Scoped to be completed within a single sprint.	Features are specific and can be directly related to analytics work.
PBI	A general term for any item in the backlog, including Epics, Features, and User Stories. It represents a unit of work to be prioritized and addressed.	Varies	Cataloging the work to be done.	Analytics engineers might encounter PBIs more often; understanding this unit of work is crucial for prioritizing work.

Concept	Description	Scope/ Size	Typical Use in Development Process	Note for Analytics Engineers
Task or Work Item	Granular units of work derived from User Stories or Features. These represent specific activities or steps required to complete a PBI, User Story, or Feature.	Granular	Breaking down work into items that can be tackled by a single person in a sprint.	Tasks or work items are the bread and butter of daily analytics work.
Subtasks	Granular breakdown of the work within a Task.	Smallest	Detailing the smallest units of work within a PBI.	Subtasks offer a detailed view of what needs to be done on a very small scale; they are often encountered in the more detailed planning and prioritization stages.

Table 10.2 – Agile tasks hierarchy

The hierarchy generally follows the flow of breaking down high-level goals (Epics) into more manageable features that are then further detailed into user-centric stories. Finally, Tasks and Subtasks provide the specific steps and activities necessary to implement the User Stories.

This hierarchy allows for the better planning, prioritization, and tracking of work in a DevOps environment. It also helps to align development efforts with business goals and ensures that each piece of work is well-defined and delivers value to the end-users or stakeholders.

Let's discuss each of these in detail:

- **Prioritization and backlog management**: In an Agile way of working, creating a backlog of tasks is usually the first step before doing sprint planning. In sprint planning, tasks are assigned to a sprint from the backlog. What needs to be considered is the priority of tasks. Knowing the priority of tasks is important to stay on track with long-term goals. Most tools provide a neat way of creating tasks on the backlog and assigning priorities to them.

- **Visibility and transparency**: Try to find a tool that provides visibility and transparency regarding the tasks and one that easily allows you to find related tasks and user assignments without losing yourself in the navigation. This saves time and reduces ambiguity. Experiment with different ways to visualize outstanding tasks and work items to find the one that works best for your team.

- **Regular status updates and reporting**: An issue and task tracking tool is useless without proper reporting functionality. In order to do regular status updates, the tool should provide functionality that supports tracking indicators, such as how long tasks have been open or in a certain state, e.g., tasks waiting on the backlog; this provides insights into the development process and helps uncover bottlenecks and improves resource allocation.

- **Integration with version control**: Some tools, such as Azure DevOps and Jira, provide an easy way to link up work items or tasks with code pushes in version control (tools such as Git). These types of tools natively integrate with version control, and this is a handy feature to streamline the development process and provide transparency regarding code development. We recommend this approach as it links up project management with code development, provides both project managers and developers with the ability to establish an end-to-end overview of the code development process, and reduces ambiguity for all parties involved.

Now that you have a better understanding of what tools are frequently used for task tracking in data teams, in the next section, we will have a look at **version control** as a way to help streamline the development process.

Managing versions with version control

In analytics engineering, we take best practices from software engineering. You might be familiar with version control already. You have probably heard of Git, GitHub, Bitbucket, and similar tools or have been using such tools for a while now. They are absolutely essential to developing code in a team, and we would also encourage version control in cases where you are the only person working on a code base.

There are several reasons why version control is important:

- Version control helps developers **keep track of changes** made to code over time, enabling them to revert to earlier versions if necessary

- It allows multiple developers to **work on the same code base simultaneously** without interfering with each other's work

- Collaboration and code review are easier; it is **easier to catch errors and improve code quality**

- By providing a history of changes, version control can **help with debugging and troubleshooting**

- It **aids in project management** by providing insights into who made what changes and when

Git is one the most popular version control systems out there. It is the most feature-rich and has strong, widespread adoption in the software engineering and data community; this is the reason we will cover it in this book. Other tools that you may have heard about include **Fossil** (https://www2.fossil-scm.org/home/doc/trunk/www/index.wiki), **Mercurial** (https://www.mercurial-scm.org/), and **Apache Subversion** (https://subversion.apache.org/).

Version control in Git is a broad topic that goes beyond the scope of this book. Therefore, we will give an introduction and an overview of certain best practices when working with Git, as well as provide branching strategies that are available to you when working within a team.

Working with Git

Git is a distributed version control system that helps track changes in your code over time. It allows multiple developers to collaborate on a project, making it easier to manage and merge changes seamlessly. "Distributed" means that the entire code base and its history are mirrored on each developer's machine. There are several copies of this code base, and they may exist on your local machine, on a colleague's machine, and on something called the **remote**, which is the central hub and serves as backups.

Whenever you are working on a local copy of the code, this is called a local repository, whereas the repository hosted on a Git server is called the **remote**. A **Git server** is a server that hosts and manages Git repositories. This can be an on-premise server or in exist the cloud.

A **Git repository** (**repo**) is a folder or directory that contains your project files, along with the version control information. Again, this is either a local repository or the remote repository, essentially being all copies of the same code base. A **Git repo** stores a complete history of changes, making it easy to track, collaborate, and revert back when needed. When you work on a project, it is most likely that the project folder is a Git repository, which means that this folder and its contents are checked in and tracked by Git. Any change made to any file within this repository is tracked.

A **Git commit** is a snapshot of your project at a specific point in time. It captures changes made to your files, and each **commit** has a unique identifier. A Git commit is an increment of work that you have contributed—a piece of code that you have added, edited, or deleted—and the process of **committing** is like adding this increment of work to the history or like your last saved version of a file. You can always revert to this commit when a mistake has been made, and you can continue developing from that point in time.

Commits help to understand a project's history and facilitate collaboration. Our general advice is to commit regularly, as this is beneficial for keeping a granular history of changes. It makes it easier to track when specific features were introduced and helps with debugging because you can more easily revert to a specific code modification. Regularly committing also reduces the likelihood of breaking code changes and makes it easier to collaborate.

Git branching

Branching in Git allows you to work on different versions of your project simultaneously. It is like creating a parallel universe for your code, where you can experiment without affecting the main project.

The **main branch** (formerly known as the **master**) is the default branch in Git. It represents the stable version of your project, or let's call it your **production** code. Developers often create feature branches to add new features or fix bugs (they are creating commits on this branch), and once tested, these changes are merged back into the main branch so that they become part of the production code or that the data become accessible to downstream applications. A feature branch is a separate branch created for developing a specific feature or fixing a particular issue. It allows developers to work on changes on an isolated copy of the main branch without affecting the main branch. Once the feature is complete, the branch can be merged back into the main branch. A **Git merge** is used to integrate changes from one branch into another. Essentially, it's a way to combine the history and work from different branches, reconciling divergent development paths.

The best practice for this when working in a team is through a **pull request** (**PR**). You might encounter the term **merge request** (**MR**) as well; these terms are used interchangeably.

In the next section, we will dive deeper into pull requests. For now, it is important to remember that branches may exist locally only if created by a developer. Once they are pushed to the remote or uploaded to the Git server, they become available to others as well, and, as such, they become available to be merged into the remote **main/master branch**.

Figure 10.1 illustrates how merging works in Git; a feature branch, iss53 (Issue 53), which has two commits is merged into the master branch, and the head of the master branch points to the latest commit (C6):

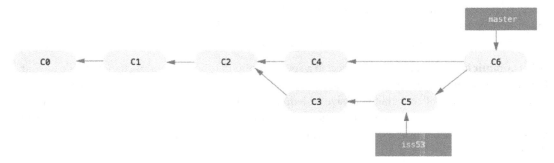

Figure 10.1 – An illustrated Git merge

An important feature Git provides is reverting to a previous commit. Git provides a timeline of changes known as the **commit history**. If something goes wrong, you can recover history by reverting to a specific commit or branch. This feature ensures that you can always return to a known, **stable state**.

This is the beauty of Git: being able to revert to a previous state so that whenever a bug has been introduced into the code, you can always go back to a previous version when the code was working fine and edit the code to remove the bug.

Now that you have a basic understanding of Git, let's look at a proposed development workflow for an analytics engineer.

Development workflow for analytics engineers

When collaborating on a project or Git repo, it is important that all colleagues follow the same approach to committing and pushing code. This facilitates collaboration and avoids confusion.

A typical workflow could include the following steps:

1. **Create a local branch**: Before making changes, create a new branch for your feature or fix.

2. **Commit changes**: Make changes to your files and commit them locally. Commits serve as checkpoints in your development.

3. **Push to remote**: Push your local branch to the remote repository on platforms such as GitHub, making your changes accessible to others.

4. **Open a PR**: If working in a team, create a PR to merge your feature branch into the main branch. This allows others to review your changes.

5. **Review and merge**: Collaborators review your code in the PR. Once approved, merge the feature branch into the main branch.

6. **Pull from main**: Regularly pull the latest changes from the main branch to keep your local environment up to date.

7. **Continuous integration/continuous deployment (CI/CD)**: CI/CD automates the testing and deployment processes. CI ensures that changes are tested automatically, whereas continuous deployment automates the deployment of code to production environments. This ensures a smoother and more reliable development pipeline.

This is a workflow that is best suited for our work as analytics engineers, as it allows us to effectively collaborate on a code base with other developers. There is a clear set of steps involved to make sure that the code pushed is transparent and reviewed properly before being integrated into production code, and this method reduces the probability of bugs being introduced.

We encourage you to read more about Git, as this is just a brief introduction to version control with Git. Have a look at some of the advanced and powerful features of Git such as cherry-picking changes, placing Git hooks in your scripts that execute after specific Git events, stashing changes without committing them, and rebasing commits. Here is the link to Git documentation: (`https://git-scm.com/doc`).

Best practices when using Git

Let us assume you get a task assigned to you as an analytics engineer and let us say this task is the implementation of a new dbt model. One of the best practices we can give you is to use feature branching.

Feature branching involves creating a new branch from the main branch specifically for a new feature, keeping your work isolated from the main branch so that you do not alter the production code. Therefore, this allows for independent development and easier code review.

Some general best practices when it comes to using Git in your development workflow are the following:

- Commit often and be descriptive in your commit messages; after all, this is not only about transparency to others, but it is also about making it easier for yourself and others to trace back any errors introduced in the code base.

- Regularly pulling changes from the main branch helps resolve conflicts promptly.

- When merging code to the main branch, use PRs.

We will provide a template PR that you can use for your projects in the *Reviewing Code* section of this chapter. We will see why PRs are such an essential part of DevOps and how to properly set up a pull request template for use with your projects.

Branching strategies when working with dbt

Luckily, dbt Labs, the company behind dbt, has provided us with another nice illustration of a useful Git workflow for data teams. Note that this is not exclusive to working with dbt; it is generalizable to working with other data transformation tools as well.

In the following image, you can see a suggestion for a basic Git workflow when working with dbt, which is based on the typical workflow introduced previously:

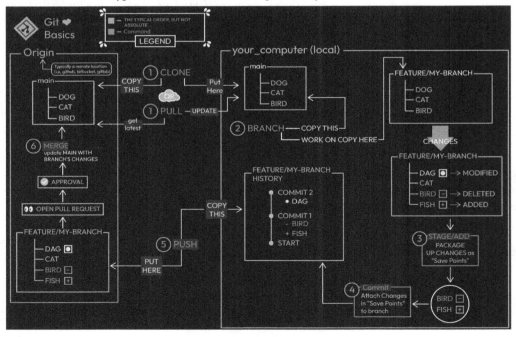

Figure 10.2 – A basic Git workflow for dbt (Source: https://www.getdbt.com/
analytics-engineering/transformation/git-workflow#:~:text=The%20basic%20
Git%20flow%20%23,another%20cloud%2Dbased%20Git%20provider.)

The workflow steps shown in *Figure 10.2* are as follows:

1. **Clone the codebase**: Begin your local development by cloning the repository you're working on. Use `git clone` to create a local copy, and `git pull` to update it periodically.

2. **Create a development branch**: Instead of modifying the main branch, establish a separate branch for your development work using a Git branch. This approach allows for experimentation without permanent consequences.

3. **Stage file updates**: After modifying files, stage them for a commit, which acts as a logical save point. This is done with the Git stage command (`git add .`).

4. **Commit staged changes locally**: Once satisfied with the staged changes, commit them to your branch using `git commit`. These changes are local until pushed to the remote repository.

5. **Push changes and open pull requests**: Share your work with your team by pushing commits with `git push`. To integrate your changes into production, open a pull request for code review. For collaboration without merging, push your branch and have colleagues pull it.

6. **Merge changes with master code base**: After approval, merge your branch into the main branch with `git merge`, signaling readiness for production. Remember, this action makes your local clone outdated.

7. **Update your local clone**: Finally, keep your local repository up to date with the main branch, especially after your or your colleagues' changes are merged, by using `git pull`.

We will now move our focus to applying coding standards.

Working with coding standards

Coding standards are a set of guidelines that help ensure that code is readable, maintainable, and consistent across a team or organization. By adhering to coding standards, analytics engineers can create more efficient, scalable, and reliable code, ultimately leading to a better understanding of the code and faster development times.

> **Note**
>
> This chapter features code snippets designed to showcase best practices. However, executing these snippets may need extra setup, not covered in this book. Readers should view these snippets as illustrative examples and adapt the underlying best practices to their unique scenarios.

Have a look at the following Python function definition:

```python
def add_numbers(a,b) :
c = a+b;return c
```

Here is the same code but in a different formatting:

```
def add_numbers(a, b):
    c = a + b
    return c
```

What do you notice about the format of the code and how it is written? You probably think that the latter is a nicer way of writing this code, right? Turns out that in the top code block, there are multiple issues:

- A lack of consistent indentation
- No spaces around the operators
- An unnecessary semi-colon at the end of the line
- No spaces after commas in the function parameters

When we write code, we want it to be consistent so that it is easier to interpret. The way code is written is called the **formatting** of the code or the **code format**. Developers may have their idiosyncrasies when it comes to writing code and employing different standards: you might have noticed that when looking at other people's code. Improper formatting generally makes it harder to debug code, understand the functionality and scope of the code, and build on top of it. It creates ambiguity and confusion when sifting through the code, especially when you are just getting onboarded on a new project and getting yourself acquainted with the code base.

Later on, we will see that there are certain standards within the Python and SQL community that we can adhere to to ensure consistency in formatting.

Let's look at writing SQL; sometimes, you will encounter one-lined SQL statements such as the following:

```
SELECT name,address FROM customers WHERE country='USA'AND age>25;
```

A more readable way of writing this code would be this:

```
SELECT name, address
FROM customers
WHERE country = 'USA' AND age > 25;
```

As you can see, nothing could be more frustrating than encountering code that is not properly formatted. Without clear guidelines, it can be challenging to ensure consistency and quality in analytics engineering. This is where coding standards come in.

Enforcing these standards can be done through code reviews and automated tools. Code reviews allow team members to check each other's code for adherence to the standards. Automated tools can also be used to check for adherence to the standards automatically.

Let us look at some industry standards: PEP8 and ANSI.

PEP8

PEP8 is a set of guidelines for writing Python code that is easy to read and understand. It covers topics such as code layout, naming conventions, and programming style. The goal of PEP8 is to make code more consistent and readable, which makes it easier for other developers to work with and maintain. By following PEP8, your code will be more organized, easier to understand, and more maintainable in the long run.

Some features of PEP8 are the following:

- **Indentation**: When you start a new line in your code, use four spaces to show where it belongs. Don't use tabs because they might not look the same on every computer.
- **Line length**: Try to keep each line of your code less than 79 characters long. For comments, aim for 72 characters. This helps people read your code without scrolling too much.
- **Imports order**: When you bring in pieces of code from other places, organize them in three groups: first, Python's own stuff; second, things made by others; and third, your own creations.
- **No extra spaces**: Avoid putting extra spaces where they're not needed. This keeps your code clean and tidy.
- **String quotes**: Be consistent with the type of quotation marks you use for strings. Whether it's single or double quotes, pick one style and stick with it.
- **Special names**: If you use special names that start and end with a double underscore (dunder names), put them in the right place in your code.
- **Naming things**: Give your variables names that make sense. Use lowercase with underscores between words (snake_case) for variables and start each word with a capital letter (CamelCase) for classes.
- **Comments**: Write comments that are clear, and do not write too many. Save longer explanations for the documentation inside your code (called docstrings).

These are just some examples of the substandards within PEP8, and we highly encourage you to have a look at the official documentation (`https://peps.python.org/pep-0008/`) on PEP8 to become better acquainted with proper Python formatting.

ANSI

By itself, **American National Standards Institute (ANSI)** is more of a framework for database implementation than a strict standard on how to write SQL code. Therefore, it is important to note that while ANSI offers guidelines, SQL does not have a specific guideline analogous to PEP8 for Python, making consistency across SQL dialects dependent on the database system and vendor practices.

ANSI, therefore, is a set of guidelines for how relational databases should be structured and queried, not necessarily how to format your SQL. It was developed by the ANSI in collaboration with the **International Organization for Standardization (ISO)**, and it defines a common syntax for accessing and manipulating data stored in a database.

The standard includes a wide range of features, such as data types, operators, functions, and commands, that make it possible to create complex queries and manage large amounts of data efficiently. By adhering to the ANSI SQL standard, developers and database administrators can ensure interoperability and portability across different database systems, which can save time and reduce costs in the long run.

Some ANSI features are the following:

- Standardized syntax for portability so that the SQL syntax is fairly standard across database vendors
- Basic querying (SELECT, FROM, WHERE)
- Joins for combining data
- Subqueries for complex operations
- Data manipulation (INSERT, UPDATE, DELETE)
- Data definition (CREATE, ALTER, DROP)
- Access control (GRANT, REVOKE)
- Transaction support (ACID properties)
- Indexes for performance enhancement
- Date, time, math, and string functions
- Aggregate functions for data summarization

You might already be acquainted with these features if you frequently use SQL statements such as SELECT, WHERE, GROUP BY, GRANT, and REVOKE. ANSI ensures that SQL is consistent and, thus, portable between database systems. Think of data migration use cases where data needs to be moved from one database to another; this is a use case you might encounter as an analytics engineer. ANSI provides a standard to which most SQL dialects across different database systems and vendors mostly adhere. This ensures that functions, data types, and data definition/manipulation languages are portable between database systems.

For us analytics engineers, it is not that important to understand the full scope of ANSI; rather, we should be aware of differences in SQL syntax between different database vendors and which syntax is portable and not portable (does not strictly adhere to ANSI) when migrating and refactoring code for portability. Think of quoted identifiers, data type assignment differences, date and time functions, string concatenation, and others. It is important to be aware of the extent to which your SQL code is cross-compatible with other database systems.

We encourage you to read about ANSI and get acquainted with some SQL standards (`https://blog.ansi.org/sql-standard-iso-iec-9075-2023-ansi-x3-135/`) so that you know when certain keywords in SQL are general or specific to a certain SQL implementation of a database vendor you are using.

Next, we will introduce linters, which help to keep your SQL code consistent and adhere to at least some pre-defined, bespoke standard.

Linters

Linters can help in writing robust and clean code that adheres to certain formatting requirements, as stipulated by coding standards, such as that of PEP8 for Python. Linters are programs written specifically to flag errors in code formatting and they can also fix them for you. They are installed as extensions to your text editor and will flag errors in your code as you write.

As analytics engineers, we will use Python to automate tasks, build CI/CD pipelines, and use Python in other data engineering tasks. It is of paramount importance that our code is readable by other colleagues, as this makes it easier to maintain and debug in the future. As such, since linters are so important for maintaining a **healthy** and **well-formatted** code base, it should be almost illegal not to use them, and we strongly encourage their usage.

Some examples of linters include **Pycodestyle**, **Flake8**, **Black**, **Autopep8**, and **yapf**. Flake8 (`https://flake8.pycqa.org/en/latest/`) and Black (`https://pypi.org/project/black/`) are quite popular. We would recommend tools such as Black, as they format and check your code automatically and comply with the PEP8 standard.

When it comes to doing formatting checks on SQL, **SQLfmt** and **SQL Fluff** are the most popular linters, especially when used with a tool such as dbt:

- **Sqlfmt**: This is a linter that comes pre-configured, meaning that you cannot specify specific formatting rules to apply; it will always format your code the same way. The tool automatically formats your SQL code based on a pre-defined set of formatting rules. Its main focus is on the presentation and layout of the code, ensuring consistent indentation, line breaks, and spacing. However, it does not analyze your code for errors or bugs, nor does it consider any coding issues beyond formatting. You can explore more on sqlfmt here: `https://sqlfmt.com/`.

- **SQLFluff**: SQLFluff is a linter and code formatter; it is a tool used to analyze your code to identify potential issues and bugs and follow coding standards. It formats your code according to a customizable set of rules, ensuring consistent coding practices. SQLFluff also helps keep your SQL code well formatted and aligned with styling best practices. SQLFluff documentation can be found here: `https://sqlfluff.com/`.

You can use either sqlfmt or SQLFluff to format your code as long as you are consistent. When choosing one of them, keep in mind the following:

- SQLFluff is a tool that analyzes and formats SQL code and checks your code for errors/bugs, allowing for customizable rules. This is a helpful feature if you do have clearly defined formatting rules within your setting that you want the code to adhere to.

- Use sqlfmt to only have your code well formatted without analyzing it for errors and bugs. Sqlfmt is a straightforward tool that does not require you to define the rules you want and makes sure that your SQL is always formatted in a consistent manner throughout your code base.

Remember that consistency in formatting is important, so choose one and stick with the linter of your choice. Make sure that other developers contributing to the code base also make use of this linter with the same configuration. This can be configured in pre-commit hooks.

Pre-commit hooks

Git commits are small increments of code modifications that you have saved to your branch, as you have read before. **Pre-commit hooks** are commands that are written in a pre-commit script (essentially, a YAML file) and are executed before a commit is made.

Pre-commit hooks are configured as follows:

1. **Install** `pre-commit`: This Python package manages all your hooks. Install it globally or within your project's virtual environment.

2. **Configure hooks**: Create a `.pre-commit-config.yaml` file in your project's root directory. Here, you'll define the hooks you want to use, their versions, and any specific configurations.

3. **Integrate with an existing workflow**: Ensure your team understands and integrates these hooks into their daily development workflow for maximum effectiveness.

In general, they allow developers to enforce certain checks or tasks to ensure that the committed code meets specific standards or criteria. In the context of linting your code, pre-commit hooks are often used to enforce code formatting standards by using tools such as Black (for Python) and an SQL formatter, such as sqlfmt. This is their most common use, as you can see in the following code snippets:

```
repos:
-   repo: https://github.com/psf/black
    rev: stable
    hooks:
    - id: black
      language_version: python3.6
```

The preceding example shows a pre-commit command for linting with Black, which does formatting checks on your Python code before you commit:

```
repos:
- repo: https://github.com/offbi/pre-commit-dbt
  rev: v1.0.0
  hooks:
  - id: dbt-docs-generate
  - id: check-model-has-properties-file
    name: Check that all models are listed in a YAML file
    files: ^models/
  - id: check-model-has-tests
    name: Check that all models have tests
    files: ^models/
```

The second example shows a pre-commit hook from the `pre-commit-dbt` package that allows you to do some checks on the integrity of your dbt project, such as checking for the proper naming conventions of models, checking if tests are included, and seeing if there is a corresponding property file.

Although including pre-commit checks in the development workflow is optional, we would highly encourage you to use pre-commit hooks to test your code before committing; although, keep in mind that these checks might increase development times and, as such, they can be frustrating for developers. In our experience, it is better not to overdo it

Pre-commit hooks are a handy feature in the context of code review, which we will introduce next.

Reviewing code

Code reviews provide a critical safeguard to ensure code quality. They are essential for data teams to collaborate effectively and ensure high-quality coding practices. They provide a framework for team members to evaluate code together, identify potential issues, and share knowledge.

By fostering a culture of learning, code reviews enable individuals to learn from one another, ultimately improving the collective expertise of the team. Additionally, they reinforce accountability by ensuring compliance with coding standards, data privacy protocols, and best practices. Overall, code reviews are crucial for creating robust, reliable, and high-performing data solutions.

Pull requests – The four eyes principle

A **pull request** (**PR**) or **merge request** is a feature in Git that facilitates collaborative development and code review. The purpose of a PR is to propose changes made in one branch (typically, a feature branch) to be merged into another branch (often, the main or master branch).

PRs are an example of a method that helps with reviewing code before it is merged to the main branch of your repository. The **four eyes principle** in code review is a fundamental practice that emphasizes the importance of having multiple sets of eyes scrutinize code changes before they are integrated into a code base.

This principle asserts that no single developer should have the sole responsibility of reviewing and approving their code. Instead, a second person, or a pair of eyes, should independently scan the code. A proper PR template ensures all developers go through the same checklist before merging into the main branch.

How to open a PR

PRs are commonly opened and managed through Git hosting platforms such as GitHub, GitLab, Bitbucket, Jira, and Azure DevOps. You have seen before that some of these tools are used for task tracking and project management, but some of them are also used for hosting Git repositories. We have mentioned before that tasks and work items can be linked to Git branches and commits, which is a powerful feature of these platforms.

The specifics of opening a PR may vary slightly between platforms, but the general process involves creating a branch, making changes, tagging colleagues, and initiating a review for code inclusion.

A starter PR template

At a minimum, a PR should require a review by a colleague who preferably works on the same code base. Some features of a good PR include the following:

- **Title and description**: Clearly states the purpose and changes.
- **Related issues or User Stories**: References relevant tasks/work items. This can be easily done in tools such as Jira and Azure DevOps.
- **Code changes**: Specify the added, modified, or deleted code.
- **Review checklist**: Includes code quality and functionality.
- **Deployment considerations**: Notes special deployment steps.
- **Performance and security**: Highlights relevant considerations.
- **Backward compatibility**: Addresses compatibility concerns (if any).
- **Documentation updates**: Specifies if the documentation was changed.
- **Dependencies**: Lists any affected external dependencies.
- **Reviewer requests**: Mentions specific reviewers (if any).

Take a look at the default PR template at `https://learn.microsoft.com/en-us/azure/devops/repos/git/pull-request-templates?view=azure-devops#default-pull-request-templates`. This template illustrates a PR template in Azure DevOps, where the submitter is presented with a review checklist and can check off requirements before submitting a PR.

You can see that the template warns developers to check whether the code builds without any errors (this can be automatically checked using a pipeline, which is a topic for the next chapter) and whether unit tests have been added to test the functionality of the code. Having a PR template with a checklist is an ideal way to alert developers about their responsibility to double-check their commits before they are merged to a branch. The preceding example highlights a best practice in doing so, where pre-requisites can be ticked off as you prepare your merge. This neatly ties in with our earlier discussion of the four eyes principle: the importance of having another reviewer scrutinize code changes before they are integrated into a code base.

A PR checklist only goes as far as alerting the developer to certain preconditions before merging, but it does not prevent a developer from sidelining this and merging anyway.

We still need an automated way of catching bugs, testing the functionality of our code, and deploying it to production, regardless of a human review, and this is exactly where CI/CD come into play.

Continuous integration/continuous deployment

Perhaps you have come across this term before. **Continuous integration** and **continuous deployment**, also known as **CI/CD**, is a practice used in software development to enhance the speed and quality of the software delivery process. It is an automated approach that involves the CI of code changes and testing to ensure the early detection of issues and faster delivery of software updates.

The benefits of CI/CD are multifold. It helps to reduce the likelihood of introducing new bugs into the code base, as well as ensuring that the code changes are always in a releasable state. This means that code updates can be deployed more frequently, which, in turn, leads to faster feedback loops, and ultimately, better customer satisfaction.

From an analytics engineering perspective, an example of CI/CD in action is the development of models in dbt. In this scenario, as soon as a developer pushes a code change to a shared repository, a series of automated tests are triggered to ensure that the code compiles and runs properly, meaning that the dbt model that you developed can actually materialize and that the code is properly formatted. If any issues arise, the developer is alerted immediately, allowing them to fix the issue before it progresses further down the pipeline.

Developers can use pull requests as a way to collaborate and review each other's code changes before they are merged into the main branch or production version of your code base, as we have seen before. This helps to ensure that all changes are properly reviewed and tested before they are integrated into the code base to prevent bugs from appearing in production.

Now, a pull request is definitely useful to prevent buggy code from being deployed into production and messing things up. However, you can imagine that when reviewing code from a colleague, you might not always be able to review everything; you might overlook some bugs or idiosyncrasies in the code, even more so if you are not entirely familiar with the particular feature being worked on by your colleague.

This is where CI/CD comes into place, whereby we automate some of the code integration, testing, and deployment as an extension to reviewing code in a PR. With CI/CD, we can be sure that code follows our coding standards and actually executes without errors. These are things that we cannot really test for by solely reviewing a PR.

You can see the benefit of CI/CD. In the next chapter, *Continuous Integration and Deployment*, we will have a more in-depth look at CI/CD and how to implement it in the realm of analytics engineering. Since this is a complex topic, we believe it deserves a chapter on its own.

Now, let's look at writing documentation for your project.

Documenting code

Documentation is the holy grail when maintaining a code base. This should sound familiar; how often have you found yourself reviewing or having to work with a new code base, and there is little to no documentation on how things work? It is every engineer's nightmare in this field of work. When we talk about documentation, we not only talk about code comments or technical documentation but also conceptual documentation that describes what certain code does on a higher level.

In fact, as mentioned in the book *Docs for Developers: An Engineer's Field Guide to Technical Writing* (`https://docsfordevelopers.com/`), we can distinguish between several types of documentation:

- Code comments
- READMEs
- Getting started
- Conceptual documentation

Let's talk about each of them in detail.

Documenting code in dbt

As an analytics engineer, we recommend several handy tools for documenting your code. Tools such as dbt allow you to place documentation alongside your code, such as in the following cases:

- Documenting model metadata such as column names, key columns, column tests, column values, descriptions, and column relationships
- Documenting Jinja and SQL logic inside of your dbt models

This is a handy feature from dbt. One of the core principles of dbt is, in fact, that documentation should be part of your code. dbt can also generate documentation for us that is based on the metadata we have added to our models in dbt. Please refer to the official documentation of dbt (`https://docs.getdbt.com/docs/collaborate/documentation`) for more detail.

The following screen capture illustrates documenting your dbt models in a resource property file, which allows you to add metadata to any resource (model or source; snapshot or seed files), and you can describe these resources and their columns. You can define datatests alongside your descriptions. You can also use these resource properties for documenting downstream uses of your data models; these are known as **dbt exposures**:

```
1    version: 2
2
3    models:
4      - name: customers
5        description: This table has basic information about a customer, as well as some derived facts based on a customer's orders
6
7        columns:
8          - name: customer_id
9            description: This is a unique identifier for a customer
10           tests:
11             - unique
12             - not_null
13
14         - name: first_name
15           description: Customer's first name. PII.
16
17         - name: last_name
18           description: Customer's last name. PII.
19
20         - name: first_order
21           description: Date (UTC) of a customer's first order
22
23         - name: most_recent_order
24           description: Date (UTC) of a customer's most recent order
25
26         - name: number_of_orders
27           description: Count of the number of orders a customer has placed
28
29         - name: total_order_amount
30           description: Total value (AUD) of a customer's orders
```

Figure 10.3 – In a schema.yml file in dbt you can add a model description, column tests, and descriptions

These `schema.yml` or `properties.yml` files (you can name them whatever you want) are files that you put in the same directory (they can be nested in subfolders) as the resource you are referring to.

Take a look at *Figure 10.4* and *Figure 10.5*, which show a markdown file that can help in documenting your code:

```
1    {% docs orders_status %}
2
3    Orders can be one of the following statuses:
4
5    | status         | description
6    |----------------|----------------
7    | placed         | The order has been placed but has not yet left the warehouse
8    | shipped        | The order has ben shipped to the customer and is currently in transit
9    | completed      | The order has been received by the customer
10   | return_pending | The customer has indicated that they would like to return the order, but it has not yet been received at the warehouse
11   | returned       | The order has been returned by the customer and received at the warehouse
12
13
14   {% enddocs %}
```

Figure 10.4 – A markdown file that can help with documenting your code

Markdown is a lightweight markup language for creating formatted text using a plain-text editor, which means it can be edited with any text editor, requires no special software, and is inherently portable and easy to manage. The beauty of markdown is that it aligns with the needs of both a technical and non-technical audience; it strikes a balance between simplicity and functionality, making it accessible for non-technical users while providing enough power for technical documentation.

Its plain text nature ensures longevity and portability, and its wide support across platforms and tools makes it an efficient choice for a range of documentation needs. The combination of these factors contributes to markdown's popularity and its reputation as an easy-to-use format for documentation.

{% docs orders_status %}

Orders can be one of the following statuses:

status	description
placed	The order has been placed but has not yet left the warehouse
shipped	The order has ben shipped to the customer and is currently in transit
completed	The order has been received by the customer
return_pending	The customer has indicated that they would like to return the order, but it has not yet been received at the warehouse
returned	The order has been returned by the customer and received at the warehouse

{% enddocs %}

Figure 10.5 – A markdown-rendered table to explain order status

Tags and meta properties are also useful when documenting your dbt resources. Tags allow you to identify models and define groupings of models, which you can run together as part of your resource selection syntax. For example, you can have resources that are tagged **hourly** or **daily**, which determine when these models should run. You can also place tags to indicate if a resource belongs to a certain group of resources, such as in the following example, where the seed file utm_mappings belongs to marketing:

```
seeds:
  jaffle_shop:
    utm_mappings:
      +tags:
        - marketing
        - hourly


# Run all models tagged "daily"
$ dbt run --select tag:daily


# Run all models tagged "daily", except those that are tagged hourly
$ dbt run --select tag:daily --exclude tag:hourly
```

Meta configs allow you to set metadata for your resources. This metadata will be compiled into the manifest.json file, which is used by dbt to generate documentation about your project. You can define it as a dictionary. You can define a model owner, document if a model contains **personally identifiable information** (**PII**) data, or the maturity of a model, just to name a few examples:

```
version: 2

models:
  - name: users
    meta:
      owner: "@alice"
      model_maturity: in dev
```

Resources descriptions, column descriptions, tests, metadata, and tags are compiled into the manifest.json file, which is used to generate a documentation page. This documentation page, which is shown at https://docs.getdbt.com/docs/collaborate/documentation, shows detailed information on our resources, the columns, tests, and descriptions that we defined, as well as a DAG lineage graph that we can use to navigate and check the lineage of our resources.

Finding the right table and columns for analytical purposes is very useful to a developer or a data analyst. Not only that, your business stakeholders will also appreciate the observability and transparency it provides (as we discussed in *swswswswswsw, Data Quality and Observability*), as they can now have a comprehensive overview of the data lineage.

As you can see, dbt has a strong documentation feature already, and the nice thing is that it is part of the code, thus it is automatically generated whenever you run the command. In the dbt Cloud, you can configure your jobs to generate documentation after each successful run.

Apart from dbt, tools such as **Confluence pages** (which integrates nicely with Jira) and **GitHub Pages** are also great, versatile tools to help you document your code in a professional manner, and we strongly suggest using these tools if you have them at your disposal. These tools are more useful for the documentation of the project itself on a higher level instead of at the code level itself, and they are useful for documentation such as getting started guides or conceptual documentation, as we will explain shortly.

Code comments

Code comments play a crucial role in software development and analytics engineering, too. They are meant to make the code more understandable to other developers and to oneself in the future. However, commenting on every single line of code can lead to over-documentation, making the code harder to read and understand. Striking a balance between writing proper inline comments and not overdoing it is key.

Properly written comments can help other developers understand the code more easily, which, in turn, leads to faster code review and bug fixing. **Inline comments** represent documentation that is part of the code. Inline comments should explain the purpose of the code block or line of code, its input and output, and any assumptions made.

For instance, if there is a conditional block that relies on a certain variable, it's important to explain what that variable represents and how it affects the code.

Code comments should be relevant, used liberally but not excessively, and brief. They reduce ambiguity about what the code does, and it provides useful context that does not exist in the code itself. Poorly written comments can lead to confusion and even introduce bugs in the code. It is important to avoid comments that simply restate what the code does, as they can become outdated and inaccurate over time.

Have a look at the following code snippet which shows a Jinja macro that supposedly calculates the lifetime value of a customer and basically sums up the order amount for a total revenue calculation per customer:

```
{% macro calculate_lifetime_value(user_id_field, order_value_field) %}
    SUM({{ order_value_field }}) OVER (PARTITION BY {{ user_id_field
}}) AS lifetime_value
{% endmacro %}

SELECT
    user_id,
    {{ calculate_lifetime_value('user_id', 'order_amount') }},
    COUNT(order_id) as total_orders
```

```
FROM orders
GROUP BY user_id
```

However, this is not immediately apparent from the following snippet; you can see there's no comment explaining the macro's purpose, parameters, or expected output. Without documentation, it's unclear without reading the macro's code directly what it does, how it should be used, or what kind of arguments it expects.

Such lack of documentation can lead to the misuse of the macro, difficulty with debugging, or challenges in extending or maintaining the code.

Take a look at *Figure 10.6*:

```
 1    with source as (
 2
 3        {#-
 4        Normally we would select from the table here, but we are using seeds to load
 5        our data in this project
 6        #}
 7        select * from {{ ref('raw_payments') }}
 8
 9    ),
10
11    renamed as (
12
13        select
14            id as payment_id,
15            order_id,
16            payment_method,
17
18            -- `amount` is currently stored in cents, so we convert it to dollars
19            amount / 100 as amount
20
21        from source
22
23    )
```

Figure 10.6 – Inline comments help you to better understand the functionality of your code

You can see that the first comment explains that a seed is used instead of referring to a dbt model for our source. The second comment explains the reasoning behind dividing the amount column by 100; it is because the amount is stored in cents and, thus, we convert it into dollars.

Code comments such as the preceding ones—even though they are simple line comments—go a long way to help developers understand the inputs and outputs of functions and the reasoning behind certain decisions, such as the division in the preceding example. Let's now have a look at **README**, the most common and most crucial form of documentation for your project.

READMEs

Code comments are not enough to document your code and the entire context with which to establish an understanding of the purpose of the code and how it works. Inline comments are helpful for documenting code in a file, but README files add another layer of documentation to a repository or project.

A README is typically a markdown-formatted text file that provides an overview of a code collection and is usually located at the top level of a code repository. It is also possible to create READMEs for significant subfolders that need further clarification or summary.

The README should include important details, such as the following:

- The code's primary functionality
- Instructions for installation
- Troubleshooting steps
- The code's maintainer
- Licensing information
- A changelog
- Basic examples
- Links to more comprehensive documentation and resources

These are the basic elements that your README should consist of. There are websites available that help you build a README file, such as `https://www.makeareadme.com/`. In any case, if you try to stick with the preceding outline as much as possible, you can be sure to capture the most essential elements of a good README file.

Documentation on getting started

To easily onboard new users, it is essential that you write clear guidelines on how to get started. It is a refreshing feeling when you can quickly set up your development environment and start working, as this reduces friction. This documentation could be part of your README, but if you want to separate code and the documentation, then writing a separate Wiki page is an option, especially if you are onboarding nontechnical users for the first time.

At the very least, the "Getting started" documentation should cover the following:

- What is the purpose of this code? How does it help solve certain problems?
- How to get started
- Some examples

Again, this could be part of your README file and, thus, be located close to your code, but writing a separate Wiki page on this topic can prove valuable when writing a more holistic document that can be generally considered to be more beginner-friendly.

Conceptual documentation

To help users comprehend the principles and notions of your project, **conceptual documentation** is essential. It explains the functionality of your project on a high-level. Although conceptual content can be subjective, it should avoid technical details that are better suited for a README file or procedural content, which we'll discuss later in this chapter.

For the conceptual content in your project, sources such as meeting notes, design documents, whiteboard diagrams, and internal documentation are highly beneficial. Ensure that when incorporating this conceptual information to a frame a procedure or tutorial, the documentation remains concise and focused.

With this type of documentation, it is important to keep the end-user in mind; this documentation is high-level and should therefore not contain too many technical details.

When designing conceptual documentation, it is important to strike a balance between simplicity and detail. By keeping the language clear and concise, beginners will find it easier to understand and navigate, which will help them feel more comfortable learning about your project. At the same time, advanced users will appreciate the inclusion of certain technical details and specific examples that demonstrate the efficiency and power of your project but do not make it too technical. By providing both simplicity and detail in your conceptual documentation, your project will be more accessible and useful to a wider range of users.

Useful tools for writing such documentation are **Confluence**, **GitHub Pages** and **Azure DevOps**, just to name a few. These tools allow you to capture crucial business documentation on a single Wiki page and allow you to add diagrams and technical details as well. They are meant for a wider audience than other forms of documentation we have seen earlier, so keep that in mind.

We will now discuss containers, which are useful to ensure that code can be run by all developers and that coding standards are respected.

Working with containers

In the rapidly evolving field of analytics engineering, the ability to maintain consistency, efficiency, and collaboration across development teams is very important. A key technology enabling this is **containerization**, exemplified by tools such as **Docker** and the use of development containers or **devcontainers** in **Visual Studio Code (VS Code)**. **Containers** are lightweight, standalone packages that contain everything needed to run a piece of software, including the code, runtime, system tools, libraries, and settings. Docker, a popular containerization platform, allows developers to package applications into containers, ensuring consistency across environments.

We will not explain Docker in detail here; instead, we will explain (on a higher level) how this technology allows us to have the same development environment for each developer. Docker uses a **Dockerfile** that contains the instructions to build images, which are used to execute code in a Docker container. We strongly encourage you to check out Docker (`https://www.docker.com/`).

Advantages of using containers

One of the significant advantages of using containers in analytics engineering is the guarantee that any developer will be able to run the project's code on any machine, without the "works on my machine" syndrome. This is crucial in a field that often deals with complex data processing tasks requiring specific versions of libraries and tools.

The introduction of devcontainers for VS Code further enhances the collaborative experience among analytics engineering teams. A devcontainer allows a developer to package a development environment into a container, which can then be shared and reused by others. This approach ensures that all team members adhere to the same coding standards and best practices defined within the team, as the container includes not just the application and its dependencies but also the specific tools and extensions needed for the project. Devcontainers can be pre-configured to include the right dependencies, linters, pre-commit hooks, and even VS Code extensions.

Using Docker and devcontainer

The following is an excerpt from the official Dockerfile that dbt provides as a starter, which you can modify to your use case. Notice how the base image includes all of the dbt adapters for specific databases:

```
##
# Generic dockerfile for dbt image building.
# See README for operational details
##


# Top level build args
ARG build_for=linux/amd64


##
# base image (abstract)
```

```
##
# Please do not upgrade beyond python3.10.7 currently as dbt-spark
does not support
# 3.11py and images do not get made properly
FROM --platform=$build_for python:3.10.7-slim-bullseye as base

# N.B. The refs updated automagically every release via bumpversion
ARG dbt_core_ref=dbt-core@v1.8.0a1
ARG dbt_postgres_ref=dbt-postgres@v1.8.0a1
ARG dbt_redshift_ref=dbt-redshift@v1.8.0a1
ARG dbt_bigquery_ref=dbt-bigquery@v1.8.0a1
ARG dbt_snowflake_ref=dbt-snowflake@v1.8.0a1
ARG dbt_spark_ref=dbt-spark@v1.8.0a1
```

The following line specifically instructs the installation of dbt-snowflake, which is the dbt adapter required for working with Snowflake:

```
FROM base as dbt-snowflake
RUN python -m pip install --no-cache-dir "git+https://github.com/dbt-
labs/${dbt_snowflake_ref}#egg=dbt-snowflake"
```

This code block from a Dockerfile installs some of the tools that you have become familiar with already, sqlfluff and pre-commit:

```
# Install sqlfluff
RUN python -m pip install sqlfluff

# Install pre-commit
RUN python -m pip install pre-commit

#Install dbt sqlfluff templater
RUN python -m pip install sqlfluff-templater-dbt
```

To configure a devcontainer in VS Code, you need a minimum of two files:

- A Dockerfile, which will build the underlying container
- A devcontainer.json file, which has the configuration for VS Code, including extensions, settings, or formatting, and any additional information should be passed over to the container during the build, for example, SSH keys forwarding for authentication with a Git provider

Devcontainers, thus, rely on Docker, with the added benefit of creating the exact same environment for all developers using that code editor, which ensures consistency.

The following excerpt from a `devcontainer.json` file in VS Code shows the reference to a Dockerfile that is used to build the container. You can see that arguments are passed to install `dbt-snowflake` and `dbt-core` at runtime. It includes an extra Docker run command that will set the environment variables defined in an `.env` file. It also includes arguments that configure the SSH agent forwarding into the container. It mounts the SSH authentication socket from the host machine into the container and sets an environment variable to use it. This allows operations within the container that require SSH authentication, such as Git operations or SSH to remote servers, to work seamlessly using the host's SSH keys:

```
{
    "name": "Existing Dockerfile",
    "build": {
        // Sets the run context to one level up instead of the
.devcontainer folder.
        "context": "..",
        "dockerfile": "../Dockerfile",
        "args": {
            "dbt-snowflake": "v1.7.1",
            "dbt-core": "v1.7.1"
        },
        "runArgs": ["--env-file","../.env",
        "-v", "${localEnv:HOME}/.ssh/ssh_auth_sock:/run/host-services/
ssh-auth.sock",
        "-e", "SSH_AUTH_SOCK=/run/host-services/ssh-auth.sock"
        ]
    },
    "forwardSSH": true,
}
```

The following snippet shows how VS Code extensions are installed in the environment; notice how the useful extension `innoverio.vscode-dbt-power-user` is installed, which is really helpful when working with dbt in VS Code, as it can auto-complete dbt code (auto-fill model names, macros, sources, and docs), preview query results (which is a really powerful feature), generate dbt models and documentation and allow you to see the lineage graph, amongst others. It also installs Black for linting Python, and it installs sqlfluff for linting SQL:

```
"customizations": {
        "vscode": {
            "extensions": [
                "ms-python.python",
                "ms-python.black-formatter",
                "mhutchie.git-graph",
                "esbenp.prettier-vscode",
                "mechatroner.rainbow-csv",
```

```
                    "snowflake.snowflake-vsc",
                    "samuelcolvin.jinjahtml",
                    "dorzey.vscode-sqlfluff",
                    "innoverio.vscode-dbt-power-user"


        ]
    },
```

Figure 10.7 shows the configuration of SQLFluff; putting these settings in the devcontainer configuration ensures these linting rules are set by default when starting the container:

```
"sqlfluff.experimental.format.executeInTerminal": true,
"editor.formatOnSave": false,

"sqlfluff.config": "${workspaceFolder}/.sqlfluff",
"sqlfluff.dialect": "snowflake",
"sqlfluff.env.environmentVariables": [
  {
    "key": "example_key",
    "value": "example_value"
  }
],
"sqlfluff.env.customDotEnvFiles": [
  "${workspaceFolder}/example.env"
],
"sqlfluff.env.useDotEnvFile": true,
"sqlfluff.excludeRules": ["L009"],
"sqlfluff.executablePath": "/usr/local/bin/sqlfluff",
"sqlfluff.ignoreLocalConfig": false,
"sqlfluff.ignoreParsing": false,
"sqlfluff.rules": [],
"sqlfluff.suppressNotifications": false,
"sqlfluff.workingDirectory": "",
/* Linter */
"sqlfluff.linter.arguments": [],
"sqlfluff.linter.run": "onType",
"sqlfluff.linter.diagnosticSeverity": "error",
"sqlfluff.linter.diagnosticSeverityByRule": [
  {
    "rule": "L010",
    "severity": "warning"
  }
],
```

Figure 10.7 – Sqlfluff configuration in devcontainer.json

Devcontainers are powerful tools to ensure consistency in the development workflow within the team, which combines all the useful best practices we introduced earlier, such as linting, unit testing, and pre-commit hooks, to ensure consistency and efficiency in your code base.

Limitations of containers

Docker ensures consistency across different environments. But, as you have seen, topics such as SSH key forwarding and generally forwarding credentials from the host to a virtual environment might be tricky sometimes.

Deploying and managing a large-scale analytics environment with Docker can be complex. Orchestrating multiple containers, managing dependencies, ensuring high availability, and scaling resources efficiently require additional tools (e.g., Kubernetes) and expertise.

Therefore, even though Docker or devcontainers in Visual Studio Code solve the problem of consistency in a development workflow, you might introduce more unnecessary technical complexity for your project.

We know this is a lot of information to digest, but we're almost there!

In the final section, let us have a look at the burden of rewriting code when these standards are not adhered to.

Refactoring and technical debt

Refactoring means rewriting code to adhere to certain best practices or pre-defined standards without changing the behavior of the code. As analytics engineers, we will more often than not be confronted with legacy code that might not always be easily maintainable due to complexity; it might not have been tested properly, resulting in indeterministic outputs, or it might not be very performant or is even costly to run.

This burden of rewriting code ties in with what is called **technical debt**. Technical debt refers to the implied cost of additional rework caused by choosing an easy (or quick) solution now instead of using a better approach that would take longer. This debt will oftentimes result in slower development times and increased bugs down the road.

In the context of analytics engineering, technical debt accumulates when data models, ETL jobs, or analytics code bases are built with shortcuts or are not adequately updated to reflect new understandings of the data or business requirements. This debt can lead to slower development times, increased bugs, or difficulties in adapting to new data sources or analytical needs.

Here are some examples of technical debt:

- **Hard-coded values**: Hard-coded dates or business logic in data transformation scripts can create technical debt by requiring manual updates whenever these values change rather than designing the system to dynamically adapt to such changes.

- **Ignoring data quality**: Skipping the implementation of data quality checks or not addressing known data inconsistencies can accumulate technical debt, as future analytics might be based on faulty assumptions or incorrect data.

- **Lack of documentation**: Failing to document the data pipeline, data models, or the rationale behind specific transformations can create technical debt. New or existing team members may struggle to understand or modify the pipeline, leading to errors or inefficiencies.

You can imagine a scenario where you inherit a code base that has stored procedures, and the goal is to migrate towards using dbt as your data modeling and transformation tool. The functionality of the code remains the same, except, now, you have to switch from SQL-stored procedures to the modeling paradigm of dbt. Moreover, it could be the case that this 'old' code is not that performant, and you need to make it more efficient by optimizing the SQL.

What often helps is having legacy code and dbt code side by side in your code editor, and, with the advent of the use of Github Copilot and other LLM's that help with programming, it is easier to turn long, badly formatted SQL into clean and performant code.

This is how dbt approaches refactoring:

1. Migrate your legacy SQL code (unchanged); make sure it runs and produces an identical output.
2. Implement dbt sources (as opposed to raw references).
3. Choose a refactoring strategy.
4. Implement clean CTEs
5. Separate transformation logic into standardized data model layers.
6. Audit the output (often using the `audit_helper` dbt package).

What probably will take the longest is Step 5, and this is the most crucial step to get right. Step 6 proposes the use of the `audit_helper` package, which is handy when it comes to checking the output of both your old and new models to check if the tables match in terms fo the number of columns, records, and uniqueness. These results are materialized as tables in your data warehouse; it is a transparent way to track progress of refactoring.

dbt also has a helpful guide and separate course on how to refactor legacy SQL to dbt, which is worth checking out (`https://docs.getdbt.com/guides/refactoring-legacy-sql?step=5`).

Technical debt can be mitigated by adhering to regular code reviews, including automated checks such as unit tests and code formatting and review processes, such as opening PRs, as we saw earlier. Regularly checking back on your code and reviewing it also helps to prevent the accumulation of technical debt.

Summary

Working on code together in a team can be challenging; you have seen the complexity of topics such as project organization, task tracking, version control, code formatting, and review and documentation. Your code base is like a living organism, and therefore, maintaining the health of your code base to ensure continuity and consistency in quality can be challenging.

In this chapter, we discussed team member responsibilities, issue and task tracking tools, version control, coding standards, code review, and documentation. You now have a better understanding of the importance of these concepts to ensure proper code quality and make collaborating with team members a lot easier and more error-prone. You also got to know certain tools that can help us to better manage team resources, time, code quality, and the easy onboarding of new users.

In the next chapter, we will have a more detailed look into continuous integration/continuous deployment and delivery, which helps to automate the review process of code.

11
Automating Workflows

In the previous chapter, you got acquainted with challenges surrounding ownership and accountability in a development team, ensuring coding standards are adhered to and task tracking. We had a look at how to do a code review and got to know some best practices around writing documentation for easily onboarding new colleagues. We briefly mentioned **Continuous Integration/Continuous Deployment** or **CI/CD** as a way to do functionality tests and formatting checks on your code and deploy changes into production in an automated fashion. In this chapter, you will learn about data orchestration and automating workflows, and we will give you all the details you need to know to successfully build a CI/CD pipeline as an analytics engineer.

By the end of this chapter, you will have gained a comprehensive understanding of several key concepts and practices. Firstly, you will understand the critical role of CI/CD within the realm of DataOps. Additionally, you will have a clear grasp of the various components that make up CI, as well as those that constitute CD. Furthermore, you will be able to distinguish between continuous deployment and continuous delivery. Lastly, you will acquire the skills necessary to effectively implement CI/CD in the dbt Cloud environment.

In this chapter, we are going to cover the following main topics:

- Introducing DataOps
- Orchestrating data pipelines
- Continuous integration
- Continuous deployment
- Continuous delivery
- Implementing CI/CD

Introducing DataOps

DataOps is a relatively new term and is derived from the more prominent term **DevOps**, which has been around for quite some time now. This term hails from software engineering and refers to the practices that aim to automate and streamline the software delivery process, making it faster, more reliable, and more efficient.

DevOps and DataOps are related. DevOps is a set of practices that emphasizes collaboration and communication between development and operations teams. The goal of DevOps is to streamline the software development and deployment process, enabling teams to release software faster and more reliably.

The key elements of DevOps include **continuous integration (CI)**, **continuous delivery**, and **continuous deployment (CD)**. CI involves regularly merging code changes into a central repository and testing this code, while CD involves automating the deployment of code changes.

With the increasing importance of data in today's world, a new term has emerged – DataOps – which is derived from the principles of DevOps. DataOps is a methodology that applies the same principles of collaboration, automation, and monitoring to the management of data, enabling organizations to quickly and efficiently derive insights from their data.

Therefore, DataOps is a set of practices that focuses specifically on data-related activities, such as analytics engineering. The goal of DataOps is to streamline the data pipeline from source to consumption, enabling teams to make data-driven decisions faster and more reliably.

The key elements of DataOps include **data integration**, **data quality**, and **data governance**. Data integration involves bringing together data from various sources, while data quality involves ensuring that the data is accurate and consistent. Data governance involves establishing policies and procedures for managing and using data.

Another important element is the automation of development and deployment. This refers to automating CI/CD pipelines, in the next few sections, we will specifically focus on and discuss what the **CI** and **CD** stand for, and why **CI/CD** is so important to ensuring code quality.

First, let's have a look at automating the process of running dbt code and some considerations around the choice of tools, regardless of code testing and deployment.

Orchestrating data pipelines

Data orchestration refers to the automated and coordinated management of data workflows across various stages of the analytics life cycle. This process involves integrating, cleansing, transforming, and moving data from diverse sources to a data warehouse, where it can be readily accessed and analyzed for insights.

We have already covered how dbt empowers data engineers and data analysts to move away from repetitive stored procedures and employ version control and testing found in traditional software engineering to help run data workflows. dbt is largely used for the transformation part of the analytics workflow.

On the other hand, the goal of data orchestration in analytics engineering is to streamline the flow of data through different tools and processes, ensuring that it is accurate, timely, and in the right format for analysis. This involves scheduling dbt jobs in the correct sequence – for example, managing dependencies between tasks, handling errors gracefully, and ensuring data quality and compliance standards are met throughout the data pipeline.

In this section, we will talk about designing an automated workflow and introduce certain tools and libraries that help automate the loading and moving of data.

First, we'll look at some considerations when designing an automated workflow.

Designing an automated workflow – considerations

When designing an automated workflow for orchestrating data, keep the following in mind:

- **Complexity versus simplicity**: Choose a tool that matches your team's skill set and the complexity of your workflows. Integration efforts will vary significantly depending on whether data is coming from APIs, databases, file systems, or cloud services.

- **Scalability**: Consider future growth in data volume and complexity. Design workflows with scalability in mind, allowing them to handle increases in data volume and complexity without significant rework.

- **Integration**: Ensure the tool integrates well with your data stack.

- **Maintenance**: Consider the effort required to maintain and update your workflows.

- **Cost**: Factor in both direct costs and the indirect costs of tool complexity and maintenance.

Scalability is largely dependent on how flexible the tool is with increased data volume or new requirements for ingesting and extracting data. Ask yourself whether the volume of your data will change in the future by a certain order of magnitude and whether your current tooling will be able to adapt to this without incurring extra costs. Second, ask whether your current setup can be ported to a different tooling and whether it is modular enough that it can easily be maintained. Check whether it's a simple exercise to update or modify parts of the workflow without impacting the entire system. Does it provide enough support for other tools in the future, if we were to change to a different tooling?

These questions will inevitably come up when deciding on an orchestration solution and are crucial to get right if you want to avoid technical debt and incur extra costs because of unforeseen maintenance.

Now that we have challenged you on how to approach automating your data orchestration, let's have a look at certain tools that integrate well with dbt and are most commonly encountered within analytics engineering teams.

dbt Cloud

In this book, we have mostly focused on **dbt** and highlighted it as our main go-to tool in the analytics engineering toolbox. In *Chapter 8, Hands-On Analytics Engineering*, you got a glimpse of the features of dbt Cloud, and you saw how to set up dbt Cloud for use with Google BigQuery. This is why we will briefly discuss the orchestration feature here. **dbt Cloud** allows you to develop and define jobs, orchestrate them, and view documentation about your project, but its range of features is largely determined by the subscription you have.

As a hosted service, dbt Cloud comes with a subscription cost, which might be a consideration for smaller teams or projects. The main benefit is that dbt Cloud offers built-in job scheduling and monitoring, eliminating the need for external orchestration tools.

We will not go into detail on how to create and schedule jobs in dbt Cloud as the process is fairly straightforward if you follow the official dbt guide (`https://docs.getdbt.com/docs/deploy/deploy-jobs`). dbt Cloud is a standalone tool and luckily, you do not need to think about provisioning and maintaining the underlying infrastructure for orchestration.

However, keep in mind that while it offers convenience, some users might prefer the control and customization that's possible and the lower price tag offered by self-hosted orchestration tools. As mentioned in *Chapter 8*, there are more sophisticated tools for job orchestration. Tools such as Airflow, Prefect, and Dagster have far better integration with other tooling compared to using dbt Cloud as your orchestration environment – for example, Airflow is configured in Python, which allows you to extend your workflow so that it includes orchestration of other notebooks or ML scripts. You can deploy and orchestrate it on whatever infrastructure you want and maintain everything in code, which is not possible with dbt Cloud.

The next tool we'll discuss is open-source and is fairly popular within the data engineering community. We will not do a deep dive into it as that would require writing another book! Rather, we will explain the basics of the tool and highlight some features that are interesting when combined with dbt. We chose to focus on Airflow as this is the most common data orchestration tool. We also encourage you to check out good alternatives such as Dagster, Prefect, and Mage, which is also an upcoming promising tool.

Airflow

You may have heard of **Apache Airflow**, which is the most commonly encountered open-source tool for orchestrating data pipelines. It is frequently hailed as the *Swiss Army knife* of data engineering. Airflow allows you to author, schedule, and monitor workflows. It is highly customizable and can integrate with many data processing frameworks, databases, and cloud services (`https://airflow.apache.org/`).

A great benefit of sticking with Airflow is its widespread use within the data engineering and analytics community. There is plenty of documentation and integrations available with other tools and it is a highly flexible tool that uses Python to define highly complex workflows. It has a rich UI that enables monitoring and managing workflows.

Making use of Airflow in orchestrating your dbt jobs requires having dbt and Airflow be installed in the same environment, such as a Docker container. Airflow uses a database to track task status and manage metadata. You'll need a running instance of a compatible database (for example, PostgreSQL, MySQL, and so on) and configure Airflow to use it so that this metadata can be stored. This can be useful to track task completion and failure over time.

When it comes to using Airflow with dbt, the most important thing to get right is workflow design, specifically task dependencies and error handling. You need to understand the dependencies between your dbt models to properly orchestrate them in Airflow tasks. This includes knowing which models need to be built before others can be run. Also, you need to plan for how to handle errors in your dbt runs, including retries, alerts, and potentially skipping or marking tasks as failed.

Airflow relies on **operators**. Operators are the building blocks of workflows as they define the individual tasks that make up a DAG, similar to a DAG in dbt.

Each operator represents a single task in a workflow, specifying what action to perform when that task is executed. Operators are designed to do one thing well and can be combined in a DAG to perform complex workflows. There are several types of operators in Airflow, each serving different purposes. We will not dive into all the operators available, but the most common ones are **action operators**.

These operators execute a specific action or task, such as running a Python function, executing a SQL query, or sending an HTTP request. Here are some examples:

- **BashOperator**: This executes a Bash command or script. This can be used to run a `dbt build` command, for example, as dbt Core is used with the command line.

- **PythonOperator**: Executes a Python function.

- **HttpOperator**: Sends an HTTP request.

> **Note**
> This chapter features code snippets designed to showcase best practices or usage. However, executing these snippets may need extra setup, not covered in this book. Readers should view these snippets as illustrative examples and adapt the underlying best practices to their unique scenarios.

The following code snippet illustrates the use of a simple `BashOperator` for the simple task of running `dbt run -models`. This will run all dbt models under the `models` directory:

```python
from pendulum import datetime
from airflow.decorators import dag
from airflow.operators.bash import BashOperator

PATH_TO_DBT_PROJECT = "<path to your dbt project>"
PATH_TO_DBT_VENV = "<path to your venv activate binary>"

@dag(
    start_date=datetime(2023, 3, 23),
    schedule="@daily",
    catchup=False,
)
def simple_dbt_dag():
    dbt_run = BashOperator(
        task_id="dbt_run",
        bash_command="source $PATH_TO_DBT_VENV && dbt run --models .",
        env={"PATH_TO_DBT_VENV": PATH_TO_DBT_VENV},
        cwd=PATH_TO_DBT_PROJECT,
    )
simple_dbt_dag()
```

The downside of using a default `BashOperator` is that for debugging purposes, you have no observability on task execution – that is, on what went wrong in dbt. If a single model fails in a large project, you will not have observability of what failed, and it can be costly to rerun everything. You will have to check your `run_results.json` artifact file (which is a log file that's generated after each dbt run and contains metadata on model execution) to see what has gone wrong.

Luckily, there is a specific operator that better integrates with dbt. This operator can execute dbt Cloud jobs, poll for status, and download job artifacts and, under the hood, leverages the dbt Cloud Administrative API to trigger jobs. We will explain the features of this API in more detail later.

You can use `DbtCloudRunJobOperator` to trigger a run of a dbt Cloud job. By default, the operator will periodically check on the status of the executed job to terminate with a successful status every pre-defined number of seconds or until the job reaches a certain timeout length of execution time (`https://airflow.apache.org/docs/apache-airflow-providers-dbt-cloud/stable/operators.html`):

```python
trigger_job_run1 = DbtCloudRunJobOperator(
    task_id="trigger_job_run1",
    job_id=48617,
```

```
        check_interval=10,
        timeout=300,
    )
```

The preceding code snippet illustrates the use of this operator, where it triggers a certain job with `job_id` 48617 in dbt Cloud and has a timeout set (which is also a configurable parameter when calling the API) to limit execution time.

The biggest limitation here is that you have to use dbt Cloud. Essentially, this operator just calls dbt Cloud under the hood. It has some parameters that can help you monitor your run better compared to just using `BashOperator`, such as certain polling parameters, but there is a better alternative available!

The better alternative is **Cosmos**, which is an open-source library that dynamically generates DAGs from other tools or frameworks for Airflow. In *Chapter 9, Data Quality and Obervability* (*Figure 9.4*), we saw that DAGs are a way to visualize data transformation: each node in this chart represents a model, and thus it helps understand how tables are related to each other. In the context of Airflow, a DAG collects all tasks together, organized with dependencies and relationships to say how they should run, in which order they should run, and what tasks depend on each other. Cosmos automatically creates Airflow tasks from dbt models.

Here are the benefits of using Cosmos with Airflow and dbt Core:

- Using Airflow's data-aware scheduling and Airflow sensors to run models that depend on other events can be useful.

- Each dbt model can be turned into a task, complete with Airflow features such as retries and error notifications, as well as full observability into past runs directly in the Airflow UI.

- We can run dbt tests on tables created by individual models immediately after a model has completed. We can catch issues early and configure some other data quality tools to run alongside dbt tests.

- We can run dbt projects using Airflow connections instead of dbt profiles. We can store all your connections in one place, directly within Airflow, or by using a secrets backend. This centralizes secrets and connection details, which makes them easier to maintain.

- It leverages native support for installing and running dbt in a virtual environment to avoid dependency conflicts with Airflow.

Have a look at the following code snippet, which imports the necessary packages from Airflow and Cosmos, including `PostgresOperator` and `DbtTaskGroup`, to trigger a dbt run and subsequently query this model in Postgres:

```
from airflow.decorators import dag
from airflow.providers.postgres.operators.postgres import
PostgresOperator
from cosmos import DbtTaskGroup, ProjectConfig, ProfileConfig,
```

```
ExecutionConfig

# adjust for other database types
from cosmos.profiles import PostgresUserPasswordProfileMapping
from pendulum import datetime
import os

YOUR_NAME = "<your_name>"
CONNECTION_ID = "db_conn"
DB_NAME = "<your_db_name>"
SCHEMA_NAME = „<your_schema_name>"
MODEL_TO_QUERY = "model2"
# The path to the dbt project
DBT_PROJECT_PATH = f"{os.environ['AIRFLOW_HOME']}/dags/dbt/my_simple_
dbt_project"
# The path where Cosmos will find the dbt executable
# in the virtual environment created in the Dockerfile
DBT_EXECUTABLE_PATH = f"{os.environ['AIRFLOW_HOME']}/dbt_venv/bin/dbt"
```

Notice the DBT_PROJECT_PATH environment variable, which points to your dbt project, as well as DBT_EXECUTABLE_PATH, which points to your dbt installation. You can see how rather straightforward it is to get started with orchestrating your dbt models from Airflow with Cosmos. The following snippet shows the remainder of the definition of the DAG:

```
profile_config = ProfileConfig(
    profile_name="default",
    target_name="dev",
    profile_mapping=PostgresUserPasswordProfileMapping(
        conn_id=CONNECTION_ID,
        profile_args={"schema": SCHEMA_NAME},
    ),
)

execution_config = ExecutionConfig(
    dbt_executable_path=DBT_EXECUTABLE_PATH,
)


@dag(
    start_date=datetime(2023, 8, 1),
    schedule=None,
    catchup=False,
    params={"my_name": YOUR_NAME},
```

```
)
def my_simple_dbt_dag():
    transform_data = DbtTaskGroup(
        group_id="transform_data",
        project_config=ProjectConfig(DBT_PROJECT_PATH),
        profile_config=profile_config,
        execution_config=execution_config,
        operator_args={
            "vars": '{"my_name": {{ params.my_name }} }',
        },
        default_args={"retries": 2},
    )

    query_table = PostgresOperator(
        task_id="query_table",
        postgres_conn_id=CONNECTION_ID,
        sql=f"SELECT * FROM {DB_NAME}.{SCHEMA_NAME}.{MODEL_TO_QUERY}",
    )

    transform_data >> query_table

my_simple_dbt_dag()
```

Notice how simple the DAG is – it leverages the `DbtTaskGroup` class to create a task group from the models in your dbt project. The dependencies between dbt models are turned into dependencies between Airflow tasks automatically. This saves a lot of time if you had to define this yourself. All we had to specify was `profile_config` and `execution_config`, which specify which profile to use for connection and the path to the dbt executable. Cosmos will parse your dbt project files to define a DAG for you. Moreover, we can also run a query on Postgres using `PostgresOperator`, which allows us to combine several tasks into one workflow.

Now that you have a better understanding of the considerations involved in automating data workflows and recognize the added flexibility of using a tool such as Airflow, let's dive into another important workflow that helps us automate the testing of our data: CI.

Continuous integration

CI is part of **CI/CD**, a practice hailing from software engineering and DevOps. CI allows developers to test their code before code is merged into production, in an automated fashion.

Integration

The term **integration** in CI refers to the process of combining code changes from multiple contributors into a shared unified code base. The key principle behind CI is to automate the process of merging code changes regularly and consistently, thereby reducing the risk of merge conflicts that may arise when integrating changes made by different team members.

Merge conflicts arise when code from different branches is merged, and certain code or functionality is present in one branch but not in the other, where you may have different lines of code. When you build on a separate feature branch, the code will probably have diverged from what is in the main branch.

Before code is merged to production, this could be your main or master branch in your version control. We want to make sure that our code or code from our colleagues runs without errors. First and foremost, we want to prevent bugs from entering our production code and be able to consistently and promptly deploy or ship code to production. This is the very foundation of CI/CD.

Remember, it is not guaranteed that code that successfully runs on your machine will also run in a different environment, so you can see why it is necessary to test your code in an isolated environment – that is, to verify that your code also works in and across different environments.

Moreover, when collaborating with colleagues on the same code base, we want to make sure that all the code that is merged to the main branch is well-tested before this happens.

This is why we want to have an isolated environment where we can run our code and that of our colleagues before it is merged into production. In this environment, we will do some checks to make sure that errors within new code pushes are caught, the output of certain function calls is consistent with expectations, and that code is properly and consistently formatted.

Continuous

The term **continuous** in CI emphasizes the automated nature of the integration process. Instead of waiting until the end of a development cycle to integrate code changes, CI encourages developers to integrate their work continuously throughout the development process. This helps in identifying and fixing integration issues quickly and early on, preventing the buildup of conflicts and errors, which can be challenging to resolve later in the development life cycle.

In short, when code changes are made, we would like to test these out in smaller chunks or batches and iteratively. This saves on total development time and ensures that only specific code changes are tested in increments so that we don't have to do tests on our code all at once. This makes it easier to test code and integrate code into the main branch continuously. To accomplish this, CI pipelines are used, which we will introduce later in this chapter.

Now, let's have a look at what potential integration issues you could face when developing code. These are precisely the issues we want to catch in a CI pipeline.

Handling integration issues

The most common integration issue is that the code does not behave as we expected. The code might not produce the result we want, or the code simply does not run due to errors that we need to address first. In this section, we'll look at some errors that you might encounter when integrating or running your code and ways to remedy them. Note that compilation and runtime errors are quite general, while database and dependency errors are more specific to dbt.

A divergence in code formatting, issues with code functionality, or bad adherence to certain best practices can all occur. Think of SQL limitations across databases, such as the use of recurrent **common table expressions (CTEs)**, inconsistent use of casing or indentation in SQL, a Python function that you wrote as part of a CI pipeline that does not have deterministic output (unexpected output), or a dbt model not having a corresponding entry in a source.yml file. These issues can be spotted using some tools that we will now introduce.

Compilation and runtime errors

Compilation or runtime errors are the most common errors. **Compiling code** refers to the process of translating source code written in a high-level programming language (for example, SQL, Jinja, Python, and so on) into machine code or an intermediate representation. This process is performed by a compiler that's specific to the programming language.

Before code runs, it compiles, so the first thing we will catch is any **compilation errors**.

Now, let's go back to working with dbt. When you have a SQL syntax error, your code will not compile. The compiler is unable to parse this SQL or Jinja, which means the database cannot create a query plan for execution as it does not recognize the SQL commands, and an error is thrown. Thus, compilation errors occur when code syntax is not valid or it is not semantically correct: database objects referenced in the query may not exist.

Generally, this is the first thing you would want to check as part of an integration test in a CI pipeline: whether the code compiles and runs without errors. The following table illustrates the steps dbt takes when you run a command such as dbt run:

1. First, it checks whether there is a dbt project file and the connection to your data warehouse based on your profiles.yml file. If there is no dbt project, no connection profile, or an invalid project YAML file, a runtime error is thrown.

2. Second, it checks if Jinja snippets and YAML files are valid as these are compilation errors. If a YAML file does not have a valid structure, dbt will not be able to understand the project structure, such as your project metadata, data warehouse connection, and model and column definitions. There can also be issues with the way your dbt models are referenced by other models. If a circular dependency is detected, dbt will not be able to deduce which models to run first.

3. The last possible error is a database error, which dbt defines as an error that is returned by your data warehouse, usually a compilation error by its nature, as 90% of the time it is a SQL syntax error.

Table 11.1 depicts the types of errors that may occur in dbt:

Step	Description	Error Type
Initialize	Check that this is a dbt project, and that dbt can connect to the warehouse	Runtime error
Parsing	Check that the Jinja snippets in `.sql` files are valid and that `.yml` files are valid	Compilation error
Graph validation	Compile the dependencies into a graph and check that it's acyclic	Dependency error
SQL execution	Run the models	Database error

Table 11.1 – Types of errors from the dbt guide that you may encounter

Therefore, make sure you always run your dbt models locally in your development environment before committing them.

Pre-commit hooks

A good practice is to make use of **pre-commit hooks**, which we briefly introduced in the previous chapter in the context of linting.

Have a look at the following code snippet, which shows a typical compilation error in dbt. This command runs the `customers` model; however, this model depends on another model called `stg_customer`, which was not found. This means that the model does not exist in the data warehouse yet as it has not been built before. You need to make sure you run the model first before attempting to run any subsequent models. This can easily be resolved by using the + sign in front of the model selection syntax. In this case, that would be `dbt run -s +customers`, and it will run upstream dependencies:

```
$ dbt run -s customers
Running with dbt=0.17.1

Encountered an error:
Compilation Error in model customers (models/customers.sql)
```

`model.jaffle_shop.customers` (`models/customers.sql`) depends on a node named `stg_customer`, which wasn't found.

Pre-commit hooks are automated checks that run before each commit, ensuring that certain conditions are met before your code is committed to the repository. This avoids errors being committed to your branch.

As you saw in the previous chapter, automating linting checks with pre-commit hooks is one possibility, but you can do plenty of other useful checks on your dbt repository, such as checking the integrity and validity of your code, as well as checking if there are any compilation errors and if it adheres to some standards that you can configure.

For example, with the `dbt-checkpoint` hook (`https://github.com/dbt-checkpoint/dbt-checkpoint`), you could verify the following when committing a new model:

- Does the model have an entry in a property (schema) YAML file?

- Does the source have a description?

- Does the model name abide by a certain naming convention?

- Does the model have several tests defined?

This is just a small selection; there are a variety of other checks you can do with this hook, from checking whether models, sources, and macros have object and column descriptions to running the dbt compile command before committing to make sure your code compiles, as we have seen in the previous section. This hook allows a dbt developer to automate some basic and advanced checks on your dbt development work, we encourage you to check out this pre-commit hook.

Another handy package that you can install as a dbt package is `dbt-project-evaluator` (`https://dbt-labs.github.io/dbt-project-evaluator/latest/`). This package allows you to check your dbt project for adherence to best practices on modeling, testing, documentation, structure, performance, and governance. Since this is a package instead of a hook, it will build models in your data warehouse that each represent a misalignment and run a test on them to check and give an alert. Additionally, you can opt for logging these misalignments by adding the following line to `dbt_project.yml`:

```
on-run-end: "{{ dbt_project_evaluator.print_dbt_project_evaluator_
issues() }}"
```

This will print any issues to the log output for you to check.

Some other useful hooks can be found in `pre-commit-hooks` (`https://github.com/pre-commit/pre-commit-hooks`), which contains out-of-the-box hooks that you can use to check if your YAML files have the correct syntax, for example, and `SQLFluff`, which you have already seen before, which allows you to run a linting check before committing.

With this, you've seen how pre-commit hooks are quite powerful and almost a necessity when developing in dbt as they can help catch errors even before committing your work. Alternatively, they can also be integrated as part of a CI pipeline, which we will introduce later. This means that you do these checks in a later stage before merging to main, with the advantage being it might speed up development time because you won't have to wait for hooks to run before committing.

These hooks allow you to test or even modify your code (such as `SQLFluff fix` or the `generate-missing-sources` hook). Be careful, though, as this means that a hook will modify your code and this might result in unwanted behavior. You should experiment to see what works before committing to automating fixes.

Next, we will discuss unit tests, which can help verify the functionality of specific functions, methods, and modules within your code base. Pre-commit hooks are valuable in themselves, but adding unit tests can go a long way in testing the code itself so that functions and modules work as intended.

Unit tests

Perhaps you have already heard of this practice. **Unit tests** also come from the field of software engineering. Unit tests are small, automated tests that are designed to verify the correctness of specific functions, methods, or modules within a software application. Each unit test focuses on a discrete piece of functionality, isolating it from the rest of the code base to ensure that it behaves as intended.

In analytics engineering, this means that we would like to test the output of specific functions and methods in SQL and Python. A handy package for this is `Pytest`. You will see an example of a unit test later when we introduce the CI pipeline. Every function that you make serves a specific purpose. As such, you expect it to be consistent when it comes to its output:

- **Correctness of output**: Ensuring that the function returns the correct result for a given set of input values. This is fundamental to verify that the function performs its intended task correctly.

- **Edge cases**: Testing how the function behaves with edge case inputs, such as empty strings, null values, or extreme numerical values. This is crucial for ensuring the robustness and reliability of the function.

- **Error handling**: Making sure that the function handles errors or unexpected inputs properly, including whether it throws exceptions or errors as expected. Good error handling is essential for the stability of the code.

- **Data types and formats**: Verifying that the function handles different data types appropriately and returns data in the expected format. This is important for the function to interact correctly with other code dependencies and to handle various input scenarios.

In *Chapter 10, Writing Code in a Team*, you saw an example of a unit test. Now that you better understand the purpose of pre-commit hooks and unit tests, let's examine the importance of code formatting.

Code formatting

As you saw in the previous chapter, integrating code from different branches when collaborating oftentimes results in challenges in dealing with inconsistencies around code formatting. We have already seen that there are certain standards we can all adhere to, so long as we are consistent. You have gotten acquainted with certain Python packages that can check and fix code formatting issues for us. This is precisely what we can leverage in a CI pipeline. Officially, as you saw in the previous chapter, we call this process **linting code**. Remember SQLFluff and sqlfmt? These are great linters for SQL that help ensure coding standards are adhered to.

Generally, what is important to understand here is that this code integration is not a one-time event but an ongoing and iterative process that helps identify and resolve integration issues early in the development lifecycle.

So, how do we automate the process of testing for these issues? This is where CI/CD pipelines come in.

First, let's have a look at the CI pipeline and its components and how they can help automate the testing process.

Automating testing with a CI pipeline

CI checks can be automated in a **CI pipeline**. The purpose of a CI pipeline is to check code for any bugs and prevent faulty code from being merged into the main branch. Whenever changes are made to the code base, whether that be a change in a dbt SQL model or YAML configuration file in a repository, for example, this pipeline is triggered to run and test the code. We can have particular steps specifically for the type of checks we have defined previously: compilation tests, unit tests, and formatting checks.

Pipelines are, more often than not, written in YAML. Firstly, YAML's human-readable simple format makes it exceptionally easy to understand and edit, even for those who are not deeply familiar with programming. It also makes them somewhat portable to other CI/CD tools and platforms. Many CI/CD tools, such as Jenkins, GitLab CI, and GitHub Actions, natively support YAML for pipeline definitions. This widespread support ensures that YAML-based pipelines can be easily transferred, shared, or adapted across different systems with minimal modifications.

Pipeline scripts are executed in specialized environments managed by what are known as agents. An **agent** is a software instance that executes the pipeline tasks defined in your scripts. VMs are often used as the underlying infrastructure for both hosted and self-hosted agents.

In a hosted scenario, the CI/CD service provider manages these VMs, ensuring they are available and meet the necessary specifications for running the pipelines. In a self-hosted setup, the organization is responsible for provisioning and maintaining these VMs. VMs offer the advantage of creating isolated and reproducible environments for running CI/CD tasks, ensuring consistency across runs, and mitigating the *"it works on my machine"* problem.

Therefore, agents can be hosted or self-hosted:

- **Hosted agents** are provided and managed by the CI/CD service platform (for example, Azure Pipelines or GitHub Actions). They offer convenience as they are pre-configured and maintained by the service provider.

- **Self-hosted agents** are set up and maintained by the organization using them. They provide more control over the environment where the CI/CD pipelines run, allowing customization to meet specific requirements or to use resources that are not available in the hosted option.

A **CI pipeline** is usually triggered the moment a **pull request** (**PR**) is opened, which, as you learned in the previous chapter, is essentially a request that's opened by a developer to merge code from the feature branch you worked on into the main branch so that it becomes part of production code.

Therefore, a CI pipeline checks a new code push for any bugs or formatting issues, regardless of whether the PR has been already reviewed by a colleague or not. Therefore, you can imagine that this saves time for a reviewer as there is no value in reviewing a PR if this pipeline fails.

The following example CI pipeline is in Azure DevOps. First, it installs the requirements, then does linting or code formatting using `sqlfmt`, and finally runs the CI Python script and cleans up the temporary schema that was generated in the data warehouse. This CI pipeline is defined in a YAML file, similar to how dbt properties and configurations are defined, and can be placed in a dedicated subdirectory in your dbt repository:

```
steps:
  - checkout: self
    fetchDepth: 0
    persistCredentials: true

  - task: UsePythonVersion@0
    inputs:
      versionSpec: 3.9
    displayName: "Use Python 3.9"
    enabled: true

  - bash: |
      python3 -m pip install --upgrade pip
      python3 -m pip install --force-reinstall
shandy-        sqlfmt[jinjafmt]==0.19.1
    displayName: Install requirements
  - bash: |
      sqlfmt --diff models macros
    displayName: Checking SQL Format

  - bash: |
```

```
      python3 .pipelines/scripts/dbt_runner/main.py --method ci
    env:
      DBT_API_KEY: $(DBT_API_KEY)
    name: DBT_SLIM_CI
    displayName: Run DBT Slim CI and poll status

  - bash: |
      python3 .pipelines/scripts/dbt_runner/main.py --method clean_up_
ci
    env:
      DBT_API_KEY: $(DBT_API_KEY)
      DBT_RUN_ID: $(DBT_SLIM_CI.DBT_RUN_ID)
    displayName: Cleanup (cancel running dbt jobs + drop temp schema)
    condition: always()
```

In the preceding CI pipeline script, we first make sure we install the right dependencies – in this case, the `sqlfmt` linter. Only after this step is executed is the code run or compiled.

A CI pipeline triggers the running of a CI job in dbt Cloud or in an agent itself. In the latter case, you will have to make sure the agent knows where your code is located, so you will have to have a Git `clone` command in the pipeline to clone your dbt repository into the environment.

In this particular case, the dbt Cloud API is used to trigger the run in dbt Cloud, since dbt Cloud has our job definitions and is used to orchestrate our jobs. Therefore, you will only see a bash command that runs a Python script with the necessary arguments that trigger a CI job run in the cloud. Later in this chapter, you will see how this is done in more detail.

Separate schema

CI jobs run in a **temporary dedicated schema** in your development environment. This makes the execution isolated from your main development schema to avoid overwriting any models in your data warehouse. Once the pipeline succeeds, this temporary schema is dropped as it is tied to a specific CI pipeline run, and it is not relevant anymore. You will notice that there is a last cleanup step in the CI/CD pipeline example we will give later. This ensures that the temporary schema is dropped so that it does not clog up your data warehouse. A temporary schema is created by default when using the native integration between dbt Cloud and GitHub, GitLab, or Azure DevOps, but you need to be on the Enterprise plan for this. A workaround is to create a Jinja macro that generates a schema each time a PR is opened.

> **Note:**
>
> A **temporary schema** for a CI job run is created by default when using the native integration between dbt Cloud and GitHub, GitLab, or Azure DevOps if you use dbt Cloud for your orchestration, but you need to be on the Enterprise plan for this. A workaround can be found in the dbt Cloud Administrative API, which has a `schema_override` field in the payload that you can configure (`https://docs.getdbt.com/dbt-cloud/api-v2-legacy#tag/Jobs/operation/triggerRun`).

To mimic the behavior of the native integration, which relies on a Git webhook, we can supply `PR_ID`, which is usually an environment variable that you can then use in the `schema_override` setting. This is how it is referenced in an Azure DevOps pipeline:

```
- name: DBT_JOB_SCHEMA_OVERRIDE
    value: dbt_slim_ci_pr_$(PR_ID)
```

If you are not using dbt Cloud, you will have to generate the temporary CI schema yourself. Please refer to this page to see how this can be configured: `https://docs.getdbt.com/docs/build/custom-schemas`.

Having a dedicated schema allows you to run those specific models that were changed in the feature branch. We will learn how to configure the process of building only modified models later, but having only those models in a dedicated temporary schema for each pipeline run makes it easy to debug and saves on compute costs and running time. You can imagine that when pipeline configuration settings are changed, a specific dbt command in your CI is changed, or that when you do a rerun of a failed CI pipeline and you want each pipeline run to be traced back, having this schema be created and dropped for every run is beneficial for clarity in tracing back CI runs.

A Git repository has multiple feature branches and several open pull requests, which causes the code to run in an isolated environment in the production database (a temporary schema or database, as it is called by some database vendors). Once the PR is merged, contingent on a successful CI run, the code is merged into `main`, and subsequently it can be deployed to production. This can also be automated in the CD part of the pipeline and is something we'll look at later.

A CI job can be executed in the production database in a temporary schema. This is not a prerequisite, and the CI job can also be configured to run in a temporary schema in your development database or a separate database or a staging database. As you can imagine, it doesn't matter where this code is tested; eventually, this code will be deployed to production through the CD pipeline and it all comes down to design decisions that work for your team. What we can recommend is running CI models in a temporary schema in your development environment. This makes logical sense as this code still has to undergo testing before it touches the production database. In addition to that, you can argue that the production database should only contain production data, and no model testing should be done there as it might impact running times when using the same underlying compute engine.

Now that you have a better understanding of the necessity of a CI pipeline, let's look at the components of this pipeline.

Pipeline stages, jobs, and steps

The pipeline can consist of several stages, steps, or jobs. In both Azure DevOps and GitHub Actions, these components (stages, jobs, or steps in Azure DevOps and workflows or jobs and steps in GitHub Actions) provide a structured way to define and manage the tasks involved in software development and deployment processes. This structure helps in organizing CI/CD workflows into manageable, logical, and reusable segments, making them more understandable and maintainable.

A **job** can consist of multiple steps to be executed together; therefore, a job is nothing more than a grouping of steps that do a certain action, such as linting, running the code, or executing unit tests. The following is just an example of a conceptual CI/CD workflow:

- **CI stage**: In this stage, the linting, compiling, running, and unit testing of code are all steps that occur sequentially, but they are logically grouped into jobs:

  - **Linting (job/step)**: Popular linters such as Black, SQLFluff, and sqlfmt can check the Python or SQL code for issues in formatting. If the code does not adhere to a predefined standard, the linter will throw an error and give you details on which line of code in which particular files the formatting is wrong.

  - **Compiling/running (job/step)**: Compiling or running the code ensures the code executes. In this stage, you run the command-line arguments that make your code compile or run. In the case of dbt, this would default to executing `dbt compile`, `dbt run`, or `dbt build`.

  - **Unit tests (job/step)**: You can have unit tests in your CI pipeline that check the output of certain functions in your Python scripts or dbt macros so that they behave as expected.

- **CD stage**: In this stage, a deploy job is run to build the models in a specific environment:

  - **Deploy to a development environment (job)**: A deployment job builds the modified models in the development environment

  - **Deploy to a production environment (job)**: A deployment job builds the modified models in the production environment so that they're available to downstream applications

The CD stage deploys the models that were tested in the CI stage to your environments. In this case, we deploy to a development and production environment, but you might encounter an intermediary testing or acceptance environment as well. Deploying your models in this case means running a dbt job that uses a `dbt run` or `dbt build` command to build those models in these environments. Remember that each CI run has a temporary schema that is dropped after the run. In this case, this temporary schema is created and dropped in the development environment as that is the environment where our code is tested before it's deployed to production.

wwHowever, after these dbt resources have been tested upon completion of a CI run, they still need to be deployed to the "main" schema of your development and production environments as they do not exist there yet. This corresponds to the main branch of your code, which you can also refer to as your "production" code, as we saw earlier.

If a particular stage in a CI pipeline fails, such as because of an error in the code and the code does not compile, or formatting is wrong, the pipeline will throw an error and will stop executing, signaling that the CI tests have failed and thus the code is not yet ready to be merged to production.

Let's take a look at *Figure 11.1*, which shows the CI and CD stages and their jobs and steps:

```yaml
stages:
  - ${{ if ne(variables['Build.SourceBranch'], 'refs/heads/main') }}:
    - stage: CI
      displayName: "CI"
      jobs:
        - job: ci
          displayName: CI
          timeoutInMinutes: 360
          steps:
            - template: ./task/ci.yml
    - stage: CD_DEVELOPMENT
      displayName: "CD_DEVELOPMENT"
      dependsOn: CI
      variables:
        DBT_RUN_ID: $[ stageDependencies.CI.ci.outputs['DBT_SLIM_CI.DBT_RUN_ID'] ]
      jobs:
        - deployment: cd
          environment: trns-dbt-development
          displayName: CD
          timeoutInMinutes: 360
          strategy:
            runOnce:
              deploy:
                steps:
                  - template: ./task/cd.yml
                    parameters:
                      environment: dev
```

Figure 11.1 – A CI/CD pipeline with CI and CD stages, along with their jobs and steps defined

Here, we can see that the pipeline consists of a `ci` (CI) and `cd` (CD_DEVELOPMENT), respectively, with jobs that call other pipelines (`.task/ci.yml` and `.task/cd.yml`) that execute steps sequentially. In this case, you can see that pipelines can call other pipelines as well, making it easier to debug code as your CI and CD are now decoupled.

Figures 11.2, 11.3 and *11.4* provide examples of this pipeline structure, illustrating a CI stage and CD stage; a CD job, and a CI Python script that triggers a CI job along with the steps in separate pipeline files, all of which are referenced:

```yaml
steps:
  - checkout: self
    fetchDepth: 0
    persistCredentials: true

  - task: UsePythonVersion@0
    inputs:
      versionSpec: 3.9
    displayName: "Use Python 3.9"
    enabled: true

  - bash: |
      python3 -m pip install --upgrade pip
      python3 -m pip install --force-reinstall shandy-sqlfmt[jinjafmt]==0.19.1
      python3 -m pip install -r .pipelines/scripts/powerbi_bim_parser/requirements.txt
    displayName: Install requirements

  - bash: |
      sqlfmt --diff models macros
    displayName: Checking SQL Format

  - bash: |
      python3 .pipelines/scripts/dbt_runner/main.py --method ci
    env:
      DBT_API_KEY: $(DBT_API_KEY)
    name: DBT_SLIM_CI
    displayName: Run DBT Slim CI and poll status

  - bash: |
      python3 .pipelines/scripts/dbt_runner/main.py --method clean_up_ci
    env:
      DBT_API_KEY: $(DBT_API_KEY)
      DBT_RUN_ID: $(DBT_SLIM_CI.DBT_RUN_ID)
    displayName: Cleanup (cancel running dbt jobs + drop temp schema)
    condition: always()
```

Figure 11.2 – The CI pipeline with linting and compilation steps

Here, you can see the CI pipeline with steps that were referenced by the CI job. You will observe that linting, compilation, and running the steps are separate bash commands.

The very first step is to install the necessary dependencies for the code to run. Remember that this script will run in an isolated environment, in an agent (a virtual environment). Every time this pipeline is triggered, an agent needs to be provisioned to run the code. By default, this environment does not have the necessary libraries installed.

Notice the command that's used in the second step called `Checking SQL format`:

```
sqlfmt -diff models macros
```

This command will run `sqlfmt` on the models and macros in the models and macros directories, respectively, and it will print a diff of changes that `sqlfmt` would make to format a file. Note that it will not format the file for you.

The second step uses a Python script to trigger a CI job run. Since our CI job is defined in dbt Cloud, we need to provide the `$(DBT_API_KEY)` environment variable as an argument. Also, notice the `-method ci` argument, which will run the `ci` function in the Python script.

The last command cancels any running jobs and drops any artifacts that remain after the job run – for example, the temporary schema that was made for running this CI pipeline. Remember that such a temporary schema is created just for building the dbt resources (models, seed files, sources, and macros) that were changed. Later, you will see how this can be accomplished by using a command-line argument on the `dbt build` command:

```
parameters:
  - name: environment
    type: string

steps:
  - checkout: self

  - task: UsePythonVersion@0
    inputs:
      versionSpec: 3.9
    displayName: "Use Python 3.9"
    enabled: true

  - bash: |
      python3 .pipelines/scripts/dbt_runner/main.py --method cd --env ${{ parameters.environment }}
    env:
      DBT_API_KEY: $(DBT_API_KEY)
    name: DBT_CD
    displayName: Run DBT Slim CD on ${{ parameters.environment }} and poll status

  - bash: |
      python3 .pipelines/scripts/dbt_runner/main.py --method clean_up_cd
    env:
      DBT_API_KEY: $(DBT_API_KEY)
    displayName: Cleanup (cancel running dbt jobs)
    condition: always()
```

Figure 11.3 – The deployment job (CD) with two steps – running and cleaning up

Figure 11.3 shows the CD pipeline with steps that were referenced by the CD job. You can see that the deployment run and cleanup were triggered as separate steps.

The following figure shows that the CI function uses the `DbtCloudRunner` class to call the API and trigger a CI run; the `-fail-fast` argument is added for efficiency here. To stop the CI pipeline as soon as there is an error, we do not need to wait until the end of pipeline execution if linting failed, for example:

```python
def ci():
    runner = get_runner()
    job_id = int(os.environ["DBT_CI_JOB_ID"])
    git_branch = os.getenv("DBT_JOB_GIT_BRANCH", None)
    schema_override = os.getenv("DBT_JOB_SCHEMA_OVERRIDE", None)
    azure_pull_request_id = int(os.environ["PR_ID"])
    steps_override = [
        "dbt build -s +state:modified+ --fail-fast",
    ]

    run_id = runner.run_job(
        job_id=job_id,
        job_cause="CI triggered job",
        git_branch=git_branch,
        schema_override=schema_override,
        steps_override=steps_override,
        azure_pull_request_id=azure_pull_request_id,
    )

    # setting env var in Azure DevOps
    logging.info(f'##vso[task.setvariable variable=DBT_RUN_ID;isOutput=true]{str(run_id)}')

    run_status_link = runner.get_status_link(run_id=run_id)

    logging.info(f"Job running! See job status at {run_status_link}")

    runner.poll_run_status(run_id=run_id)
```

Figure 11.4 – The CI function in the Python script triggers the CI job in dbt Cloud

Let's look at all these CI steps in a little more detail to better understand the considerations of having such tests in your pipeline.

Linting

We would like to point out that doing **linting** should be optional in a CI pipeline, depending on the importance you attach to code formatting versus speed of development, but we do strongly encourage enforcing it. You should already know by now from the discussion in the previous chapter that tools such as Black, SQLFluff, and Prettify are quite valuable in enforcing a coding standard and flagging errors in formatting. We encourage you to play around with different linters in a CI pipeline.

Why do we regard linting as optional? Isn't it always good to do linting? Well, this all depends on the amount of code you will write. Generally, there is a *trade-off* between development speed and code quality rigor. If speed is of the utmost essence, you might want to reconsider doing linting when working on a large enough code base that it becomes a speed bottleneck in your development process, especially if you have a lot of custom rules defined.

Therefore, perhaps you only want to do linting on certain sections of your code – perhaps you only want to check the formatting of your most essential code, such as your dbt models. If you are more lenient on development speed, however, you could lint all dbt project files, any YAML configuration files you use in your repository, and any Python files you may have. This is where tools such as Black, SQLFluff, and Prettify come in handy, as you saw in *Chapter 10*.

You can play around with the severity of the error: for instance, you can configure sqlfmt and SQLFluff to only give a warning upon encountering a formatting issue; this will not throw an error that stops pipeline execution. Thus, the CI pipeline can continue running while it logs the warnings for you to be aware of.

To configure the severity of an error in SQLFluff, have a look at the following snippet:

```
[SQLFluff]
warnings = LT01, LT04
```

This will only throw a warning for those rules and the file will not fail.

A best practice we recommend is to configure your linting tool to throw an error if a linting rule is broken. This makes it stricter when it comes to not allowing formatting issues to be introduced into production, instead of merely giving warnings. You can even let your linting tool not only flag these issues but also fix them. However, we wouldn't recommend doing this as this can result in unwanted behavior where code is changed not by the developer but within a pipeline. The tool will *quietly commit* such a fix and the developer might not be completely aware of this. It is far better to only flag these errors so that the developer can have a double look and actually fix these errors and run the pipeline again.

> **Note:**
> We have put the linting step before compiling/running the code. This is entirely optional, and we leave it up to you to either do linting or run the code first. Linting code first focuses on checking the formatting before even running the code, if that is the emphasis you put on code quality. Linting usually takes far less time than actually compiling and running the code, so we get that out of the way first. The reasoning is that building the code first, which takes relatively the longest amount of time in your pipeline, is a waste of time as the code can still be formatted incorrectly. Then, you will have to go back to the code and fix any linting errors anyway.

Needless to say, it is perfectly plausible that you would first want to execute the code before you do linting. If the code does not take a lot of time to run, then at least you know the code runs and linting might not be your highest priority in the pipeline.

Compiling and running

In this step, you run the command-line arguments that make your code run. In the case of dbt, this would default to executing `dbt compile`, `dbt run`, or `dbt build`. If the pipeline fails at this point, you can be certain that your code does not execute. There will be either a compilation error or a runtime error, as you have seen before. Perhaps the way your dbt project is configured is wrong in that it cannot resolve dependencies or the syntax of one of your models is wrong. This would be a compilation error because the SQL cannot be compiled. Perhaps a reference to an upstream dbt model breaks because the model does not exist in your database schema yet since you forgot to run it. In any case, you should debug the logs of your dbt run to check the cause of the error. Check out the official documentation on debugging logs for more details: `https://www.getdbt.com/dbt-learn/lessons/debugging-dbt#1`.

Configuring unit tests with Pytest

As we have seen, unit tests are an essential part of the software engineering life cycle, and we encourage you, as an analytics engineer, to adopt such practices as well. Unit tests check if the output of functions adheres to the expected output. This prevents code ambiguity and ensures code behaves as expected when given certain inputs. This ensures a certain degree of code reliability. In this section, we will provide an example.

For instance, you can test whether a function returns the expected output. Here is an example of testing whether an email is valid with the `pytest` Python library:

```
import re

def is_valid_email(email):
    pattern = r"[^@]+@[^@]+\.[^@]+"
    return re.match(pattern, email) is not None

# Test for is_valid_email function
@pytest.mark.parametrize("email,expected", [
    ("test@example.com", True),
    ("invalid-email", False),
    ("another.test@domain.co", True),
    ("", Fal
```

To run these tests, you would simply run `pytest` in your terminal in the directory where your test file is located. Pytest automatically discovers tests and runs them, providing a detailed report of the results.

You can extend this to performing unit tests on your dbt models. For this, there are several repositories worth checking out – there's even a repo (`https://github.com/pgoslatara/dbt-beyond-the-basics?tab=readme-ov-file#dbt-artifacts-and-pytest`). You can do advanced testing that parses dbt artifact files such as `manifest.json`. You can test naming conventions on dbt models and columns and check the integrity of your dbt modeling. There is another repo (`https://github.com/yu-iskw/dbt-unittest`) that allows you to unit test dbt macros as well. We encourage you to check them out and see if some of the tests are applicable and valuable to your use case.

Now that you have a better understanding of the CI process, let's have a look at CD.

Continuous deployment

In analytics engineering, CD refers to the automated process of deploying all changes in data models, scripts, and configurations to the production environment, post-testing. This practice ensures that new features, bug fixes, and updates are swiftly and reliably deployed into production, usually on the condition that the CI pipeline has been completed successfully. Therefore, in essence, a deployment job *deploys* the modified models into production. As you can imagine, this defaults to running a dbt build or run command, just like any other dbt job. The subtle difference is in the naming – a *deployment* job is a dedicated job that is only ever called after a CI job.

Let's break it down:

- **Deployment**: The *deployment* aspect of CI/CD refers to deploying changes in your dbt models, YAML configuration files, and any changes you have committed to your development feature branch. Essentially, with *deployment*, we mean running your dbt models in a production environment. After your code has been tested in a CI pipeline for formatting using a linter, and any compilation or runtime errors and code integrity checks have been performed using a unit testing library, the code can be deployed to production on the condition of a successful CI pipeline run. When we say deploying code, it can mean any of the following things:

  - Building a newly added dbt model in production

  - Rebuilding a dbt model because you added a column dbt test

  - Rebuilding your entire dbt project (running all dbt models, seeds, tests, and so on) because an important seed file or macro has been changed

  - Adding a new line of code with updated logic to a dbt model

  - Fixing a bug in a dbt model

- For example, let's you have built a new dbt model. This model is available in your dbt development environment, specifically in your development schema, but not yet in the production environment. Deploying this model means building this dbt model in your production environment so that it is available to downstream applications.

- **Continuous**: Similar to CI, the term continuous in CD emphasizes the automated nature of the deployment process. When code changes have been tested, we would like to immediately deploy them. The reasoning is the same as with a CI pipeline – it makes it easier to spot errors in code, and code adjustments can easily be tracked because it is increment-based.

We will now move our focus to the CD pipeline.

The CD pipeline

Similar to how a CI pipeline automates the process of testing code modifications, a **CD pipeline** automatically deploys code to the production environment. A CD pipeline automates the running or rebuilding of dbt models and project configuration files in one or more production environments after they have been tested in a CI pipeline run.

Integration and deployment in practice

At this point, you might be wondering how we ensure only the changed models and their dependencies are tested and rebuilt, instead of everything. If we just run `dbt build` or `dbt run`, this will run all models by default, just like any other job. Rebuilding all dbt models if we just changed a single line of code in our feature branch for a single model is wasteful in terms of compute costs and development time. How do we know what has been changed and what has not?

If you introduced a new model, fixed a bug, changed a configuration file, or added a dbt test to a column in a model, the scope of change determines what upstream and downstream models need to be run to successfully deploy these changes to production. You might be tempted to think that only a single changed model needs to be deployed to production, but think about model dependency in dbt. For instance, if you update essential logic in a single staging model, you also want to rebuild downstream models to reflect this change in logic because you expect the structure of the data to change. If you update a project configuration file, a seed file, or a macro that is used by many models, this will update all these models and their dependencies.

Similarly, if you add a test to an intermediate or mart model, ideally, you want to backfill the tables and run all dependencies to verify if the dbt test works as expected. Have a look at *Figure 8.16* again in *Chapter 8*, *Hands-On Analytics Engineering*, for a reminder on dbt model dependency.

Therefore, in dbt, we need a way to check our current production environment state regarding the incoming change – the change you have pushed from your feature branch and want to merge to the main branch. Luckily, there is a way to do this. This check is called state deferral, and we will discuss this next.

State deferral

With the `state:modified+` argument that we add to a dbt build command, we make sure that dbt only runs modified models and their downstream dependencies (the + sign in a dbt selector command means downstream).

How does dbt know which models were changed? For that, you need to supply the path to your `manifest.json` file, which is a dbt artifact file that describes all the dbt nodes in your project (models, tests, macros, and so on), including all node configurations and resource properties. This file is used to produce dbt docs, which is the documentation feature of dbt, and it is used for state comparison.

The key thing with **state comparison**, also called **state deferral**, is that dbt checks two manifest files to see if they match up. If one of them has newer models (or newly modified models), then upon running the following command, dbt will exclusively run the modified models only:

```
dbt build state:modified  --defer --state path/to/artifacts
```

This combination of commands and arguments will allow us to enable *Slim CI*. This helps us only run models that have been newly created in our feature branch.

This also applies to developing in the dbt Cloud IDE: you can configure state deferral here to avoid rerunning models that were not modified, speeding up development. Please have a look at the following documentation for more on this interesting feature: https://docs.getdbt.com/best-practices/best-practice-workflows#run-only-modified-models-to-test-changes-slim-ci.

Defer is a powerful feature that makes it possible to run a subset of models or tests in a sandbox environment without having to first build their upstream parents. This can save time and computational resources when you want to test a small number of models in a large project. Defer requires that a manifest from a previous dbt invocation be passed to the `--state` flag or `env` variable. Together with the `state: selection` method, these features enable **Slim CI**.

Remember that state deferral is only possible because dbt models are **idempotent**: given the same manifest and the same raw data, dbt will always output the same result.

> **Idempotency, as explained by dbt**
>
> "One of the greatest underlying assumptions about dbt is that its operations should be stateless and idempotent. That is, it doesn't matter how many times a model has been run before, or if it has ever been run before. It doesn't matter if you run it once or a thousand times. Given the same raw data, you can expect the same transformed result. A given run of dbt doesn't need to "know" about any other run; it just needs to know about the code in the project and the objects in your database as they exist right now."

There are caveats around state comparison, which can be found here: https://docs.getdbt.com/reference/node-selection/state-comparison-caveats.

Now that you have a better understanding of state deferral and how the `manifest.json` artifact file is used for this purpose, let's move our focus to Slim CI/CD.

Slim CI/CD

Slim CI was a term introduced by dbt itself in an article at `https://discourse.getdbt.com/t/how-we-sped-up-our-ci-runs-by-10x-using-slim-ci/2603` from 2021, although now, it has become the default way of doing CI and generally, the term has lost the *Slim* prefix. It is a smart way of doing CI, as we like to put it.

A defining characteristic of a Slim CI pipeline is that a Slim CI run only tests dbt models that have *actually been modified*. It makes use of the state deferral command introduced previously.

As we have seen, if you only run a `dbt run` or `dbt build` command in your CI pipeline, it will build all models. If you just changed some code line in an upstream model in your feature branch, you do not want to build all model dependencies as this can result in slower development times and is wasteful when it comes to cloud compute costs for both testing and deploying.

The same logic applies to deploying your dbt models in a CD pipeline after you have tested them in your CI pipeline – you only want to rebuild those models that were changed (the same models that were also tested in your CI run); there is no need to rebuild existing models that have not changed. The same command introduced earlier is used here as well.

You could call this whole process **Slim CI/CD**, but this has now become the default for dbt and in the future, this term might not be relevant anymore.

Let's take a look back at our Stroopwafelshop, which we introduced in *Chapter 8*, *Hands-On Analytics Engineering*. Let's take a closer look at the scenario.

Stroopwafelshop has expanded its geographic reach by acquiring another shop called Pepernotenshop. This Dutch sweet delicacy is a nice addition to their product offering.

You have been assigned the task of remodeling the data in the data warehouse. To do this, you need to integrate the data from Pepernotenshop. Specifically, your task is to update the sales table with an explicit `eur_amount` column. Since Pepernotenshop also sells in the US and sales amounts were given in USD, these need to be converted into euros. For this, you have been told there is a new source table available with fxrates (currency exchange rates). Also, the products table needs to be enriched with data from Pepernotenshop's products. For now, you will have to read from both systems instead of combining the data at once.

Let's assume you previously had added intermediate and marts layer models called `int_fact_sales`, `fact_sales`, `int_dim_product`, and `dim_product`.

You proceed to update the existing dbt model, `stg_sales`, and change its name to `stg_sales_stroopwafels` because it only contains the sales records of stroopwafels sales. You proceed to add a new staging model called `stg_sales_pepernoten`, which reads from a newly ingested source table coming from the `Pepernotenshop` database, which contains the sales records for `pepernoten` sales.

You add `stg_fx_rates` and `fact_fx_rates` based on the new currency exchange rates table. In `int_fact_sales`, you update the logic to union the two sales tables we defined previously into one consolidated table. You add the `eur_amount` column by converting the USD amounts into euros based on the `fact_fx_rates` table that you joined on. You also update the products table in the same way, by appending records from Pepernotenshop's product table.

What models will be tested in the CI pipeline, and which ones will have to be built in the CD pipeline?

With the command we introduced previously (`dbt build state:modified+ --defer --state path/to/artifacts`), we will only run modified models and their dependencies. Have you guessed them? In this case, the modified models are `stg_sales_pepernoten`, `stg_sales_stroopwafels`, `stg_products_stroopwafels`, `stg_products_pepernoten`, `stg_fx_rates`, `fact_fx_rates`, `int_fact_sales`, `fact_sales`, `int_dim_product`, and `dim_product`.

The staging models (all the models that start with the `stg-` prefix) will have to be rerun for the following reasons:

- We added the new staging model, `stg_sales_pepernoten`
- `Stg_sales` was renamed to `stg_sales_stroopwafels`
- We added `stg_fx_rates` for our currency rates
- We added `stg_products_stroopwafels`, which contains our new stroopwafel products

As you can see, the intermediate and mart models will also be run – remember the + sign in `state:modified+`. Since we have modified the staging models, any downstream models, such as `int_dim_product`, `dim_product`, `fact_fx_rates`, `int_fact_sales`, and `fact_sales` will therefore also be rerun, regardless of whether some of them have not been modified themselves. The `employees` table will not be tested or deployed since we have not modified it.

The next section will introduce you to implementing a CI/CD pipeline in dbt Cloud.

Configuring CI/CD in dbt Cloud

There are several ways to configure CI/CD in dbt Cloud. First, we will take a look at CI configuration, followed by CD configuration.

CI

Configuring CI/CD in dbt Cloud is quite straightforward. At the time of writing, you can make use of its native integration with GitHub, GitLab, or Azure DevOps, which requires you to be on the Enterprise plan for dbt Cloud, though you can use the Administrative API (`https://docs.getdbt.com/docs/dbt-cloud-apis/admin-cloud-api`) to trigger a CI job run, which is helpful if you are not on the Enterprise plan but wish to orchestrate CI and CD jobs from within dbt

Cloud nevertheless. This API can be called from within your CI pipeline in GitHub Actions, GitLab, or Azure DevOps. There is insightful documentation available to get started that discusses setting up the CI job in dbt Cloud and also goes over the necessary commands and linting: `https://docs.getdbt.com/guides/set-up-ci?step=1`.

Note that the Administrative API is available to you by default if you are on the Teams or Enterprise plan and can be used to kick off a job, download artifacts, and manage your dbt Cloud account.

You need to have a dedicated environment that's separate from your production deploy environment and have a dedicated CI job with the command (`state:modified+`) we introduced in Slim CI/CD.

When a PR is opened, the PR ID and the git commit SHA that triggered the run are passed to the cloud job .

State deferral is enabled through deferring to a pre-defined production environment by default. Without this, we cannot make use of Slim CI. The `manifest.json` artifact file is taken from your production environment. It keeps the latest version of the last successful run of any deploy job as this represents the latest state of the project. Then, dbt compares it to the `manifest.json` file in the code push in your PR, and dbt can deduce which models to run.

There is also an option to trigger the run through opening a PR, which also creates a temporary schema for running the models, starting with `dbt_cloud_pr` followed by the `PR_ID` value coming from the service you are using.

When a PR has already been opened and you continue to push commits to the remote from your local development environment, this will trigger another pipeline run every time. This will create a queue of pipeline runs. Ideally, you want to cancel the previous stale run in favor of the latest run. This is handled by dbt Cloud and is called **smart cancellation**.

Another feature that's offered is the possibility of **concurrent runs**. **Concurrency** means that when multiple developers have a PR open at the same time and are pushing code, the CI runs can run in parallel without having to wait for each other.

Official documentation for concurrent CI checks

We recommend checking out the official documentation (`https://docs.getdbt.com/docs/deploy/continuous-integration#concurrent-ci-checks`) as this workflow is subject to change. The documentation on setting up CI in dbt Cloud can be found at `https://docs.getdbt.com/docs/deploy/ci-jobs` and `https://docs.getdbt.com/docs/deploy/continuous-integration`.

CD

A separate deploy job can be configured specifically as part of a CI/CD workflow that is triggered through the dbt Cloud Administrative API, though you can use an existing production job run with a step-override parameter passed to it that overrides the steps in the job. In any case, you will have to trigger these jobs from the Administrative API from within a pipeline. This setup can be customized to your tastes.

For example, if you have a GitHub Actions pipeline, you can make an API call to trigger a deploy job after a merge to the main branch is completed. If you opt to use an existing deploy job, be sure to override the job steps of the job (these are commands that the job executes).

The following code illustrates how this is done. You can see the individual steps that are part of a CD pipeline; they cause a CD pipeline to run via a Python class called `DbtCloudRunner`, which makes use of the Python requests library to call the dbt Cloud Administrative API:

```python
def cd(env: str):
    runner = get_runner()
    if not env:
        raise ValueError("Environment must be provided through --env
flag")

    if env == "dev":
        job_id = int(os.environ["DBT_DEVELOPMENT_JOB_ID"])
        git_branch = os.getenv("DBT_JOB_GIT_BRANCH", None)
    else:
        job_id = int(os.environ["DBT_PRODUCTION_JOB_ID"])
        git_branch = "main"

    steps_override = [
        "dbt seed --full-refresh",
        "dbt build -s state:modified+ ",
    ]

    run_id = runner.run_job(
        job_id=job_id,
        job_cause="CD triggered job",
        git_branch=git_branch,
        steps_override=steps_override,
    )
    # setting env var in Azure DevOps
    logging.info(f'##vso[task.setvariable variable=DBT_RUN_
ID;isOutput=true]{str(run_id)}')

    run_status_link = runner.get_status_link(run_id=run_id)
```

```
logging.info(f"Job running! See job status at {run_status_link}")

runner.poll_run_status(run_id=run_id)
```

There is also an option to trigger the run through opening a PR, which also creates a temporary schema for running these models, beginning with the name `dbt_cloud_pr` and followed by the identifier of the PR, which in the case of the native integration is provided through the Git webhook.

Take a look at *Figure 11.5*, which shows the `DbtCloudRunner` python class. This handles API calls for us. It allows us to fetch job metadata and artifacts, and it also triggers dbt Cloud job runs:

```python
import json
import logging
import time
from urllib.request import Request, urlopen


class DbtCloudRunner:
    """
    Helper class to run dbt jobs in dbt cloud using the dbt API version 2
    """

    run_status_map = {
        1: "Queued",
        2: "Starting",
        3: "Running",
        10: "Success",
        20: "Error",
        30: "Cancelled",
    }

    def __init__(
        self,
        *,
        api_base: str,
        api_key: str,
        account_id: str,
        project_id: str,
    ):
        self.api_base = api_base
        self.api_key = api_key
        self.account_id = account_id
        self.project_id = project_id
        self.req_headers = {
            "Authorization": f"Token {self.api_key}",
            "Content-Type": "application/json",
        }
        self.base_url = f"{self.api_base}/api/v2/accounts/{self.account_id}"
```

Figure 11.5 – The DbtCloudRunner Python class

Figure 11.5 shows the `run_job` method of the `DbtCloudRunner` class. It is responsible for triggering dbt Cloud job runs:

```python
def run_job(
    self,
    *,
    job_id: int,
    job_cause: str,
    git_branch: str = None,
    git_sha: str = None,
    schema_override: str = None,
    steps_override: str = None,
    azure_pull_request_id: int = None,
) -> int:
    """
    Runs a dbt cloud job using the dbt cloud API

    :param job_id: dbt cloud job identifier
    :param job_cause: reason for running the job
    :param git_branch: (optional) git branch to run the job from, either git_branch or git_sha can be provided
    :param git_sha: (optional) git sha to run the job from, either git_branch or git_sha can be provided
    :param schema_override: (optional) schema override to run the job with
    :param steps_override: (optional) steps override to run the job with, should be an array of dbt commands
    :param azure_pull_request_id: (optional) identifier of the Azure DevOps pull request
    :return: dbt cloud run identifier
    """
    if git_branch and git_sha:
        raise ValueError("Either git_branch or git_sha can be provided, not both")

    req_job_url = self._get_job_url(job_id=job_id)
    req_payload = {"cause": job_cause}
    if git_branch:
        req_payload["git_branch"] = git_branch.replace("refs/heads/", "")
    if git_sha:
        req_payload["git_sha"] = git_sha
    if schema_override:
        req_payload["schema_override"] = schema_override.replace("-", "_")
    if steps_override:
        req_payload["steps_override"] = steps_override
    if azure_pull_request_id:
        req_payload["azure_pull_request_id"] = azure_pull_request_id

    data = json.dumps(req_payload).encode()
    request = Request(
        method="POST", data=data, headers=self.req_headers, url=req_job_url
    )

    with urlopen(request) as req:
```

Figure 11.6 – The run_job method of the DbtCloudRunner class

Now that you have a proper understanding of CI and CD, let's have a look at a slightly different alternative to this called continuous delivery.

Continuous delivery

Continuous delivery also involves testing any code change, whether it's a new feature, bug fix, or experiment, and preparing it for release to a production environment. However, the actual deployment to production in continuous delivery is a manual step, requiring a human decision to make the final push. The goal of continuous delivery is to ensure that software can be reliably released at any time, creating a stable, reliable, and repeatable process for releasing software. The benefits include having a deployable product after every change and more reliable software delivery. This approach also eases the pressure on the decision to release as the product is always ready for deployment.

First, let's understand how continuous delivery and CD are different.

Continuous delivery versus continuous deployment

Continuous deployment (CD) and continuous delivery, while closely related in the realm of software development, particularly in automated deployment pipelines, are distinct practices with key differences. Continuous delivery is much less common nowadays in data teams working with the modern data stack, but it might sometimes be practiced within bigger development teams that work with release cycles. This is the reason we're briefly mentioning it here.

Continuous delivery typically aligns with a more traditional release schedule found in traditional software engineering. It maintains the practice of keeping software in a state where it can be released to production at any time, but the actual deployment is a controlled and scheduled process. Releases are often done regularly, such as once or twice a week, depending on the organization's workflow, policies, and needs.

This approach allows teams to bundle several changes or features together for a scheduled release and allows them to perform final checks or preparations before deploying to production. This ensures that extra attention is paid to the quality of the product and that there are no bugs or security issues with the release.

While there are clear benefits to a release schedule, it can also slow down development if the team's working velocity is higher than its release cycle. This is the crucial difference between an automated CI/CD pipeline and continuous delivery.

CD, on the other hand, allows for a more dynamic and ongoing release process. In this model, changes that have been approved, and pass all automated tests, are deployed to production automatically without the need for a scheduled release. This can result in multiple deployments per day, making it a more ad hoc and continuous approach. CD is highly efficient in environments where rapid iteration and frequent updates are necessary and where there is a high level of confidence in the automated testing and deployment processes. The potential downside is that developers, especially on larger teams, can have a hard time keeping up with a high velocity of changes on parts of the codebase that they are not involved in.

The evolution of CD as a standard practice for many teams can be attributed to several key factors. Firstly, advancements in CI/CD tooling, such as GitHub Actions and Azure Pipelines, provide integrated testing and deployment capabilities directly within code repositories instead of requiring external tooling. Additionally, the blurring of lines between Operations and Development roles, coupled with the adoption of Agile methodologies, has further cemented CD's role in the software development life cycle.

In modern teams, features are not only developed but also deployed by the development team, who then assume responsibility for any issues or errors that may emerge. This shift in responsibility empowers developers to oversee the entire development cycle, reducing their reliance on a separate Operations team and promoting a more integrated approach to software development.

Summary

In this chapter, we saw how integrating and deploying your code can be automated. We also discussed how analytics engineering is leveraging existing practices from software engineering when it comes to using CI/CD for automated tests and deployment to ensure code quality and delivery promptly. Testing code for formatting, compilation errors, and unit testing functions and macros is an essential part of testing your code before deploying to production.

In this chapter, we introduced the paradigm of DataOps, its ideas and principles, and how it is strongly influenced by practices from software engineering. Then, we introduced the concept of CI, discussed the necessity of testing your code for formatting issues, compilation and runtime errors, and covered unit testing your functions and macros. Next, we talked about CD, the concept of state comparison and idempotency, and enabling Slim CI/CD runs in dbt Cloud using state deferral to reduce costs and time. Lastly, we briefly touched upon continuous delivery as an alternative to CD – that is, release cycles that are triggered manually based on a more thorough review.

By now, you should have a good understanding of how code is reviewed, tested, deployed, and documented. In the next chapter, you will learn how to gather business requirements for your project.

Part 5:
Data Strategy

This section comprises two pivotal chapters, guiding you in strategically harnessing the value of data. This knowledge helps practitioners gain buy-in from stakeholders and integrate their solutions into the organization's way of working. To conclude, we also have an *Epilogue* with a summary of the book and some tips to kickstart your career as an analytics engineer.

This section has the following chapters:

- *Chapter 12, Driving Business Adoption*
- *Chapter 13, Data Governance*
- *Chapter 14, Epilogue*

Driving Business Adoption

Until now, we have focused on the technical skills essential to an analytics engineer's work. However, the success of these professionals also depends on correctly identifying business requirements and ensuring the adoption of data projects.

Gathering requirements is the first step of any product development project. At this stage, soft skills such as clear communication, active listening, and project management are fundamental. By correctly identifying business priorities and quick wins, data teams eventually deliver relevant data products that the business embraces.

In this chapter, we will discuss the following topics:

- Defining analytics translation
- Scoping analytics use cases
- Ensuring business adoption

Defining analytics translation

In 2018, the consulting firm McKinsey introduced the **analytics translator** role as a new must-have for companies (`https://www.mckinsey.com/capabilities/quantumblack/our-insights/analytics-translator`). According to this article, analytics translators are essential to generate impact from data initiatives.

Analytics translators possess skills ranging from project management and business domain knowledge to technical literacy. They bring use cases forward from ideation to deployment and adoption, which makes gathering business requirements one of their main responsibilities. Ultimately, analytics translation is a set of practices that help companies develop valuable data products.

In *Figure 12.1* (sourced from *Xebia*, `https://pages.xebia.com/whitepaper-data-democratization`), the responsibilities of analytics translators and analytics engineers are plotted in relation to the data supply chain; this time expanding the similar diagram displayed in *Chapter 1, What is Analytics Engineering?*:

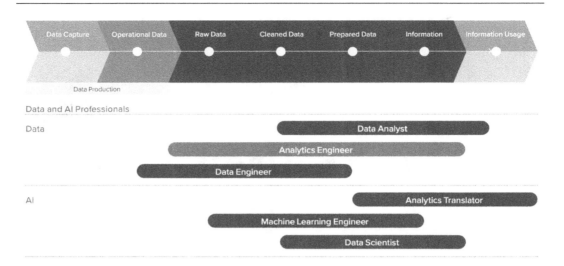

Figure 12.1 – The data supply chain and the roles of analytics translator and engineer

Analytics translators monitor how the business consumes data products, translating the requirements to analytics engineers, data analysts, data scientists, and data engineers. This process ensures that the development of data products, such as self-service analytics reports or ML models, is aligned with the business needs.

While the value of analytics translation is undeniable, not every company has this role division in place. This forces other data professionals to gather business requirements, as they are generally in touch with stakeholders and uniquely positioned to identify opportunities.

Whether a company has an analytics translator or not, the **analytics value chain** can help data professionals identify requirements. Within this framework, the business value is always the starting point for data use cases.

The analytics value chain

Similar to the data supply chain seen in *Figure 12.1*, the analytics value chain describes the process of extracting value from data. It focuses on how data can be transformed into analytics products and lead to insights that will optimize actions. These actions ultimately contribute to business value.

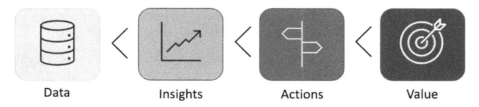

Figure 12.2 – The data analytics value chain

In *Figure 12.2*, going from right to left, we can ask the following questions:

- **Value**: What is the value for the business?
- **Actions**: Which actions can be optimized to create value?
- **Insights**: Which **Key Performance Indicators** (**KPIs**) and metrics should be tracked to inform these actions?
- **Data**: What data is necessary to produce these insights?

When working on analytics engineering products, it is important not to lose sight of the end goal: added business value. A transformation pipeline in dbt can adhere to all possible best practices, but if it doesn't serve a clear purpose, its value is halted. Therefore, for an analytics engineer, business acumen is as important as technical depth to translate business requirements into valuable data products.

The last two points in the list (**Insights** and **Data**) are related to technical aspects and require working hand in hand with data professionals. As illustrated in *Chapter 8, Hands-On Analytics Engineering*, analytics engineers collaborate closely with data analysts to develop data models and transformations. It is fundamental to communicate with the analyst or scientist responsible for building the data product that will provide the insights. If data is missing or source schemas require changes, communication with data engineers is also essential.

Now that we are familiar with the analytics value chain, we will discuss the framework to scope use cases.

Scoping analytics use cases

To identify the scope of analytics use cases, there are several key steps involved. The first important step is to identify the stakeholders involved in the project.

Identifying stakeholders

Identifying stakeholders ensures that the solution developed aligns with the expectations and needs of different parties.

First, let's make the distinction between primary users and secondary stakeholders. Primary users, such as department heads or company executives, consume the data product directly. Secondary stakeholders, such as managers in other departments, impact the project indirectly.

Primary and secondary stakeholders require different levels of interaction and have different expectations. The **stakeholder map** allows us to map these in greater detail. It divides the relationship between a party's influence and interest into four quadrants.

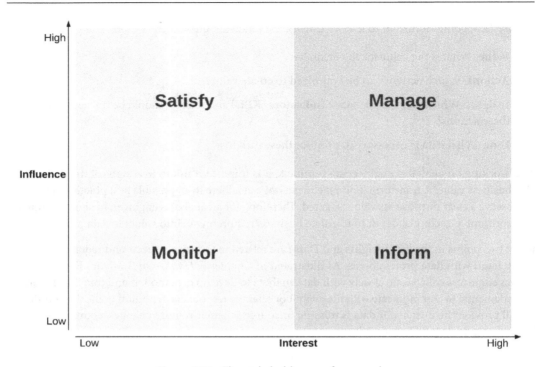

Figure 12.3 – The stakeholder map framework

As illustrated in *Figure 12.3*, stakeholders can be classified as follows:

- **Manage** (high interest and high influence): These primary users and other directly affected parties must be informed constantly and managed closely to meet their expectations

- **Inform** (high interest and low influence): These secondary stakeholders need to be informed, and their feedback is important to the project's success

- **Monitor** (low interest and low influence): Similar to the **Inform** quadrant, they need to be informed, but not as closely

- **Satisfy** (low interest and high influence): Unlike stakeholders that need to be monitored, these parties require directed actions that meet their feedback

Mapping the use case parties according to these four quadrants helps develop clear communication, engagement, and trust in the project.

Ideating analytics use cases

Use case ideation focuses on the value added to encourage a business pull rather than a technical push. However, to build a use case, you must eventually consider what needs to be done technically.

Collecting ideas

Use case ideation is, ideally, handled by dedicated analytics translators. In their absence, data analysts, product owners, and analytics engineers may take on this responsibility.

Collecting ideas in collaboration with business stakeholders ensures covering the entire value chain and avoiding technical pushes from the data team that are unactionable or misaligned with business priorities.

In mature organizations, the business is empowered to bring valuable analytics use cases to the data team. In that case, the data team can take a passive stance in ideating new use cases by, for instance, providing a form and inviting stakeholders to submit their requests.

Often, however, stakeholders need some guidance from data specialists. Analytics engineers can organize or participate in ideation workshops where they gather business needs across the organization. They can help stakeholders identify the type of insight they need, use case success metrics, underlying data, and possible increments. This is an excellent moment to encourage stakeholders to generate ideas and worry about evaluating their feasibility later. For analytics engineers, actively collecting business needs also ensures that their foundational work is future-proof from a business perspective. For instance, they don't have to develop a transformation pipeline that will need to be redone in a few months to facilitate a use case that could have been anticipated. In that sense, business savviness and domain knowledge are crucial analytics engineering skills.

Defining use cases

Based on the data value chain from *Figure 12.2*, a use case describes the following:

- **Business value and value proposition**: What value do you expect to create for the business, and what is the value proposition for your end users? For example, increased sales and improved user experience.

- **Success metrics**: How will you measure the success of this use case? You need to be precise in what you want to optimize for to avoid increasing one metric and decreasing another, leading to a neutral or negative impact on the business down the line. For example, you might increase the conversion rate but decrease the average basket size.

- **Business action**: What actions will the stakeholders take based on the provided insights? For example, re-designing the shopping cart of your e-commerce website.

- **Insights**: What insight do you need to take the action that will create value? For example, the performance of different design options for your shopping carts over time.

- **Data**: What data needs to be available to generate the insight? For example, website user behavior and sales.

You may be able to identify several use cases in the process. Not all use cases may need to be adopted at the same time. Some use cases may be good to have while some may be essential for business success. We will now see how to prioritize these use cases.

Prioritizing use cases

To prioritize use cases and even change requests as you iterate on a solution, you can consider two dimensions: **impact** and **effort**.

The matrix in *Figure 12.4* illustrates how use cases can be categorized in terms of prioritization:

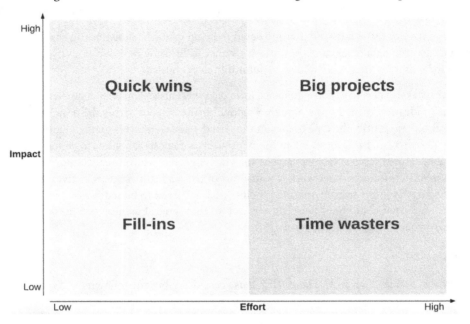

Figure 12.4 – The impact/effort matrix framework

Impact can be assessed together with business stakeholders and in alignment with your organization's strategy. To evaluate impact, you can estimate the expected improvement in your business's KPIs. Additionally, you may want to consider the risk of not achieving the desired impact, for example, having stakeholders misinterpreting your results or not adopting your solution.

Effort can be measured by data specialists and technical experts involved in designing the solution. As an analytics engineer, you will have to investigate the availability of data, its quality, its readiness, and how to expose it.

For example, imagine your data team is trying to prioritize the following tasks based on the requests of a marketing team in an e-commerce company. The stakeholders are interested in three data products:

- A customer segmentation model that will improve promotional email targeting
- A dashboard with marketing campaign KPIs
- A predictive ML model to evaluate customer churn

As an analytics engineer, you provide modeled datasets for these products, and your product owner asks you to calculate the impact and effort for each one. To do that, you rate these three requests from 1 (low) to 5 (high) in impact and effort.

Let's imagine that for the first two data products, data is already ingested, and there is some transformation implemented in dbt. In the case of the customer segmentation dataset, you need additional metrics and transformations. For the predictive ML model request, new data must be ingested, and new dbt models must be created.

With that, we can calculate the impact/effort scores and check where they fit in the matrix from *Figure 12.4*:

```
Customer segmentation: impact (5) * effort (4) = 20
Dashboard: impact (4)* effort (2) = 8
Predictive ML model: impact (2) * effort (5) = 10
```

Following *Figure 12.4*, the customer segmentation model is mapped as a *big project*, the dashboard as a *quick win*, and the predictive ML model as a *time-waster*. Consequently, apart from use cases with high effort and low impact (time-wasters), all use cases should be considered for prioritization.

Now that we have discussed analytics use cases in detail, we must ensure that they are adopted in practice.

Ensuring business adoption

A data product only has value if its users successfully adopt it and make decisions based on it. For that, the analytics product should be known by its users and easily actionable.

Most data professionals are familiar with agile frameworks and know the importance of working incrementally, getting feedback, and documenting their work for better collaboration, transparency, and continuity. This section incorporates these techniques into analytics use cases to ensure business adoption.

Working incrementally

A typical struggle for analytics engineers, inherent to the fact that they stand between business and engineering, is balancing creating business value quickly while ensuring the quality of their solution. Developing quickly can come at the expense of a robust and future-proof solution, creating technical debt that will slow down the team in the future.

To ensure both the speed of delivery and the quality of the product, analytics engineers should work incrementally. During use case ideation, they help define increments that will showcase value with minimum effort and allow you to pivot or even stop the development of a use case if necessary. The key to designing good increments is identifying the smallest valuable steps that lead to the final product. This allows us to test feasibility, prove the solution's value, and gather feedback as early as possible.

Gathering feedback

Analytics engineers gather requirements during the ideation phase and must also gather feedback from their stakeholders as frequently as possible during the development phase. Regular input from stakeholders is crucial to developing a user-friendly and actionable product.

Sharing progress with business stakeholders early and frequently minimizes the risk of misunderstandings and facilitates transparent communication. Moving from conceptual discussions to tangible outcomes will result in more concrete and valuable feedback for the data team.

During this phase, the product may be part of a user acceptance environment that allows stakeholders to test functionalities and validate the data before moving to production. Some BI tools, such as Power BI, allow separating environments or workspaces into development, user acceptance, and production. This way, analytics engineers can develop and test changes on dashboards, underlying datasets, or pipelines without impacting production dashboards.

Knowing when to stop developing

Often, analytics use cases remain in testing for too long or increase indefinitely in complexity to accommodate constant changes that add little value. To avoid getting trapped in this cycle and to manage expectations, the data team must, together with the business owners, agree on the deliverable before entering the industrialization phase and set a **Definition of Done** (**DoD**).

The DoD describes all the criteria the product must satisfy to be accepted by the end users or stakeholders.

The DoD of an analytics use case may include the following:

- **Peer reviews**: Peers (such as analysts and engineers) review the solution and check for malfunctions or data quality issues
- **User tests**: End users get access to the solution in testing and give feedback to developers on readability, relevance of visuals, data quality, and accessibility
- **Data quality monitoring and alerting**: Proper monitoring and alerting of the data exposed to end users should be in place so the data team can be proactive in case bugs or data quality issues appear
- **Data quality tests, security tests, and continuous integration builds**: When deploying to production, tests and CI builds should pass before the code is merged
- **Documentation updates**: The solution is documented end to end to ensure continuity and facilitate interpretability and usage

A clear DoD enables teams to converge to acceptable product deliverables.

Communicating your results

Once your solution is in production, make it visible. The data team can organize a demo to inform the business of the existence of a new product, explain how to use it, and showcase its value. This demo can be co-organized with the business owners of the use case to increase buy-in. To facilitate the discoverability of your analytics products, you can create a catalog as simple as a SharePoint web page linking to relevant resources for your stakeholders.

During the ideation phase, the business and the development team have identified success metrics for the use case. Now is the time to measure impact. For instance, in the case of a dashboard, the data team should monitor usage metrics and get back to its stakeholders to confirm whether the solution meets the use case's expected value. Value tracking is crucial to make informed investment decisions in the future.

Documenting business logic

Business logic is the way the solutions developed adhere to business rules, which define constraints on certain aspects of an organization. For instance, the way to create categories of products constitutes a business rule. For analytics use cases, business logic is how these rules are enforced within the different stages of the data supply chain – from ingestion to serving data. In the example of product categorization, the business logic may be translated into a **CASE WHEN** statement (to handle if/ then logic in SQL). Other examples include filtering out invalid, duplicate, or incomplete records, classifying data as sensitive to comply with data privacy regulations, or applying exchange rates to convert to different currencies.

For the sake of clarity, note that business rules are different from business requirements. Business requirements indicate the specifications of the data product, such as the frequency of updates for a dashboard, the availability of certain metrics, or the presence of specific features.

Documenting business logic is crucial for continuity, collaboration, interpretability, and trust, contributing greatly to adopting analytics products. Business logic should not only be captured in the code but also documented in a central place such as Confluence, making it available and clearly outlined to all stakeholders involved.

Proper documentation allows data analysts to autonomously use the data transformed by analytics engineers, and business stakeholders to easily and correctly interpret the data exposed. In a nutshell, clear business logic lowers the barrier to entry for stakeholders to adopt the solution.

Additionally, agreeing on business rules to be incorporated into business logic fosters healthy discussions among business stakeholders, especially in siloed organizations where multiple sources of truth coexist. This exercise will contribute to adopting a common language and understanding of data throughout the organization.

Summary

In this chapter, we have discussed the value of analytics translation for analytics engineering. In particular, the data analytics value chain helps scope use cases by focusing on actionable, valuable insights. Finally, we explored practical ways to increase adoption and maximize the impact of data use cases.

In the next chapter, you will learn about a crucial practice to manage and protect organizations' data assets: data governance. You will discover its objectives, methods, challenges, and how it intersects with analytics engineering.

13

Data Governance

Data governance can be irresponsibly defined as, everything you need to do to ensure data is compliant, secure, accurate, available, and valuable.

Most data professionals and technologists are rebels. Instinctively, we worry more about making something work rather than reflecting on the role of our solution in the extensive landscape of our organizations. We often enjoy novelty and working with new technology but not the administration and processes to support that work. In fact, we secretly believe most people reading this book will skip this chapter after reading the title. However, we urge you to stay a bit longer. Data governance is not the sexiest topic, but it is what separates mature data teams from the rest.

In short, doing data governance well can be challenging. It requires a lot of discipline, empathy, detail-oriented thinking, and (most often lacking) dedication. But it is probably one of the most essential activities to ensure that your work benefits your whole organization.

In this chapter, we will talk about governance. Some of the topics we will discuss are the following:

- Understanding data governance
- Applying data governance in analytics engineering
- Addressing critical areas for seamless data governance

Understanding data governance

Data governance is a comprehensive and disciplined approach to managing and protecting an organization's data assets. It involves establishing a framework encompassing people, processes, rules, policies, tools, and guidelines to ensure data quality, security, and compliance.

Any **data governance framework** should specify the interactions between its **three pillars**: people, process, and technology.

The **people** pillar involves establishing clear roles and responsibilities for individuals within the organization. This includes people who create guidelines, oversee compliance, and implement these policies in the tools we use (the last is probably you). It is crucial to have a team that understands the importance of data governance and can effectively implement and enforce the necessary policies and procedures.

The **process** pillar involves developing data lifecycle management processes that cover data creation, storage, usage, sharing, and disposal. By having well-defined processes in place, organizations can ensure that data is managed consistently and in accordance with regulatory requirements.

The **technology** pillar encompasses the tools and technologies that support data governance initiatives. This encompasses technologies specifically made for governance purposes (e.g., data catalogs) and other data tools that the team already uses (e.g., dashboarding tools or data warehousing tools).

Take the onboarding of a new employee as an example. In this situation, a good governance framework for defining data roles and access to new employees should specify the following:

- Who is responsible for granting access?
- To which tools do they need access?
- What type of access do they need?
- Who is responsible if something goes wrong?

For example, IT Senior Management sets the IT policies and procedures regarding access, including if that access is based on roles, such as **role-based access control** (**RBAC**), and how frequently access is reviewed. The IT administrators grant the access requested to the tools needed. Every quarter, an IT Manager runs an audit to review access and ensure that everything is under control. Any findings that are detected are the responsibility of the IT Manager.

Thus, data governance is a comprehensive framework that brings together people, processes, and technology to manage and protect an organization's data assets effectively. By implementing robust data governance practices, organizations can ensure data integrity, enhance data security, comply with regulations, and leverage data as a valuable strategic asset.

Governance is not unique to data

Across your organization and outside it, you will find countless examples of governance. A good example is HR. Most large organizations have a well-defined process to hire people, fire people, increase salaries, and promotions. HR departments standardize processes to avoid trouble and keep everything fair. In an ideal world, IT processes such as deploying to production or releasing new features should be governed similarly to how HR governs salary increases and promotions.

The objective of data governance

Every task in an organization can be classified as **working on the business** or **working in the business**. The former refers to working toward strategic goals, growth initiatives, and everything that will bring the business closer to a desirable state. The latter refers to the day-to-day activities required for the business to run. This can be things such as paying your employees every month or ensuring that there is fresh coffee every morning.

The **objective of governance** is to create robust frameworks around everything that needs to happen (i.e., the working in your business part) so that you have more time to work on achieving your strategic goals. In this framework, you should find policies and guidelines detailing how people, tools, and processes go together.

In the case of data, governance ensures that your business-critical data assets remain functional so that you can focus on achieving more value from your data. To exemplify this, it is not about creating new dashboards or pipelines but ensuring that the existing ones do not break.

For instance, imagine you work for a healthcare organization that manages sensitive patient data. Data governance, in this context, would involve implementing strict access controls and encryption protocols to protect patient privacy and comply with regulatory requirements such as HIPAA. It would also include establishing data quality standards to ensure accurate and reliable patient records. By having comprehensive data governance practices in place, you can ensure that healthcare professionals have access to the right information at the right time, enabling them to make well-informed decisions about patient care. This improves the overall quality of healthcare services and builds trust with patients, knowing that their personal information is secure and handled with utmost care.

Note that data governance is not a one-person assignment. It requires work and effort from every single data professional and data user. However, your tasks and responsibilities shape the parts of governance you should lead.

In the next section, we will discuss how analytics engineers can be involved in data governance projects.

Applying data governance in analytics engineering

So far, the concept of data governance might feel overwhelming or a bit fuzzy. If so, there is no need to worry. Nobody is going to ask you for a textbook definition. In fact, nobody else in your team may have ever heard of governance.

Nevertheless, even if they do not call by its name, your colleagues will often discuss the issues caused by poor governance. They will talk about how much time they waste cleaning data or their frustration when nobody fixes data quality at the source. For this reason, from now on, we will talk about governance in the way that most people understand: highlighting its main topics and demonstrating how they are relevant to your work.

Governance is interwoven into your role as an analytics engineer, especially if enabling data analysts and other data consumers is among your responsibilities. In this section, we will provide a comprehensive overview of the essential elements that data teams need to consider, from establishing data governance roles, ownership, and responsibilities to addressing data privacy and regulatory compliance.

Finally, we cannot stress enough that data governance is a team sport. In most organizations, creating governance frameworks from scratch is not your job. Hopefully, there is a data architect, CTO, InfoSec professional, or somebody better qualified for that task. However, you must understand these concepts since you will often be responsible for implementing governance within your data tools.

> **For more information**
>
> Previous chapters have covered some topics in this section in much more detail. For more information about data modeling and quality, you can revisit *Chapter 5*, *Data Modeling*, and *Chapter 7*, *Serving Data*, respectively. In this chapter, we will focus on how these areas affect your job as an analytics engineer.

Defining data ownership

Data ownership refers to the roles that humans have in a data setting. More specifically, it is about making clear what needs to happen and, more importantly, who needs to do it. Imagine there is a critical report in your organization. In a mature data team, it is always clear who is responsible when you need to do the following:

- **Create a new feature for your data product**: In the case of a report, adding one more chart or an extra column to the dataset would be the equivalent.

- **Investigate a wrong number in a dashboard**: If another team claims that the numbers in your report differ from their numbers, somebody should investigate it.

- **Fix a data pipeline that stopped working**: If the report is not up to date, somebody should repair that particular data pipeline.

- **Approve a pull request on the main branch**: If the pipeline is written with a programming language and you are using Git, you will need somebody to review the code and approve when somebody pushes new lines of code to the repository.

Assigning an owner to every data source, system, pipeline, and data product is desirable. Ideally, there is always an individual responsible and accountable for the lifetime of this data asset. This person oversees any action required for the correct functioning of the data asset, or, at the very least, this person is responsible for finding somebody else to take over.

By default, the owner tends to be the creator of a data asset (quite often, you or one of your colleagues). If you build something, you maintain it. However, this is far from a perfect system. In practice, the lead developer is busy building something new, or a person who has already left the company has done so without leaving any proper documentation.

One key difference between mature data teams and the rest is how efficiently they can transfer ownership. Ideally, inheriting a data product from its developer should be frictionless. Anybody should be able to open a script or dashboard and understand how to maintain it. However, as you can imagine, this rarely happens. Ironically, it takes a lot of hard work and experience to be fully replaceable.

Here are some examples of things that you, as an analytics engineer, can do to help:

- **Prioritize code readability**: It is okay if your code is less efficient and sophisticated as long as it is easy to understand. Avoid boilerplate code, leave comments explaining the why behind some of your decisions, use descriptive names for your variables and functions, and break your code into functions.

- **Automate documentation**: Very few people document their work, and even fewer keep documentation up to date. You can alleviate this problem with automation, from LLMs and other AI solutions that can explain how code works to tools that make documentation easier (e.g., dbt).

- **Reduce technical debt**: Spend time improving and refactoring legacy solutions. It might seem like a waste of time, but just know that this type of work happens anyway when something breaks. Regardless of when you do it, refactoring your business-critical data products pays off exponentially in terms of maintainability.

Organizations also have a role in improving the transfer of ownership. You can convince your team and management to implement the following solutions:

- **Force collaboration**: Make an effort to break silos. If you have a team of specialists, taking over each other's work is harder. However, if you force the team to work together on the same data products, they will understand each other's work more efficiently. You can accomplish this by conducting periodic initiatives such as code reviews, pair programming, or knowledge-sharing sessions.

- **Hire a data owner**: Officially appointing a data owner as a full-time or part-time job is becoming increasingly popular. For larger deployments, it is also common to see domain owners (e.g., finance data owner or marketing data owner) or system owners (e.g., data laker owner or CRM data owner).

Next up, we talk about why maintaining quality data is essential and what role analytics engineers play in ensuring the integrity of data.

Data quality and integrity

Bad quality refers to any instance when the data is missing, inaccurate, or unreliable. It is important because bad data can invalidate your insights. In the worst cases, bad data can be detrimental to your business objectives. Some examples may come in the form of the following:

- An old email address that is no longer in use
- A small typo that causes your client information to be split into multiple records
- Somebody who did not complete a survey and left some questions blank
- Failing to report that a product contains allergens (e.g., nuts or shrimp)
- Records missing when a database went offline for a couple of hours

Bad data can have multiple causes, and preventing it might not always be possible. However, regardless of the reason, data quality is one of the reasons most companies fail to leverage value out of data. Even more worrisome, bad data can lead to erroneous decisions, uncountable losses, or even death.

As an analytics engineer, you are in a privileged position to solve data quality challenges. Often, you can help your governance team by doing the following:

- **Spotting bad data**: By working with the data and the stakeholders, you learn about data issues, what causes them, and sometimes who is affected by them.
- **Creating strategies to prevent or clean bad data**: While manual work is often unavoidable, your technical knowledge should suffice to automate some of this work. With some coding skills, you can write formulas or dbt macros that help fix some of the data's flaws.
- **Implementing these strategies within the platform**: In its most basic form, this can come in the form of database constraints, fuzzy matching, dbt tests, and many other techniques. However, you may implement proper data quality and monitoring tools.
- It is not uncommon to have a component of data quality in your job. It can be as little as making data contracts and tests in dbt. But it can encompass setting up data quality tools such as **Soda** (`https://www.soda.io/`), **Monte Carlo** (`https://www.montecarlodata.com/`), **great_expectations** (`https://greatexpectations.io/`), **Anomalo** (`https://www.anomalo.com/`), or **DataFold** (`https://www.datafold.com/`), just to name a few.

Another important aspect of analytics engineering is to seamlessly manage data assets, which we discuss next.

Managing data assets

As a power user of any data tool, such as dbt or Databricks, you are a prime candidate to manage how this tool is used, especially if you work in a small organization where you will become the administrator of some of your tools. This might require thinking about cost management, access control, monitoring, or other governance-related activities.

This is not an exhaustive list of everything you need to administer a tool. However, here are some of the most common tasks:

- **User provisioning**: This entails granting licenses, creating accounts, giving a user access, and deleting users once they no longer need access. A common example is approving access requests for colleagues who need to see a dashboard.

- **Monitoring**: This means keeping track of any metric that's relevant to your data infrastructure's health. Some common examples involve cost control or investigating what your most popular reports (to prioritize them) are.

- **Access control**: This refers to limiting access to data or resources. A prime example is a dashboard that only lets you see your data. Depending on your role, you might be responsible for creating permission structures, granting licenses to a data tool, masking/encrypting sensitive information, or limiting the amount of data users can see (e.g., row-level security).

Data governance is incomplete if the professionals who interact with data on a day-to-day basis are not empowered to tackle the complexities of data, manage it effectively, and leverage insights to make impactful decisions.

Training, enablement, and best practices

No organization has enough skilled data professionals. Honestly, we might retire before the huge market gap for experienced analytics experts closes. The best you can do to alleviate this problem at your organization is to make analytics more accessible. In other words, by reducing or hiding the complexity behind your data, your coworkers can leverage the power of data with fewer hours of training.

Here are some ideas that you can try to make analytics more accessible for the rest of your team:

- **Training programs**: Create training materials, organize regular training sessions, or even create tutorials on performing common tasks by recording your screen.

- **Create templates**: Make template dashboards, SQL scripts, dbt models, or whatever your team uses. Often, it is easier for people to learn when they can learn from an existing example.

- **Make a Wiki**: Answering the same questions over and over is annoying. You can reduce the amount of frequently asked questions by creating a Wiki. This can be a page on your data catalog, a **Slack** channel, a blog, or a SharePoint page.

- **Build abstractions**: Abstraction is a computer science concept that hides data or process complexity, generally, for the benefit of the end user. Some examples of abstractions that you may be familiar with include coding libraries, **dbt macros**, **dbt packages**, stored procedures, and user-defined functions, just to name a few.

Another key aspect of data governance that we will discuss next is the importance of **data definitions**, especially when multiple stakeholders are working with the same data.

Data definitions

Organizations struggle to guarantee that data-driven decisions are always based on the same numbers. In an ideal universe, every analyst across the organization can provide the same number for basic questions such as "how many clients do we have?" or "what is our best-selling product?" We generally refer to this ideal state as a **single source of truth** (or **SSoT** for short). Unfortunately, achieving an SSoT is not as easy as it sounds.

Besides data quality issues, part of the problem is the lack of a common definition. For example, even a basic concept, such as "customer," has a lot of complexity. To understand who counts as a customer, you need to answer the following questions:

- When exactly do you become a customer? Is it when you enter a shop, when you show any intent of purchasing, when you pay, when you receive the goods, or after the window when you can return the goods passes?

- Who does not count as a customer? How about your employees who get free products? Or the people who won a free product during a contest? Do they count as customers as well?

- Who exactly is your customer? Imagine parents who buy a toy for their child. Who is the customer? The parents, the child, or both?

The answer to these questions is up to your organization, but it really does not matter what you and your team decide (there are no wrong answers). The only thing that matters is that everyone agrees on exactly the same definition of "customer."

The key to unified and consistent analytics is good governance. More specifically, documenting data definitions, metrics, data models, and anything that modifies the state of your data. There are tools specifically built for this, such as data catalogs, metrics stores, and even **dbt metrics**.

Imagine a subscription-based software company that offers different pricing plans based on the number of users. However, due to a lack of clear data definitions, the term "customer" is ambiguous across different departments. The sales team may consider anybody who signed up as a user. Finance will surely only count somebody as a user once they have provided a payment method and fully paid for the service. These inconsistencies in data definitions can lead to challenges in accurately tracking customer growth, calculating revenue, and forecasting future sales. It can also result in discrepancies in customer support metrics and hinder the company's ability to provide personalized experiences and targeted marketing campaigns.

Please note that the topics discussed here are specific to your tasks as an analytics engineer. However, some topics in data governance affect every data professional equally. Some examples involve resistance to change, colleagues who do not want to collaborate, and stakeholders who do not understand the value of following a procedure.

In the next section, we will discuss these key topics and the importance of having a data governance roadmap.

Addressing critical areas for seamless data governance

Enabling data governance at your organization is not going to be seamless. There will always be some challenges. From a lack of awareness and understanding to resistance to change and adoption, we will delve into these challenges and provide insights on overcoming them.

Resistance to change and adoption

People's resistance to change in the field of IT is extremely common, especially if your organization is not primarily or entirely online. Technology moves fast, and people must constantly adapt to new systems, processes, and tools. However, many tend to resist change due to various reasons. Some fear the unknown, some do not have enough broadband to relearn how to do their job, and some just want to maintain the status quo. Regardless of the reason, here are some strategies to address this resistance:

- **Effective communication**: It is important to communicate the reasons behind the change, its benefits, and how it aligns with the organization's goals. By providing a transparent and compelling vision, individuals are more likely to understand the purpose of the change and be motivated to embrace it. Especially if this change truly makes their work better for them.

- **Involving employees in the change process**: Honestly, many people just hate it when somebody else tells them how to do their job. However, if you rephrase this by asking them for input about improving the job, they will be more receptive. Giving them a sense of ownership and involvement makes them more likely to embrace change. This can be achieved through engaging employees in decision-making, seeking their input, and providing training and support to build their skills and confidence in the new IT systems.

- **Address any concerns or fears individuals may have regarding the change**: You can alleviate anxieties and build trust by actively listening to their feedback and addressing their apprehensions.

- **Create a culture that embraces continuous learning and innovation**: By encouraging experimentation and learning from failures, individuals will be more open to change and willing to explore new technologies and ways of working.

- **Recognize and celebrate the successes and achievements resulting from the change**: By acknowledging and rewarding individuals for their adaptability and willingness to embrace new IT solutions, organizations can create a positive feedback loop that encourages further acceptance of change.

Overcoming resistance to change in IT requires effective communication, employee involvement, addressing concerns, fostering a culture of learning, and recognizing achievements. By implementing these strategies, organizations can successfully navigate the challenges associated with change and drive positive outcomes in the IT landscape.

Engaging stakeholders and fostering collaboration

Engaging stakeholders and fostering collaboration is crucial to ensure the successful implementation of IT projects. However, resistance to collaboration and stakeholder engagement can hinder progress and limit the potential benefits that IT initiatives can bring. Here are some tips on how to gain buy-in from your stakeholders:

- **Identify and involve key stakeholders from the beginning of the project**: This includes individuals or groups whom the IT project may directly or indirectly impact. By involving stakeholders early on, their perspectives, concerns, and expertise can be considered, leading to more informed decision-making and greater buy-in.

- **Effective communication plays a vital role in engaging stakeholders and fostering collaboration**: Regular and transparent communication channels should be established to keep stakeholders informed about the project's progress, goals, and potential impacts. This can be achieved through meetings, newsletters, project updates, or dedicated communication platforms. Additionally, active listening and feedback mechanisms should be in place to ensure that stakeholders' concerns and suggestions are heard and addressed.

- **Create a culture of collaboration and teamwork**: This can be achieved by promoting a shared vision and common goals among stakeholders. Encouraging cross-functional collaboration and breaking down silos can facilitate knowledge sharing, innovation, and problem-solving. By fostering a collaborative environment, stakeholders are more likely to feel valued, engaged, and motivated to contribute to the success of the IT project.

- **Providing training and support to stakeholders can help build their skills and confidence in utilizing new IT solutions**: By offering workshops, tutorials, or one-on-one coaching, organizations can empower stakeholders to effectively use the technology, leading to increased engagement and adoption.

- **Recognizing and celebrating the contributions of stakeholders can reinforce their engagement and foster a sense of ownership**: This can be done through public acknowledgment, rewards, or incentives for their efforts and achievements. By highlighting the positive impact of stakeholder collaboration, organizations can inspire others to engage actively in future IT projects.

- **Leverage technology to facilitate stakeholder engagement and collaboration**: Using collaboration tools, project management platforms, or virtual communication channels can enhance communication, facilitate document sharing, and enable real-time collaboration among stakeholders, regardless of their geographical locations.

Engaging stakeholders and fostering collaboration is essential for the successful implementation of IT projects. By involving stakeholders from the beginning, establishing effective communication channels, promoting collaboration, providing training and support, recognizing contributions, and leveraging technology, organizations can overcome resistance and create an environment that encourages active stakeholder engagement and collaboration.

Establishing a data governance roadmap

As I mentioned before, governance separates mature data teams from the rest. For your data team to improve how it functions, creating a roadmap is vital. In this roadmap, you need to capture your organization's view on topics such as data security, data sharing, collaboration, access control, data definitions, regulatory compliance, and any other relevant governance topics to your team.

Not every topic will be equally crucial to your organization. Here are some examples:

- Data teams in highly regulated industries will probably care more about **regulatory compliance**. The analytics engineers in these industries will likely focus more on data security and data quality than their counterparts in other industries.

- Larger data teams will probably spend more time on **collaboration topics**. The analytics engineers in those teams will focus on topics such as ownership, documentation, and anything that ensures a uniform experience for any team member.

- Organizations with stakeholders resistant to using data in their decision-making process are more likely to spend their efforts **making data useful and usable**. The analytics engineers in those teams will probably run more training and workshops to engage the business.

Once you know how your team views different governance topics and what is important, expand your roadmap with concrete goals and actions that you can undertake. Some examples include the following:

- Reducing the cost of your data platform by a certain percentage

- Minimize the hours your team spends administrating tools with automation

- Write a script involving the data quality in a certain table

- Refactor and improve the most popular dashboards in your organization

Summary

Data governance refers to any task you must do to make your data compliant, secure, accurate, available, and useful. Even though organizations often ignore it, it sets mature data teams apart. It enables you to work towards your strategic goals and reduce the hours wasted maintaining and fixing existing data assets.

In this chapter, we discuss some key topics in governance, such as ownership, data quality, managing data assets, training, and data modeling. A recurrent theme is that building governance roadmaps from scratch is generally not your responsibility. However, analytics engineers are in a privileged position to understand issues with the data and have enough technical knowledge to correct them at the source.

Working on data governance is never going to be easy. You will face resistance to change and need to get buy-in from your stakeholders to ensure the success of your initiatives. However, any goal you achieve will translate into a much better experience for the rest of the data team.

Finally, we highlight the importance of building a data governance roadmap for your team. In this document, you should state your team's vision on different governance topics and include goals and actions.

14
Epilogue

Congratulations! You've made it to the last chapter of *Fundamentals of Analytics Engineering*. With this concluding chapter, we will review the fundamental insights from the book, connecting them to their practical applications. We will also share a few tips to future-proof your analytics engineering career. These include a commitment to continuous learning and skill development, active networking and community engagement, and the strategic initiative to showcase your work by building a comprehensive portfolio.

Here are the topics covered in this chapter:

- Reviewing the fundamental insights – what you've learned so far
- Making your career future-proof – how to take it further
- Closing remarks

Reviewing the fundamental insights – what you've learned so far

In these concluding remarks, we'd like to give you a big-picture view of the topics you have covered so you can see how they connect with each other. This way, you will not only review some key concepts but also learn how to apply them in real-world situations for professional development:

- **Introduction to analytics engineering (Chapters 1-2):** The first two chapters introduced the core concepts underpinning analytics engineering and the modern data stack. Remember how analytics engineers leverage software engineering best practices to model, transform, test, deploy, and document data in a reusable way, saving teams time and reducing duplicated effort. On the other hand, the modern data stack optimizes the speed of delivery, costs, and data democratization, but may lead to tool proliferation and siloed information.

- **Building pipelines (Chapters 3-7)**: These chapters equipped readers with the practical skills to navigate the intricacies of handling data and platform construction. Each chapter represents a core part of your responsibilities as an analytics engineer. These are some of the important takeaways to remember:

  - Regarding data ingestion, remember to think ahead and plan its eight steps

  - For data warehousing, consider your requirements, existing technological infrastructure, team proficiency, and budget constraints to choose the right platform offer

  - For data modeling, remember that most systems have mixed data models, and finding a pure data model with all of the desired characteristics is almost impossible

  - For data transformations, consider reusability in query processes and optimize SQL queries for modularity

  - When serving data, strive to turn vanity metrics into actionable ones and establish a balance between reusability and bespoke processes.

- **Hands-on guide** (*Chapter 8*): This chapter was a step-by-step description of all the typical tasks you will face as an analytics engineer. Before diving into all the hard work, remember to keep the business goals in mind and set clear KPIs to make yourself accountable

- **DataOps (Chapters 9-11)**: In this part of the book, the focus shifted toward refining the craft of analytics engineering through the lens of quality assurance, collaborative coding, and streamlined workflows. The emphasis extends beyond building a data pipeline that works; it revolves around establishing safety measures, reliability, and collaboration and optimizing processes for a more secure and efficient analytics workflow. Think of this knowledge as the difference between a senior analytics engineer and an aspiring analytics engineer.

- **Data strategy (Chapters 12-13)**: This part equipped readers with the tools to bridge the gap between business objectives and effective analytics implementation. Always remember to address the strategic aspects of data management, align analytics initiatives with overall business goals, and leverage data for informed decision-making. The knowledge in this section is how you can demonstrate your value to your organization and how your work can coexist with the rest of the IT infrastructure.

Next, we will share a few tips for you to advance your career in analytics engineering.

Making your career future-proof – how to take it further

If you made it this far into the book, you are probably serious about becoming an analytics engineer. We hope the knowledge in this book will make a difference in your career and future endeavors. As the cherry on top, here are three pieces of advice for a successful career as a data professional.

Tip #1 – keep learning and developing your skills

In the ever-evolving data landscape, improving your capabilities over time is a must. With the advent of artificial intelligence in data analytics, many wonder whether the traditional roles are in danger of becoming obsolete.

Although some of the new tools and models out there are impressive, the reality is that analytical professionals have a set of soft skills that are almost impossible to simulate. Some of these skills include understanding the business and its stakeholders to provide information at the right moment and context, the ability to discriminate in determining which data to ingest in the system, and handling dirty data.

The analytics engineer's core skills are so relevant that they influence the tools being developed in the space of the modern data stack. These new tools help with data ingestion, data quality, data observability, data transformation, documenting semantic information, collaborative development, orchestration, and reporting, among many other tasks.

However, the analytics engineer's skills keep evolving over time. The use of data across almost every human activity creates limitless use cases and allows us to improve our skills and expand beyond our current knowledge.

Some ways to continuously improve these skills include attending online and in-person training, reading blogs and articles about new tools, and replicating your peers' work. One way to do this is by reviewing the technical example from this book and making it grow by, for example, changing the parts that manage ingestion or exploring a different data model.

In analytics engineering, some of the most crucial skills relate to dealing with other professionals. Skills such as stakeholder management, gathering requirements, and managing expectations take time to develop, but can help you network and engage with the community.

This brings us to tip #2.

Tip #2 – network and engage with the community

One of the main ways to foster human interaction is connecting with groups whose members are also into analytics engineering. The different activities of these groups help you stay up to date with industry trends, new tools and technologies, and ways to upskill yourself. Apart from giving you knowledge, networking also gives you access to new job opportunities and great collaborations for the future.

Some of the events and groups out there are organized by vendors trying to promote products or services that can be of value to your daily work. However, many other community activities are organized by private individuals who share the same interests in analytics engineering.

To get to know and find these different groups and communities, we recommend attending industry conferences and events, which you can find on social networks such as LinkedIn, Meetup, Facebook, or X (formerly Twitter). On dbt Labs's events page (https://www.getdbt.com/events), you can find a list of in-person meetups, conferences, workshops, and online webinars.

Find out whether there are meetup groups near you that organize local events or workshops. If there is not one close to you, and you feel up to the task, try organizing one yourself and hosting these activities. You will likely need some help from vendors or sponsors, but reaching out to them will also allow you to connect with some key members of your local community.

Regarding online interactions, participating in forums and discussion boards, posting, and answering questions on your daily activities can also help you connect with other professionals facing the same challenges.

Building a strong online presence through blogging or social media will increase your chances of getting in touch with more people interested in these topics. Additionally, following relevant professionals and interacting with them through social media comments can widen your network and expose you to different points of view.

Another great way to keep up to date is by working on open-source projects. You could use them on pet projects to understand the options out there, help improve them, or even collaborate on research initiatives.

Actively participating in discussions and sharing expertise will help you develop your own point of view, challenge some practices, and learn from others' feedback and experience.

To balance your daily work with these activities, it is best to focus on the quality of interactions rather than the quantity. Always pursue networking opportunities that align with your personal and professional goals, and regularly review and adjust these interactions to ensure they support the skills you want to develop.

Finally, sharing your work with other analytics engineers can help bolster your network and gain recognition in the industry, which brings us to tip #3.

Tip #3 – showcase your work and build a portfolio

When applying for your next job, preparing a presentation for a conference, or building training for new colleagues, having a portfolio that showcases your work is invaluable. Use this book as a guide to navigate the different activities an analytics engineer performs. With these in mind, build various small projects to test new tools, technologies, and datasets.

By following conversations on social media, blogs, and other networking spaces, you'll also find hot topics. These usually try to position a specific tool, introduce a new practice, or present a novel solution to a known problem. Exploring these topics is an excellent way to gather extra inspiration for small projects.

Implementing new ideas directly in your daily work might be tempting, but it also comes with disadvantages. When you test an innovative project, you might encounter results incompatible with a formal work environment. Also, if you use confidential information to build a proof of concept, it will be challenging to share it with the community later.

This is why we suggest selecting a public dataset and developing a straightforward use case. In this mini-project, document your questions, observations, and discoveries. They will all be beneficial when revisiting the exercise or sharing it with others.

Creating a suitable space to store these projects is essential for easy access and sharing. If you're using code, platforms such as GitHub, GitLab, and Hugging Face provide functionality that simplifies the process. On the other hand, if you need to share other types of files, consider creating a data lake in the cloud or using file-sharing services with free-tier options.

Since you'll be sharing these spaces with others and competing for the community's attention, adding your details and investing in your personal brand is crucial. This will help others remember you and your work. Another vital aspect is documenting each project's purpose: a good summary of the main functionalities and motivation can help new visitors understand what to expect. Take time to write a meaningful README and create templates to showcase other skills using Markdown.

Once you have projects to share, promote your portfolio using channels including blog posts, websites, social media, articles, and your network. Ask for feedback and suggestions for improvement. This will not only help you learn and grow but also increase the visibility of your work.

Closing remarks

On behalf of every author who worked on *Fundamentals of Analytics Engineering*, we hope it has equipped you with the knowledge and skills to tackle the ever-evolving analytics landscape. Remember that analytics engineering is still in its infancy. As an early adopter, you stand at the forefront to help this field develop and have yourself an amazing career.

Make sure to come and say hello if we ever meet in person! It is always a pleasure to network with our fellow data professionals. We are also particularly curious about your work and how this book has helped you with it.

Thank you for your time!

Index

packtpub.com

Subscribe to our online digital library for full access to over 7,000 books and videos, as well as industry leading tools to help you plan your personal development and advance your career. For more information, please visit our website.

Why subscribe?

- pend less time learning and more time coding with practical eBooks and Videos from over 4,000 industry professionals
- Improve your learning with Skill Plans built especially for you
- Get a free eBook or video every month
- Fully searchable for easy access to vital information
- Copy and paste, print, and bookmark content

Did you know that Packt offers eBook versions of every book published, with PDF and ePub files available? You can upgrade to the eBook version at packtpub.com and as a print book customer, you are entitled to a discount on the eBook copy. Get in touch with us at customercare@packtpub.com for more details.

At www.packtpub.com, you can also read a collection of free technical articles, sign up for a range of free newsletters, and receive exclusive discounts and offers on Packt books and eBooks.

Other Books You May Enjoy

If you enjoyed this book, you may be interested in these other books by Packt:

Data Engineering with dbt

Roberto Zagni

ISBN: 9781803246284

- Create a dbt Cloud account and understand the ELT workflow
- Combine Snowflake and dbt for building modern data engineering pipelines
- Use SQL to transform raw data into usable data, and test its accuracy
- Write dbt macros and use Jinja to apply software engineering principles
- Test data and transformations to ensure reliability and data quality
- Build a lightweight pragmatic data platform using proven patterns
- Write easy-to-maintain idempotent code using dbt materialization

Data Engineering with Python

Paul Crickard

ISBN: 9781839214189

- Understand how data engineering supports data science workflows
- Discover how to extract data from files and databases and then clean, transform, and enrich it
- Configure processors for handling different file formats as well as both relational and NoSQL databases
- Find out how to implement a data pipeline and dashboard to visualize results
- Use staging and validation to check data before landing in the warehouse
- Build real-time pipelines with staging areas that perform validation and handle failures
- Get to grips with deploying pipelines in the production environment

Packt is searching for authors like you

If you're interested in becoming an author for Packt, please visit `authors.packtpub.com` and apply today. We have worked with thousands of developers and tech professionals, just like you, to help them share their insight with the global tech community. You can make a general application, apply for a specific hot topic that we are recruiting an author for, or submit your own idea.

Share Your Thoughts

Now you've finished *Fundamentals of Analytics Engineering*, we'd love to hear your thoughts! Scan the QR code below to go straight to the Amazon review page for this book and share your feedback or leave a review on the site that you purchased it from.

`https://packt.link/r/1837636451`

Your review is important to us and the tech community and will help us make sure we're delivering excellent quality content.

Download a free PDF copy of this book

Thanks for purchasing this book!

Do you like to read on the go but are unable to carry your print books everywhere?

Is your eBook purchase not compatible with the device of your choice?

Don't worry, now with every Packt book you get a DRM-free PDF version of that book at no cost.

Read anywhere, any place, on any device. Search, copy, and paste code from your favorite technical books directly into your application.

The perks don't stop there, you can get exclusive access to discounts, newsletters, and great free content in your inbox daily

Follow these simple steps to get the benefits:

1. Scan the QR code or visit the link below

https://packt.link/free-ebook/9781837636457

2. Submit your proof of purchase
3. That's it! We'll send your free PDF and other benefits to your email directly